微观经济学
Microeconomics

于永娟　魏　鑫◎主编

Yuyongjuan Weixin Zhubian

经济管理出版社
ECONOMY & MANAGEMENT PUBLISHING HOUSE

图书在版编目（CIP）数据

微观经济学 = Microeconomics：英文 / 于永娟，魏鑫主编 . —北京：经济管理出版社，2020.12

ISBN 978-7-5096-6434-6

Ⅰ . ①微… Ⅱ . ①于… ②魏… Ⅲ . ①微观经济学—高等学校—教材—英文 Ⅳ . ① F016

中国版本图书馆 CIP 数据核字（2020）第 255173 号

组稿编辑：王格格

责任编辑：王格格

责任印制：黄章平

责任校对：张晓燕

出版发行：经济管理出版社

（北京市海淀区北蜂窝 8 号中雅大厦 A 座 11 层　100038）

网　　址：www.E-mp.com.cn

电　　话：（010）51915602

印　　刷：北京晨旭印刷厂

经　　销：新华书店

开　　本：710mm×1000mm/16

印　　张：18.25

字　　数：327 千字

版　　次：2020 年 12 月第 1 版　2020 年 12 月第 1 次印刷

书　　号：ISBN 978-7-5096-6434-6

定　　价：69.00 元

编委会

CONTENTS

10 ⟩ Market Failure and Microeconomic Policy ·············· 239

Introduction

In this book, we'll introduce you to the toolseconomists are using to tackle some of the world's biggest challenges, from health care reform, to climate change, to lifting people out of poverty. Of course, these tools are not just for taking on causes worthy of Nobel Prizes. Economics can also help you become a savvier consumer, successfully launch a new cell phone app, or simply make smarter decisions about how to spend your time and money. Throughout this book, we promise to ask you not just to memorize theories, but also to apply the ideas you read about to the everyday decisions you face in your own life.

When people think of economics, they often think of the stock market, the unemployment rate, or media reports saying things like "the People's Bank of China issues reform to improve the quoted loan prime rate of market（LPR）" Although economics does include these topics, its reach is much broader.

Why Study Economics?

What is economics?

Economics is the study of how societies choose to use scarce productive resources that have alternative uses, to produce commodities of various kinds, and to distribute them among different groups. We study economics to understand not only the world we live in but also the many potential worlds that reformers are constantly proposing to us.In economics, resources are not just physical things like cash and gold mines. They are also intangible things, such as time, ideas, technology, job experience, and even personal relationships.

Traditionally, economics has been divided into two broad fields: microeconomics and macroeconomics. ***Microeconomics*** is the study of how individuals and firms manage resources. ***Macroeconomics*** is the study of the economy on a regional, national,or international scale. Microeconomics and macroeconomics are highly related and interdependent；we need both to fully understand how economies work.

Economics starts with the idea that people compare the choices available to them and purposefully behave in the way that will best achieve their goals. As human beings, we have ambitions and we make plans to realize them. We strategize. We marshal our resources. When people make choices to achieve their goals in the most effective way possible, economists say they are exhibiting rational behavior. This assumption isn't perfect. As we'll see later in the book, people can sometimes be short-sighted or poorly informed about their choices. Nevertheless, the assumption of rational behavior helps to explain a lot about the world.

People use economics every day, from Wall Street to Walmart, from state capitol buildings to Bangladeshi villages. They apply economic ideas to everything from shoe shopping to baseball, from running a hospital to running for political office. What ties these topics together is a common approach to problem solving.

Scarcity and efficiency

Goods are scarce because people desire much more than the economy can produce. Economic goods are scarce, not free, and society must choose among the limited goods that can be produced with its available resources. *Indeed, the concerns of economics will not go away because of the fact of scarcity and the desire for efficiency.*

Consider a world without scarcity. If infinite quantities of every good could be produced or if human desires were fully satisfied, what would be the con-sequences? People would not worry about stretching out their limited incomes because they could have everything they wanted; businesses would not need to fret over the cost of labor or health care; governments would not need to struggle over taxes or spending or pollution because nobody would care. Moreover, since all of us could have as much as we pleased, no one would be concerned about the distribution of incomes among different people or classes.

In such an Eden of affluence, all goods would be free, like sand in the desert or seawater at the beach. All prices would be zero, and markets would be unnecessary. Indeed, economics would no longer be a useful subject.

But no society has reached a utopia of limitless possibilities. Ours is a world of scarcity, full of economic goods. A situation of scarcity is one in which goods are limited relative to desires. An objective observer would have to agree that, even after two centuries of rapid economic growth, production in China is simply not high enough to meet everyone's desires. If you add up all the wants, you quickly find that there are simply not enough goods and services to satisfy even a small fraction of everyone's consumption desires. Our national output would have to be many times larger before the average Chinese could live at the level of the average doctor. Moreover, outside the China, particularly in Africa, hundreds of millions of people suffer from hunger and material deprivation.

Given unlimited wants, it is important that an economy make the best use of its limited resources. That brings us to the critical notion of efficiency. Efficiency denotes the most effective use of a society's resources in satisfying people's wants and needs. By contrast, consider an economy with unchecked monopolies or unhealthy pollution or government corruption. Such an economy may produce less than would be possible without these factors, or it may produce a distorted bundle of goods that leaves consumers worse off than they otherwise could be—either situation is an inefficient allocation of resources.

Economic efficiency requires that an economy produce the highest combination of quantity and quality of goods and services given its technology and scarce resources. An economy is producing efficiently when no individual's economic welfare can be improved unless someone else is made worse off.

The essence of economics is to acknowledge the reality of scarcity and then figure out how to organize society in a way which produces the most efficient use of resources. That is where economics makes its unique contribution.

All societies must make choices about how to use their scarce resources; the way that societies differ is in how these decisions are made. Economics is the study of how people and societies deal with scarcity. The subject of this book is microeconomics, which focuses on the economic behavior of individual decision-making units. The prefix micro, which means "small" , is somewhat misleading. To be sure, microeconomists spend a lot of time analyzing the behavior of relatively small decision makers, such as individual households and firms. However, microeconomists are equally concerned with the big picture—how these individual decisions fit together and what kind of results they produce for society. However, we exclude a systematic treatment of how the economy–wide inflation and unemployment rates move overtime (the business cycle) . These topics belong in the realm of macroeconomics, which focuses on the behavior of the economy as a whole, with less attention devoted to the activities of individual units.

What are the trade–offs?

Opportunity cost and marginal decision making

Every decision in life involves weighing the trade–off between costs and benefits. We look at our options and decide whether it is worth giving up one in order to get the other. We choose to do things only when we think that the benefits will be greater than the costs. The potential benefit of taking an action is often easy to see: You can have fun road–tripping for a month; bank customers who take out a loan have the opportunity to expand their businesses. The *costs* of a decision, on the other hand, are not always clear.

You might think it is clear—that the cost of your road trip is simply the amount of money you spend on gas, hotels, and food. But something is missing from that calculation. The true cost of something is not just the amount you have to pay for it, but also the opportunity you lose to do something else instead. Suppose that if you hadn't gone on your road trip, your second choice would have been to spend that same time and money to buy a big–screen TV and spend a month at home watching movies with friends. The true cost of your road trip is the enjoyment you would have had from owning the TV and hanging out with friends for a month. Behaving rationally, you should go on the road trip only if it will be more valuable to you than the best alternative use for yourtime and money. This is a matter of personal preference. Because people have different alternatives and place different values on things like a road trip or a TV, they will make different decisions.

Economists call this true cost of your choice the *opportunity cost, which is equal to the value of what you have to give up in order to get something.* Put another way, opportunity cost is the value of your next best alternative—the "opportunity" you have to pass up in order to take your first choice.

Another important principle for understanding trade–offs is the idea that rational people make decisions at the margin. *Marginal decision making* describes the idea that rational people compare the additional benefits of a choice against the additional costs, without considering related benefits and costs of past choices. Economists call costs that have already been incurred and can not be recovered **sunk costs.** Sunk costs *should not have any bearing on your marginal decision about what to do next.*

How will others respond?

In answering this question about trade–offs, economists commonly make two assumptions. The first is that people respond to incentives. An **incentive** is *something that causes people to behave in a certain way by changing the trade–offs they face.* A positive incentive (sometimes just called an incentive) makes people more likely to do something. A negative incentive (sometimes called a disincentive) makes them less likely to do it. For example, lowering the price of spaghetti creates a positive incentive for people to order it, because it lowers the opportunity cost— when you pay less for spaghetti, you give up fewer other things you could have spent the money on. Charging people more for pizza is a negative incentive to buy pizza, because they now have to give up more alternative purchases.

The Three Questions of Economic Organization

Because of scarcity, every society inescapably has to answer three questions:

What is to be produced?

As already stressed, in the presence of scarcity, producing more of one thing means producing less of another. A society therefore has to choose how many compact disc players, ballpoint pens, missiles, or any other commodity it is going to produce. This leads us to an important concept in economics: Opportunity cost. When more of commodity X is produced, resources are used up. These resources could have been used to produce alternative commodities. The most highly valued of these forgone alternatives is the **opportunity cost** of X. Essentially, the opportunity cost of something is *what you give up by having it.*

How is it to be produced?

In the children's story "The Three Little Pigs", we are told that a house may be constructed out of straw, sticks or brick. This illustrates the important point that even after deciding what we want to produce, we have to decide how to produce it. Should houses be constructed of wood or should brick be used instead, so that the wood can be used for fuel? Perhaps straw should be used for housing, but then less would be available for fodder for livestock. Given that all resources are scarce, society must decide which resources to allocate to the production of various commodities.

Who gets the output?

Because of scarcity, no one can have all of everything that he or she wants. Every society must develop some kind of mechanism for dividing up the output among its members. And in every society, the question of whether this mechanism leads to a "fair" distribution of the output is likely to be the subject of intense debate.

The way that our three questions are answered is referred to as ***the allocation of resources***—how society's resources are divided up among the various outputs, among the different organizations that produce these outputs, and among the members of society. Although every society has to decide how to allocate its resources, societies differ greatly in how these decisions are made. As noted earlier, in centrally planned economies these decisions are made by government bureau contrast, societies like Germany, France, the UK, the United States and Australia rely more heavily on a market system, in which resource allocation decisions are determined by the independent decisions of individual consumers and producers, without any central direction. Because the ***market system*** is the most important mechanism for resource allocation in western societies, it is the main focus of this book. Our goal is to understand how markets work, and to develop criteria for evaluating market outcomes.

An Economist's Problem–Solving Toolbox

Economic analysis requires us to combine theory with observations and to subject both to scrutiny before drawing conclusions. In this section we will see how to put theories and facts together to determine what causes what. We will also distinguish between the way things are and the way we think they should be. You can apply these tools to various situations, from personal life choices to business decisions and policy analysis.

Correlation and causation

This superstition is an exaggeration of a common human tendency: When we see that two events occur together, we tend to assume that one causes the other. Economists, however, try to be particularly careful about what causes what.

To differentiate between events that simply occur at the same time and events that share a clear cause–and–effect relationship, we use two different terms. When we observe a consistent relationship between two events or variables, we say there is a *correlation* between them. If both tend to occur at the same time or move in the same direction, we say they are positively correlated. Wearing raincoats is positively correlated with rain. If one event or variable increases while a related event or variable decreases, we say they are negatively correlated. They move in opposite directions. High temperatures are negatively correlated with people wearing down jackets. If there is no consistent relationship between two variables, we say they are *uncorrelated.*

Correlation differs from causation. *Causation* means that one event brings about the other. As the preceding examples show, causation and correlation often go together. Weather and clothing are often correlated, because weather causes people to make certain choices about the clothing they wear.

Unfortunately, correlation and causation do not always go together in a straight forward way. Correlation and causation can be confused in three major ways: Correlation without causation, omitted variables, and reverse causation.

Models

A *model* is a simplified representation of a complicated situation. In economics, models show how people, firms, and governments make decisions about managing resources, and how their decisions interact. An economic model can represent a situation as basic as how people decide what car to buy or as complex as what causes a global recession.

Because models simplify complex problems, they allow us to focus our attention on the most important parts. Models rarely include every detail of a given situation, but that is a good thing. If we had to describe the entire world with perfect accuracy before solving a problem, we'd be so overwhelmed with details that we'd never get the answer. By carefully simplifying the situation to its essentials, we can get useful answers that are approximately right.

One of the most basic models of the economy is ***the circular flow model***. The economy involves billions of transactions every day, and the circular flow model helps show how all of those transactions work together. The model slashes through complexity to show important patterns. Figure below shows the circular flow of economic transactions in a graphic format called the circular flow diagram. The first simplification of the circular flow model is to narrow our focus to the two most important types of actors in the economy, households and firms:

- *Households* are vital in two ways. First, they supply land and labor to firms and invest capital in firms. (Land, labor, and capital are called the factors of production.) Second they buy the goods and services that firms produce.
- *Firms* too are vital, but do the opposite of households: They buy or rent the land, labor, and capital supplied by households, and they produce and sell goods and services. The model shows that firms and households are tightly connected through both production and consumption.

In another helpful simplification, the circular flow model narrows the focus to two markets that connect households and firms:

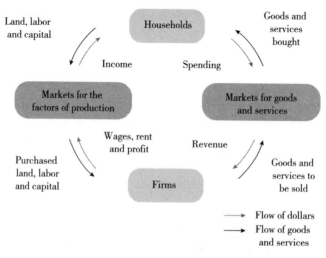

Figure 0-1 Circular flow diagram

- The *market for goods and services* is exactly what it sounds like: It reflects all of the activity involved in the buying and selling of goods and services. In this market, households spend their wages from labor and their income from land and capital, and firms earn revenue from selling their goods and services.
- The second market is the market for the factors of production. Here, households supply land, labor, and capital, and firms hire and purchase or rent these inputs.

The model puts all of this together. The transactions we have described are part of two loops. One is a loop of inputs and outputs as they travel throughout the economy. The inputs are the land, labor, and capital firms use to produce goods. The outputs are the goods and services that firms produce using the factors of production. We have already said that good models can leave out details that are not crucial, and focus on the important aspects of a situation.To be useful, a model should also do three things:

A good model predicts cause and effect. The circular flow model gives a useful description of the basics of the economy. Often, though, we want to go further. Many times we want a model not only to describe economic connections but also to predict how things will happen in the future. To do that, we have to get cause and effect right. If your model says that A causes B, you should be able to explain why. In Chapter 3 we'll learn about a central model in economics that shows that for most goods and services, the quantity people want to buy goes down as the price goes up. Why? As the cost of an item rises but the benefit of owning it remains the same, more people will decide that the trade–off is not worth it.

A good model makes clear assumptions. Although models are usually too simple to fit the real world perfectly, it's important that they be clear about the simplifying assumptions. Doing so helps us to know when the model will predict real events accurately and when it will not. For example, we said earlier that econo– mists often assume that people behave rationally. We know that isn't always true, but we accept it as an assumption because it is approximately accurate in many situations. As long as we are clear that we are making this assumption, we will know that the model will not be accurate when people fail to behave rationally.

A good model describes the real world accurately. If a model does not describe what actually happens in the real world, something about the model is wrong. We've admitted that models are not perfectly accurate, because they are inten–

tionally simpler than the real world. But if a model predicts things that are not usually or approximately true, it is not useful. How do we tell if a model is realistic? Economists test their models by observing what happens in the real world and collecting data, which they use to verify or reject the model. In the Real Life box "Testing models against history", take a look at a model that has been tested over and over again in the last few hundred years.

Positive economics versus Normative economics

When considering economic issues, we must carefully distinguish questions of fact from questions of fairness. Positive economics describes the facts of an economy, while normative economics involves value judgments.

Positive economics deals with questions such as: Why do doctors earn more than janitors? Did the North American Free Trade Agreement (NAFTA) raise or lower the incomes of most Americans? Do higher interest rates slow the economy and lower inflation? Although these may be difficult questions to answer, they can all be resolved by reference to analysis and empirical evidence. That puts them in the realm of positive economics.

Normative economics involves ethical precepts and norms of fairness. Should unemployment be raised to ensure that price inflation does not become too rapid? Should the United States negotiate further agreements to lower tariffs on imports? Has the distribution of income in the United States become too unequal? There are no right or wrong answers to these questions because they involve ethics and values rather than facts. While economic analysis can inform these debates by examining the likely consequences of alternative policies, the answers can be resolved only by discussions and debates over society's fundamental values.

1

Demand and Supply

Learning Objectives

LO 1.1   Draw a demand curve and describe the external factors that determine demand.

LO 1.2   Distinguish between a shift in and a movement along the demand curve.

LO 1.3   Draw a supply curve and describe the external factors that determine supply.

LO 1.4   Distinguish between a shift in and a movement along the supply curve.

LO 1.5   Explain how supply and demand interact to drive markets to equilibrium.

LO 1.6   Evaluate the effect of changes in supply and demand on the equilibrium price and quantity.

LO 1.7   Calculate price elasticity of demand using the mid–point method.Explain how the determinants of price elasticity of demand affect the degree of elasticity.

LO 1.8   Calculate price elasticity of supply using the mid–point method.Explain how the determinants of price elasticity of supply affect the degree of elasticity.

LO 1.9   Calculate other elasticity of demandand interpret the sign ofthe elasticity.

1.1　Demand

Demand *is an economic principle referring to the quantity of a good that consumers are willing and able to purchase at various prices during a given period of time.* Consumers not only have desires to purchase, but also have ability to pay the price. Holding all other factors constant, an increase in the price of a good or service will decrease the quantity demanded, and vice versa. Market demand is the total quantity demanded across all consumers in a market for a given good. Aggregate demand is the total demand for all goods and services in an economy.

Seen from many variables determine the quantity of pens a person demands, **the demand schedule** is table or formula that shows you how many units of a good or service consumers are willing to purchase (demand) at various prices, other things being the same. The law of demand describes that the quantity demanded of goods will be various at every price level. Thus, demand schedule is useful to represent the quantity of demand. Here is an example of a demand schedule:

Table 1–1　Demand Schedule

Price–quantity portfolio	A	B	C	D	E	F	G
Price (¥)	0	5	10	15	20	25	30
Quantity (cone)	12	10	8	6	4	2	0

Imagine that we hold all these variables constant except the price. Let's consider how the price affects the quantity of ice cream demanded. Table 1–1 shows how many ice–cream cones Mike buys each month at different prices of ice cream. If ice cream is free, Mike eats 12 cones. At ¥5 per cone, Mike buys 10 cones. As the price rises further, she buys fewer and fewer cones. When the price reaches ¥15, Mike doesn't buy any ice cream at all. Table 1–1 is a demand schedule, a table that shows the relationship between the price of a good and the quantity demanded. (Economists use the term schedule because the Table, with its parallel columns of numbers, resembles a train schedule.)

1.1.1 Determinants of demand

What determines the quantity an individual demands? Taking lipstick for example, how much how do girls decide how much lipstick to purchase yearly, and what factors affect their decision? There are some factors girls might consider. Undoubtfully, the first determinant is the price of the goods or service itself. The second is the price of related products, including complementary or substitutes. Additionally, circumstances drive the next three determinants: Consumer incomes, buyer's tastes or preferences and their expectations of price.

(1) *Price*. It is expected that the quantity demanded goes down, as the price goes up. If the price of grapes to ¥20 per kilogram, you would buy less grapes. You might buy banana or other fruit instead. You would buy more grapes, if the price fell to ¥10 per kilogram. *The notion that the quantity demanded of goods is normally negatively related to the price is called **the law of demand***.

But price is not the only determining factor. The law of demand is true only if all other determinants don't change. This requirement for the law of demand is called ceteris paribus, which means ***"all other things being the same"*** in Latin language. In other words, the law of demand states that the quantity demanded of a particular goods falls as price rises when other things are all held equal.

(2) *Prices of related goods.* Suppose that you find that the price of pen falls in the supermarket, the law of demand states that you will buy more pen to substitute for 1, given that pencil and pen are both sweet, juicy and common fruits, which are able to satisfy similar desires. Goods like pencil and pen are called ***substitutes***. An increase in the price of one good increase the demand for substitutes of this good. Conversely, the demand for substitutes will likely increase, if the price of one good declines.

Suppose that the price of pencils becomes more expensive. You will buy less pencils according to the law of demand. Yet, in this case, you will buy less erasers as well, because eraser and pencils are often used together. Goods like pencil and pen are called ***complements***. when the price of one good increase, the quantity demanded for complements of this good will rise as well. Conversely, when the price of one good decrease, the demand for complements of this good will go down as well.

(3) *Incomes.* Undoubtfully, changes in the amount of income you earn affects your quantity demanded for goods and services. Lower income you earn, less money you spend in total. Mostly, you would have to spend less on some goods and service. A good for which, other things being the same, the demand falls as income falls, is called a *normal good*. Most goods are normal goods, meaning that an increase in income causes an increase in demand and vice versa. In last case, pen is a normal good for most people. You are likely to buy more pens when your income rises. If you already have plenty of pens, you may buy some brand–name pens when your income increases.

Not all goods are normal goods. There is, in addition, a good for which, other things being the same, a decrease in income causes an increase in demand, is called *inferior goods*. When their incomes rise, people are supposed to replace inferior goods with more expensive and appealing substitutes and vice versa. Obviously, cars are more expensive and costly than motorcycle. However, most people choose to buy a car to take the place of motorcycle, with the economy developing.

(4) *Tastes.* Obviously, consumers' tastes or preference describe what the personal likes and dislikes, determining what they want to purchase. However, why people like what they like or to agree with their preferences doesn't matter for economists, what they need to know is just how these likes and dislikes affect buyers. Some consumers will buy more pens, if they prefer using pens. Because they can get more enjoyment out of writing with a pen, which are probably based on the sense of weight, or benefit for handwriting or any number of other personal preferences. Conversely, if you dislike pen, you buy less of it.

(5) *Expectations.* Your expectations about the future—especially whether the price will go up or not—may affect your demand for a good or service today. You will stockpile now if inflation is expected in the future, resulting in an increase in current demand. Taking pen as example, you are likely to buy more pens now if the price of pens increase tomorrow or you expect to have a higher income next month. Conversely, you will buy less pens today if you expect the price to fall tomorrow.

(6) *Number of buyers.* The number of buyers measure the size of market and also affects the market demand curve. In a market, an increase in the number of potential buyers will magnify the demand, while a reduction in the number of buyers tend to reduce it. The shift of major population, such as a drop in the new–born population or an increase in immigration, are able to cause nationwide changes in demand. The demand for pens and pencils also expands when the number of teenagers and college students increases.

Table 1-2　Determinants of Demand

Determinant	Examples of an increase in demand	Examples of a decrease in demand
Consumer preferences	A"Buy American" ad campaign appeals to national pride, increasing the demand for U.S.-made sneakers.	An outbreak of *E. coli* decreases the demand for spinach.
Prices of related goods	A decrease in the price of hot dogs increases the demand for relish, a complementary good.	A decrease in taxi fares decreases the demand for subway rides, a substitute good.
Incomes	An economic downturn lowers incomes, increasing the demand for ground beef, an inferior good.	An economic downturn lowers incomes, decreasing the demand for steak, a normal good.
Expectations	A hurricane destroys part of the world papaya crop, causing expectations that prices will rise and increasing the current demand for papayas.	An announcement that a new smartphone soon will be released decreases the demand for the current model.
Number of buyers	An increase in life expectancy increases the demand for nursing homes and medical care.	A falling birthrate decreases the demand for diapers.

1.1.2　Shifts in demand curve

On the demand curve, quantity goes on the x-axis (the horizontal axis) and price on the y-axis (the vertical axis) . The result is a downward-sloping line that reflects the inverse relationship between price and quantity. The demand curve in Figure 1-1 represents exactly the same information as the demand schedule. A graph that shows the quantities of a particular good or service that consumers will demand at various prices.

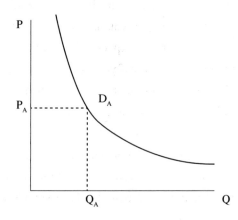

Figure 1-1　Demand curve

What happens to the demand curve when one of the five nonprice determinants of demand changes? The entire demand curve shifts, either to the right or to the left. The shift is horizontal rather than vertical, because nonprice determinants affect the quantity demanded at each price. The quantity demanded at a given price is now higher (or lower), so the point on the curve corresponding to that price is now further right (or left).

Consider what happens, for example, when the economy is growing and people's incomes are rising. The price of cell phones does not necessarily change, but more people will choose to buy a new one at any given price, causing quantity demanded to be higher at every possible price. Panel A of Figure 1-2 shows the resulting shift of the demand curve to the right, from DA to DB. In contrast, if the economy falls into a recession and people begin pinching pennies, quantity demanded will decrease at every price, and the curve will shift to the left, from DA to DC.

It is important to distinguish between these shifts in demand, which move the entire curve, and movements along a given demand curve. Remember this key point: **Shifts in the demand curve are caused by changes in the nonprice determinants of demand**. A recession, for example, would lower incomes and move the whole demand curve left. When we say "demand decreases," this is what we are talking about.

In contrast, suppose that the price of phones increases but everything else stays the same—that is, there is no change in the nonprice determinants of demand. Because the demand curve describes the quantity consumers will demand at any possible price, not just the current market price, we don't have to shift the curve to figure out what happens when the price goes up. Instead, we simply look at a different point on the curve to describe what is actually happening in the market right now.

To find the quantity that consumers will want to purchase at this new price, we move along the existing demand curve from the old price to the new one. If, for instance, the price of cell phones increases, we find the new quantity demanded by moving up along the demand curve to the new price point, as shown in panel B of Figure 1-2. The price change does not shift the curve itself, because the curve already describes what consumers will do at any price.

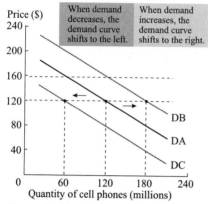

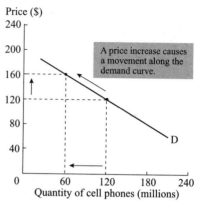

Changes in external factors cause the entire demand curve to shift. The shift from DA to DB represents an increase in demand, meaning that consumers want to buy more cell phones at each price. The shift from DA to DC represents a decrease in demand, meaning that consumers want to buy fewer cell phones at each price.

A price change causes a movement along the demand curve, but the curve itself remains constant.

(A) Shifts in the demand curve

(B) Movement along the demand curve

Figure 1-2　Movement along the demand curve versus shifts in the demand curve

To summarize, panel A of Figure 1-2 shows a shift in demand as the result of a change in the nonprice determinants; panel B shows a movement along the demand curve as the result of a change in price.

Economists use very specific terminology to distinguish between a shift in the demand curve and movement along the demand curve. We say that a change in one of the nonprice determinants of demand causes an "increase in demand" or "decrease in demand" —that is, a shift of the entire demand curve. To distinguish this from movement along the demand curve, we say that a change in price causes an "increase in quantity demanded" or "decrease in the quantity demanded." Just keep in mind that a "change in demand" is different from a "change in the quantity demanded." Observing this seemingly small difference in terminology prevents a great deal of confusion.

1.2　Supply

The concept of *supply* describes how much of a good or service producers will offer for sale under given circumstances. **The quantity supplied** is the amount of a particular good or service that producers will offer for sale at a given price during a *specified period.*

As with demand, we can find overall market supply by adding up the individual decisions of each producer. Imagine you own a factory that can produce cell phones or other consumer electronics. If the price of cell phones is ¥1100, you might decide there's good money to be made and use your entire factory space to produce cell phones. If the price is only ¥800, you might produce some cell phones but decide it will be more profitable to devote part of your factory to producing laptop computers. If the cell phone price drops to ¥550, you might decide you'd make more money by producing only lap-tops. Each producer will have a different price point at which it decides it's worthwhile to supply cell phones. This rule—*all else held equal, quantity supplied increases as price increases, and vice versa*—is called the **law of supply**. (In reality, it's costly to switch a factory from making cell phones to laptops or other goods. However, the simple version illustrates a basic truth: The higher the price of a good, the more of that good producers will want to sell.)

As with demand, supply varies with price because the decision to produce a good is about the trade-off between the benefit the producer will receive from selling the good and the opportunity cost of the time and resources that go into producing it. When the market price goes up and all other factors remain constant, the benefit of production increases relative to the opportunity cost, and the trade-off involved in production makes it more favorable to produce more. For instance, if the price of phones goes up and the prices of raw materials stay the same, existing phone producers may open new factories, and new companies may start looking to enter the cell phone market. The same holds true across other industries. If air travelers seem willing to pay higher prices, airlines will increase the frequency of flights, add new routes, and buy new planes so they can carry more passengers. When prices drop, they cut back their flight schedules and cancel their orders for new planes.

A supply schedule is a Table that shows the quantities of a particular good or service that producers will supply at various prices. *A supply curve* is a graph of the information in the supply schedule. Just as the demand curve showed consumers' willingness to buy, so the supply curve shows producers' willingness to sell: It shows the minimum price producers must receive to supply any given quantity. Figure 1-3 shows U.S. cell phone providers' supply schedule and their supply curve for cell phones.

Cell phones (millions)	Price ($)
270	180
240	160
210	140
180	120
150	100
120	80
90	60
60	40
30	20

This supply schedule shows the quantity of cell phones supplied each year at various prices. As prices decrease, suppliers want to produce fewer cell phones.

(A) Supply schedule

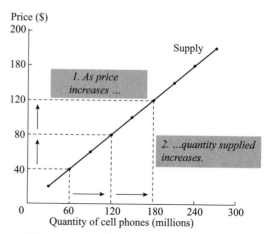

This supply curve is a graphic representation of the supply schedule for cell phones in the United States. It shows the quantity of cell phones that suppliers will produce at various prices.

(B) Supply curve

Figure 1-3　Supply schedule and the supply curve

The law of supply describes how the quantity that producers are willing to supply changes as price changes. But what determines the quantity supplied at any given price? As with demand, a number of nonprice factors determine the opportunity cost of production and therefore producers' willingness to supply a good or service. *When a nonprice determinant of supply changes, the entire supply curve will shift.* Such shifts reflect a change in the quantity of goods supplied at every price.

The nonprice determinants of supply can be divided into five major categories: Prices of related goods, technology, prices of inputs, expectations, and the number of sellers. Each of these factors determines the opportunity cost of production relative to a given benefit (i.e., the price) and therefore the trade-off that producers face. Table 1-3 shows how the supply of various products responds to changes in each determinant.

(1) *Prices of related goods.* Return to your factory, where you can produce either cell phones or laptops. Just as you chose to produce more laptops and fewer cell phones when the price of cell phones dropped, you would do the same if the price of laptops increased while the price of cell phones stayed constant.

The price of related goods determines supply because it affects the opportunity cost of production. When you choose to produce cell phones, you forgo the profits you would have earned from producing something else. If the price of that something else increases, the amount you forgo in profits also increases. For instance, imagine a farmer who can grow wheat or corn (or other crops, for that matter) on his land. If the price of corn increases, the quantity of wheat (the substitute crop) he is willing to grow falls, because each acre he devotes to wheat is one fewer acre he can use to grow corn.

(2) *Technology.* Improved technology enables firms to produce more efficiently, using fewer resources to make a given product. Doing so lowers production costs, increasing the quantity producers are willing to supply at each price. Improved technology has played a huge role in the changing popularity of cell phones. As technological innovation in the construction of screens, batteries, and mobile networks and in the processing of electronic data has leapt forward, the cost of producing a useful, consumer–friendly cell phone has plummeted. As a result, producers are now willing to supply more cell phones at lower prices.

(3) *Prices of inputs.* The prices of the inputs used to produce a good are an important part of its cost. When the prices of inputs increase, production costs rise, and the quantity of the product that producers are willing to supply at any given price decreases. Small amounts of silver and gold are used inside cell phones, for example. When the prices of these precious metals rise, the cost of manufacturing each cell phone increases, and the total number of units that producers collectively are willing to make at any given price goes down. Conversely, when input prices fall, supply increases.

(4) *Expectations.* Suppliers' expectations about prices in the future also affect quantity supplied. For example, when the price of real estate is expected to rise in the future, more real estate developers will wait to embark on construction projects, decreasing the supply of houses in the near future. When expectations change and real estate prices are projected to fall in the future, many of those projects will be rushed to completion, causing the supply of houses to rise.

(5) *Number of sellers.* The market supply curve represents the quantities of a product that a particular number of producers will supply at various prices in a given market. This means that the number of sellers in the market is considered to be one of the fixed parts of the supply curve. We've already seen that the sellers in the market will decide to supply more if the price of a good is higher. This does not mean that the number of sellers will change based on price in the short run.

There are, however, nonprice factors that cause the number of sellers to change in a market and move the supply curve. For example, suppose cell phone producers must meet strict licensing requirements. If those licensing requirements are dropped, more companies may enter the market, willing to supply a certain number of cell phones at each price. These additional phones must be added to the number of cell phones existing producers are already willing to supply at each price point.

Table 1-3　Determinants of supply

Determinant	Examples of an increase in supply	Examples of a decrease in supply
Price of related goods	The price of gas rises, so an automaker increases its production of smaller, more fuel-efficient cars.	The price of clean energy production falls, so the power company reduces the amount of power it supplies using coal power plants.
Technology	The installation of robots increases productivity and lowers costs; the supply of goods increases.	New technology allows corn to be made into ethanol, so farmers plant more corn and fewer soybeans; the supply of soybeans decreases.
Prices of inputs	A drop in the price of tomatoes decreases the production cost of salsa; the supply of salsa increases.	An increase in the minimum wage increases labor costs at food factories; the supply of processed food decreases.
Expectations	Housing prices are expected to rise, so builders increase production; the supply of houses increases.	New research points to the health benefits of eating papayas, leading to expectations that the demand for papayas will rise. More farmers plant papayas, increasing the supply.
Number of sellers	Subsidies make the production of corn more profitable, so more farmers plant corn; the supply of corn increases.	New licensing fees make operating a restaurant more expensive; some small restaurants close, decreasing the supply of restaurants.

Shifts in the supply curve

Just as with demand, changes in price cause suppliers to move to a different point on the same supply curve, while changes in the nonprice determinants of supply shift the supply curve itself. A change in a nonprice determinant increases or decreases supply, while a change in price increases or decreases the quantity supplied.

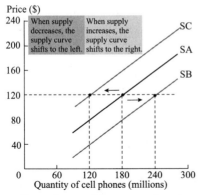

Changes in external factors cause the entire supply curve to shift. The shift from SA to SB represents an increase in supply, meaning that producers are willing to supply more cell phones at each price. The shift from SA to SC represents a decrease in supply, meaning that producers are willing to supply fewer cell phones at each price.

A price change causes a movement along the supply curve, but the curve itself remains constant.

(A) Shifts in the supply curve　　　　　　(B) Movement along the supply curve

Figure 1–4　Movement along the supply curve versus shifts in the supply curve

A change in one of the nonprice determinants increases or decreases the supply at any given price. These shifts are shown in panel A of Figure 1–4. An increase in supply shifts the curve to the right. A decrease in supply shifts the curve to the left. For instance, an improvement in battery technology that decreases the cost of producing cell phones will shift the entire supply curve to the right, from SA to SB, so that the quantity of phones supplied at every price is higher than before. Conversely, an increase in the price of the gold needed for cell phones raises production costs, shifting the supply curve to the left, from SA to SC.

As with demand, we differentiate these shifts in the supply curve from a movement along the supply curve, which is shown in panel B of Figure 1-4. If the price of cell phones changes, but the nonprice determinants of supply stay the same, we find the new quantity supplied by moving along the supply curve to the new price point.

1.3　Market equilibrium

We've discussed the factors that influence the quantities supplied and demanded by producers and consumers. To find out what actually happens in the market, however, we need to combine these concepts. The prices and quantities of the goods that are exchanged in the real world depend on the interaction of supply with demand.

Bear with us for a moment as we point out the obvious: There is no sale without a purchase. You can't sell something unless someone buys it. Although this point may be obvious, the implication for markets is profound. When markets work well, the quantity supplied exactly equals the quantity demanded.

Graphically, *this convergence of supply with demand happens at the point wherethe demand curve intersects the supply curve, a point* called the **market equilibrium**. The price at this point is called the **equilibrium price**, and the quantity at this point is called the **equilibrium quantity**. We can think of this intersection, where quantity supplied equals quantity demanded, as the point at which buyers and sellers "agree" on the quantity of a good they are willing to exchange at a given price. At higher prices, sellers want to sell more than buyers want to buy. At lower prices, buyers want to buy more than sellers are willing to sell. Because every seller finds a buyer at the equilibrium price and quantity, and no one is left standing around with extra goods or an empty shopping cart, the equilibrium price is sometimes called **the market–clearing price**.

1.3.1　Reaching equilibrium

Figure1-5 shows two graphs, one in which the starting price is above the equilibrium price and the other in which it is below the equilibrium price. In panel A, we imagine that cell phone suppliers think they'll be able to charge $160 for a cell phone, so they produce 240 million phones, but they find that consumers will buy only 60 million.（We can read the quantities demanded and supplied at a price of $160 from the demand and supply curves.）*When the quantity supplied is higher than the quantity demanded,* we say that there is a **surplus** of phones, or an **excess supply**. Manufacturers are stuck holding extra phones in their warehouses; they want to sell that stock and must reduce the price to attract more customers. They have an incentive to keep lowering the price until quantity demanded increases to reach quantity supplied.

In panel B of Figure 1-5 we imagine that cell phone producers make the opposite mistake—they think they'll be able to charge only $40 per phone. They make only 60 million cell phones, but discover that consumers actually are willing to buy 240 million cell phones at that price. *When the quantity demanded is higher than the*

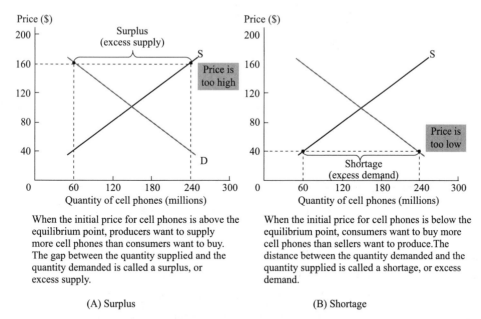

When the initial price for cell phones is above the equilibrium point, producers want to supply more cell phones than consumers want to buy. The gap between the quantity supplied and the quantity demanded is called a surplus, or excess supply.

When the initial price for cell phones is below the equilibrium point, consumers want to buy more cell phones than sellers want to produce.The distance between the quantity demanded and the quantity supplied is called a shortage, or excess demand.

(A) Surplus

(B) Shortage

Figure 1–5   Reaching equilibrium in the market for cell phone

quabtity supplied, we say there is *a shortage*, or *excess demand.* Producers will see long lines of people waiting to buy the few available cell phones, and will quickly realize that they could make more money by charging a higher price. They have an incentive to increase the price until quantity demanded decreases to equal quantity supplied, and no one is left standing in line.

Thus, at any price above or below the equilibrium price, sellers face an incentive to raise or lower prices. No one needs to engineer the market equilibrium or share secret information about what price to charge. Instead, money–making incentives drive the market toward the equilibrium price, at which there is neither a surplus nor a shortage.

1.3.2   Changes in equilibrium

We've seen what happens to the supply and demand curves when a nonprice factor changes. Because the equilibrium price and quantity are determined by the inter– action of supply and demand, a shift in either curve will also change the market equilibrium. Some changes will cause only the demand curve to shift; some, only the supply curve. Some changes will affect both the supply and demand curves.

To determine the effect on market equilibrium of a change in a nonprice factor, ask yourself a few questions:

A. Does the change affect demand? If so, does demand increase or decrease?

B. Does the change affect supply? If so, does supply increase or decrease?

C. How does the combination of changes in supply and demand affect the equilibrium price and quantity?

HINT

Remember,when we say that supply or demand increases or decreases, we're referring to a *shift in the entire curve*,not a movement along it,which is a change in quantity demanded.

i. ***Shifts in demand.*** We suggested earlier that landline service is a substitute for cell phones and that if the price of landline service suddenly skyrockets, then demand for cell phones increases. In other words, the demand curve shifts to the right. The price of landline service probably doesn't affect the supply of cell phones, because it doesn't change the costs or expectations that cell phone manufacturers face. So, the supply curve stays put. Figure 1–6 shows the effect of the increase in landline price on the market equilibrium for cell phones. Because the new demand curve intersects the supply curve at a different point, the equilibrium price and quantity change. The new equilibrium price is $120, and the new equilibrium quantity is 180 million.

We can summarize this effect in terms of the three questions to ask following a change in a nonprice factor:

A. Does demand increase/decrease? Yes, the change in the price of landlines phone service increases demand for cell phones at every price.

B. Does supply increase/decrease? No, the change in the price of landline phone service does not affect any of the nonprice determinants of supply. The supply curve stays where it is.

C. How does the combination of changes in supply and demand affect equilibrium price and quantity?

The increase in demand shifts the demand curve to the right, pushing the equilibrium to a higher point on the stationary supply curve. The new point at which supply and demand "agree" represents a price of $120 and a quantity of 180 million phones.

ii. ***Shifts in supply.*** What would happen if a breakthrough in battery technology enabled cell phone manufacturers to construct phones with the same battery life for less money? Once again, asking How will others respond? helps us predict the market response. We can see that the new technology does not have much impact on demand: Customers probably have no idea how much the batteries in their phones cost to make, nor will they care as long as battery life stays the same. However, cheaper batteries definitely decrease production costs, increasing the number of phones manufacturers are willing to supply at any given price. So, the demand curve stays where it is, and the supply curve shifts to the right. Figure 1–6 shows the shift in supply and the new equilibrium point. The new supply curve intersects the demand curve at a new equilibrium point, representing a price of $80 and a quantity of 180 million phones.

Once again, we can analyze the effect of the change in battery technology on the market for cell phones in three steps:

A. Does demand increase/decrease? No, the nonprice determinants of demand are not affected by battery technology.

B. Does supply increase/decrease? Yes, supply increases, because the new battery technology lowers production costs.

C. How does the combination of changes in supply and demand affect equilibrium price and quantity?

The increase in supply shifts the supply curve to the right, pushing the equilibrium to a lower point on the stationary demand curve. The new equilibrium price and quantity are $80 and 180 million phones.

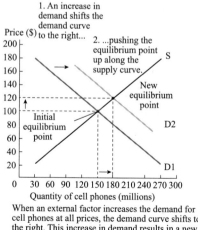

When an external factor increases the demand for cell phones at all prices, the demand curve shifts to the right. This increase in demand results in a new equilibrium point. Consumers purchase more cell phones at a higher price.

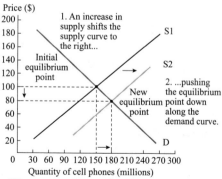

When an external factor affects the supply of cell phones at all prices, the supply curve shifts. In this example, supply increases and the market reaches a new equilibrium point. Consumers purchase more phones at a lower price.

Figure 1–6   Shift in demand and supply for cell phones

Table1-4 summarizes the effect of some other changes in demand or supply on the equilibrium price and quantity.

Table 1-4　Effect of changes in demand or supply on the equilibrium price and quantity

Example of change in demand or supply	Effect on equilibrium price and quantity	Shift in curve
A successful "Buy American" advertising campaign increases the demand for Fords.	The demand curve shifts to the right. The equilibrium price and quantity increase.	
An outbreak of E. coli reduces the demand for spinach.	The demand curve shifts to the left. The equilibrium price and quantity decrease.	
The use of robots decreases production costs.	The supply curve shifts to the right. The equilibrium price decreases, and the equilibrium quantity increases.	
An increase in the minimum wage increases labor costs.	The supply curve shifts to the left. The equilibrium price incrcases, and the equilibrium quantity decreases.	

iii. *Shifts in both demand and supply.* In our discussion so far, we've covered examples in which only demand or supply shifted. However, it's possible that factors that shift demand (such as a hike in landline cost) and supply (such as an improvement in battery technology) in the market for cell phones could coincidentally happen at the same time. It's also possible that a single change could affect both supply and demand.

For instance, suppose that in addition to reducing the cost of production, the new battery technology makes cell phone batteries last longer. We already know that cheaper batteries will increase supply. As we saw before with increases in supply, price decrease while the quantity increases. Asking how consumers will respond allows us to see that the improvement in battery life will also increase demand, because longer–lasting batteries will make a cell phone more valuable to consumers at any given price. As a result, both the demand curve and the supply curve shift to the right. Panel A and B of Figure 1–7 both show that the effect of a double change is a new equilibrium point at a higher price and a higher quantity.

When supply and demand move in the same direction, we can predict the direction of the change in quantity but not the direction of the change in price. When supply and demand move in opposite directions, the change in price is predictable, but not the change in quantity. Applying this reasoning to opposite shifts in supply and demand—when one increases but the other decreases—is trickier. To find out what buyers

An increase in supply and demand shifts both curves to the right, resulting in a higher quantity traded. However, the direction of the price shift depends on whether supply or demand increases more.

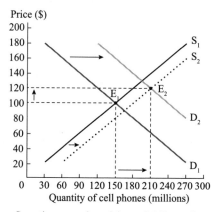

Sometimes, supply and demand shift together. In this example, both curves shift to the right, but demand increases more. At the new equilibrium point, E₂, consumers purchase more cell phones at a higher price.

(A) Demand increases more

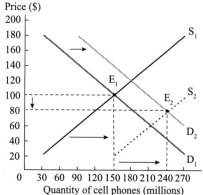

Sometimes, supply and demand shift together. In this example, both curves shift to the right, but supply increases more. At the new equilibrium point, E₂, consumers purchase more cell phones at a lower price.

(B) Supply increases more

Supply change	Demand change	Price change	Quantity change	
Decrease	Decrease	?	↓	Predicting changes in price and quantity when supply and demand change simultaneously
Decrease	Increase	↑	?	
Increase	Increase	?	↑	
Increase	Decrease	↓	?	

Figure 1–7   Shift in both demand and supply

and sellers "agree" on, try rephrasing what it means for demand to increase. One way to say it is that consumers are willing to buy a higher quantity at the same price.

Another way to say it is that consumers are willing to pay a higher price to buy the same quantity. So, when demand increases and supply decreases, buyers are willing to pay more for the same quantity; also, sellers are willing to sell the same quantity only if they receive a higher price. The opposite is true when demand decreases and supply increases. Buyers are willing to buy the same quantity as before only if the price is lower, and sellers are willing to supply the same quantity at a lower price. Because the two groups can "agree" on a lower price at any given quantity, we can predict that the price will decrease.

1.4 Elasticity

1.4.1 Price elasticity of demand

Price elasticity of demand is defined as the measure of elasticity of demand based on price which is derived by dividing the percentage change in quantity ($\Delta D/D$) by percentage change in price ($\Delta P/P$) .

Price elasticity of demand = % change in demand / % change in price

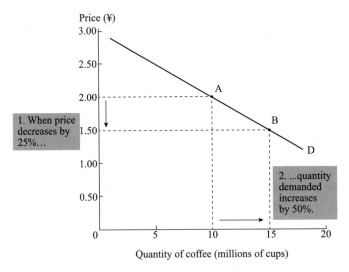

Figure 1-8　Elasticity of the demand for coffee

Point elasticity and arc elasticity

Point elasticity of demand is *the ratio of percentage change in quantity demanded of a good to percentage change in its price calculated at a specific point on the demand curve.*

Point elasticity of demand is actually not a new type of elasticity. It is just one of the two methods of calculation of elasticity, the other being arc elasticity of demand. All major measures of elasticity i.e. (price) elasticity of supply, income elasticity, cross elasticity of demand/supply have their point elasticity and arc elasticity versions even though point elasticity method is simpler and more popular method.

In order to understand the difference between point elasticity and arc elasticity, let's consider the market for public transportation in Market XYZ. Let's assume that if cost of a trip changes from $2 (P_0) to $3 (P_1) , passenger demand per day falls from 0.5 million (Q_0) to 0.4 million (Q_1) .

Elasticity of demand is defined as the percentage change in quantity demanded divided by percentage change in price:

Equation 1-1

$$E_d = \Delta Q\% / \Delta P\%$$

The percentages are most commonly defined with reference to P_0 and Q_0 and this gives us the price elasticity of demand for public transportation of -0.4.

$$E_d = \Delta Q\% / \Delta P\% = (0.4 - 0.5) \ / 0.5$$

$$E_d = \frac{\Delta Q\%}{\Delta P\%} = \frac{(0.4 - 0.5)}{0.5} \div \frac{(\$3 - \$2)}{\$2}$$

$$= -0.1 \times \frac{\$2}{0.5} = -0.4$$

Now, imagine if the price movement is opposite i.e. if price decreases from ¥3 to ¥2 and passenger demand increases. In this case, the calculation of elasticity of demand would be as follows:

$$E_d = \frac{\Delta Q\%}{\Delta P\%} = \frac{(0.5 - 0.4)}{0.4} \div \frac{(\$2 - \$3)}{\$3}$$

$$= -0.1 \times \frac{\$3}{0.4} = -0.75$$

Just using a different starting point for the price movement has caused a roughly 100% increase in elasticity which doesn't sound right. The formula for the price elasticity itself shows that the elasticity of demand at a point on a curve depends on the ratio of change in quantity demanded to change in price and on the ratio of initial price and quantity at the point on the curve on which we want to calculate elasticity. If the difference between P_0 and P_1 or Q_0 and Q_1 is high, our estimate for price elasticity will not be accurate.

Arc elasticity

One way to address the sensitivity of point elasticity to starting price and quantity is to calculate the arc elasticity. The arc elasticity of demand is calculated by finding percentage based on average of the starting and closing prices and quantities. The arc price elasticity of demand for the public transport in Market XYZ would be -0.55:

$$E_d = \frac{Q_1-Q_0}{\frac{(Q_1+Q_0)}{2}} \div \frac{P_1-P_0}{\frac{(P_1+P_0)}{2}}$$

$$= \frac{0.4-0.5}{\frac{(0.4+0.5)}{2}} \div \frac{\$3-\$2}{\frac{(\$3+\$2)}{2}} = \frac{-0.1}{0.45} \div \frac{\$1}{\$2.5} = -0.55$$

The arc elasticity method of elasticity calculation is also called ***mid–point method.***

Where the change in price or quantity demanded is large, arc elasticity method is an improvement on the point method of calculation. However, where the change is small, point elasticity of demand is preferred.

Equation 1-2

$$E_d = dQ/dP \times (P/Q)$$

Where dQ/dP is the first derivative of the demand curve/function. It measures the change in quantity demanded for very small change in price at price P. Since dQ/dP can be calculated at an exact point on a curve, the above equation gives a better estimate of elasticity.

Different level of elasticity

At the extremes, demand can be perfectly elastic or perfectly inelastic. When demand is **perfectly elastic**, the demand curve is horizontal, as shown in panel A of Figure 1–9. This graph indicates that *consumers are very sensitive to price, because demand drops to zero when the price increases even a minuscule amount.*

When demand is *perfectly inelastic*, the demand curve is vertical, as shown in panel B of Figure 1–9. In this case, *the quantity demanded is the same no matter what the price.*

These two extremes rarely occur in real life. Between these two extremes, elasticity is commonly divided into three quantifiable categories: Elastic, inelastic, and unit–elastic. When the absolute value of the price elasticity of demand is greater than 1, we call the associated ***demand elastic***. With elastic demand, a given percentage change in the price of a good will cause an even larger percentage change in the quantity demanded. For example, a 40 percent change in price might lead to a 60 percent change in the quantity demanded. Panel A of Figure 1–9 illustrates elastic demand.

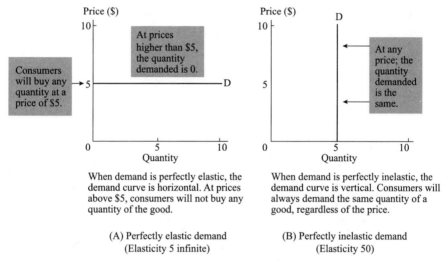

When demand is perfectly elastic, the demand curve is horizontal. At prices above $5, consumers will not buy any quantity of the good.

When demand is perfectly inelastic, the demand curve is vertical. Consumers will always demand the same quantity of a good, regardless of the price.

(A) Perfectly elastic demand
(Elasticity 5 infinite)

(B) Perfectly inelastic demand
(Elasticity 50)

Figure 1–9   Perfectly elastic and perfectly inelastic demand

When the absolute value of the price elasticity of demand is less than 1, we say that demand is ***inelastic***. With inelastic demand, a given percentage change in price will cause a smaller percentage change in the quantity demanded. For example, a 40 percent change in price might lead to a 20 percent change in the quantity demanded. Panel B of Figure 1–10 illustrates inelastic demand.

If the absolute value of elasticity is exactly 1—that is, if a percentage change in price causes the same percentage change in the quantity demanded—then we say that demand is unit–elastic. In this case, a 40 percent change in price leads to a 40 percent change in the quantity demanded. Panel C of Figure 1–10 illustrates unit–elastic demand.

Determinants of price elasticity of demand

The underlying idea here is that consumers are more sensitive to price changes for some goods and services than for others. Why isn't price elasticity of demand the same for all goods and services? Many factors determine consumers' responsiveness to price changes. The availability of substitutes, relative need and relative cost, and the time needed to adjust to price changes all affect price elasticity of demand.

(1)*Availability of substitutes.* Recall from Chapter 3 that substitutes are goods that are distinguishable from one another, but have similar uses. When the price of a good with a close substitute increases, consumers will buy the substitute instead. If close substitutes are available for a particular good, then the demand for that good will be more elastic than if only distant substitutes are available. For example, the price elasticity of demand for cranberry juice is likely to be relatively elastic; if the price gets too high, many consumers may switch to grape juice.

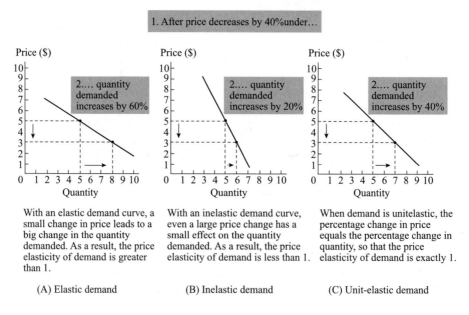

Figure 1–10   Elastic, inelastic, and unit–elastic demand

(2)*Degree of necessity.* When a good is a basic necessity, people will buy it even if prices rise. The demand for socks probably is not very elastic, nor is the demand for home heating during the winter. Although people may not like it when the prices of these goods rise, they will buy them to maintain a basic level of comfort. And when prices fall, they probably won't buy vastly more socks or make their homes a lot hotter.

In comparison, the demand for luxuries like vacations, expensive cars, and jewelry is likely to be much more elastic. Most people can easily do without these goods when their prices rise. Note, however, that the definition of a necessity depends on your standards and circumstances. In Florida, air conditioning may be a necessity and heating a luxury; the opposite is likely to be true in Alaska.

(3) *Cost relative to income.* All else held equal, if consumers spend a very small share of their incomes on a good, their demand for the good will be less elastic than otherwise. For instance, most people can get a year's supply of salt for just a few dollars. Even if the price doubled, a year's supply would still cost less than $10, so consumers probably would not bother to adjust their salt consumption.

The opposite is also true: If a good cost a very large proportion of a person's income, like going on a luxury three–week vacation to the beach, the demand for the good will be more elastic. If the price of rooms at high–end beach–front hotels doubles, then a lot of people will decide to do something else with their vacations.

(4) *Adjustment time.* Goods often have much more elastic demand over the long run than over the short run. Often, adjusting to price changes takes some time. Consider how you might react to an increase in the price of gasoline. In the short run, you might cancel a weekend road trip, but you would still have to do the same amount of driving as usual to school, work, or the grocery store. Over a year, however, you could consider other choices that would further reduce your consumption of gas, such as buying a bus pass or a bicycle, getting a more fuel-efficient car, or moving closer to work or school.

(5) *Scope of the market.* A major caveat to the determinants just described is that each depends on how you define the market for a good or service. The price elasticity of demand for bananas might be high, but the price elasticity of demand for fruit could still be low, because there are more substitutes for bananas than for the broader category of fruit. Similarly, although water might have a very low–price elasticity of demand as a basic necessity, the demand for bottled water could be extremely elastic.

1.4.2 Price elasticity of supply

Price elasticity of supply is the size of the change in the quantity supplied of a good or service when its price changes. Price elasticity of supply measures producers' responsiveness to a change in price, just as price elasticity of demand measures consumers' responsiveness to a change in price.

Equation 1-3

Es=percentage change in quantity supplied/percentage change in price

There is one important difference between the elasticities of supply and demand: The price elasticity of demand is always negative, and the price elasticity of supply is always positive. The reason is simple: The quantity demanded always moves in the opposite direction from the price, but the quantity supplied moves in the same direction as the price.

In extreme cases, we can also describe supply as being perfectly elastic (if the quantity supplied could be anything at a given price, and is zero at any other price) , or perfectly inelastic (if the quantity supplied is the same, regardless of the price) .

As with the price elasticity of demand, we can describe the price elasticity of supply using three categories:

● *Elastic*, if it has an absolute value greater than 1.

● *Inelastic,* if it has an absolute value less than 1.

● *Unit–elastic*, if it has an absolute value of exactly 1.

Determinants of price elasticity of supply

(1) *Availability of inputs.* The production of some goods can be expanded easily, just by adding extra inputs. For example, a bakery can easily buy extra flour and yeast to produce more bread, probably at the same cost per loaf. Increasing the supply of other goods is more difficult, however, and sometimes is impossible. If the price of Picasso paintings goes up, there isn't much anyone can do to produce more of them, since we cannot bring the artist back to life.

In other words, the elasticity of supply depends on the elasticity of the supply of inputs. If producing more of a good will cost a lot more than the initial quantity did, because the extra inputs will be harder to find, then the producer will be reluctant to increase the quantity supplied. Higher and higher prices will be needed to convince the producer to go to the extra trouble.

(2) *Flexibility of the production process.* The easiest way for producers to adjust the quantity supplied of a particular good is to draw production capacity away from other goods when prices rise, or to reassign capacity to other goods when prices fall. Farmers may find this sort of substitution relatively simple: When corn prices are high, they will plant more acres with corn; when corn prices are low, they will reassign acres to more profitable crops. Other producers have much less flexibility. If you own a company that manufactures specialized parts for Toyota, you might need to buy new machinery to begin making parts for Ford, let alone switch to another type of product entirely.

(3) *Adjustment time.* As with demand, supply is more elastic over long periods than over short periods. That is, producers can make more adjustments in the long run than in the short run. In the short run, the number of hotel rooms at Disneyland is fixed; in the medium and long run, old rooms can be renovated and new hotels can be built. Production capacity can also increase or decrease over time as new firms start up or old ones shut down.

1.4.3　Other elasticity

1.4.3.1　Cross–price elasticity of demand

Cross–price elasticity of demand describes how the quantity demanded of one good change when the price of a different good changes.

Cross–price elasticity of demand =% change in Q_A /% change in price of Q_B

If CPE > 0, then the two goods are substitutes. For example: Coke and Pepsi

If CPE < 0, then they are compliments. For example: Bread and Butter

If CPE = 0, then they are unrelated. For example: Bread and Soda

(1) *Substitute products. When two goods are **substitutes**, we expect their cross–price elasticity of demand to be positive.* That is, an increase in the price of one will cause an increase in the quantity demanded of the other. On the other hand, a decrease in the price of one good will cause a decrease in the quantity demanded of the other. Just how elastic it is depends on how close the two substitutes are. If they are very close substitutes, a change in the price of one will cause a large change in the quantity demanded of the other, so that cross–price elasticity will be high. If they are not close substitutes, cross–price elasticity will be low.

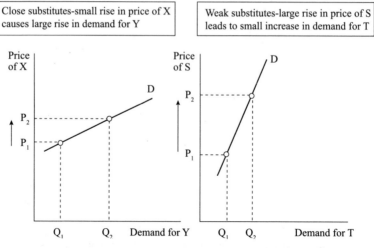

Figure 1-11   Cross Price Elasticity of Demand – Substitutes

（2）*Complementary products.* If in case one good is complementary to the other good, then a decrease in the price of one good will lead to an increase in demand for the complementary good. The stronger the relationship between the two products, the higher will be the coefficient of cross–price elasticity of demand. For example, game consoles and software games are examples of complementary goods. It is to be noted that the cross elasticity will be negative for complementary goods.

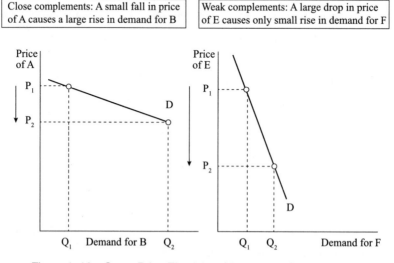

Figure 1-12   Cross Price Elasticity of Demand – Complements

（3）*Unrelated products.* In case there is no relationship between the goods, then an increase in the price of one good will not affect the demand for the other product. As such, unrelated products have a zero–cross elasticity. For example, the effect of changes in taxi fares on the market demand for milk.

1.4.3.2   Income elasticity of demand

Income elasticity of demand refers to the sensitivity of the quantity demanded for a certain good to a change in real income of consumers who buy this good, keeping all other things constant. The formula for calculating income elasticity of demand is the percent change in quantity demanded divided by the percent change in income. With income elasticity of demand, you can tell if a particular good represents a necessity or a luxury.

Wat is the formula for calculating income elasticity of demand?

The formula for calculating income elasticity is:

Equation 1-4

Income elasticity of demand =% Change in demand /the % change in income

(1) *Explain normal goods.* Normal goods have a positive income elasticity of demand so as consumers' income rises more is demanded at each price i.e. there is an outward shift of the demand curve.

Normal necessities have an income elasticity of demand of between 0 and +1 for example, if income increases by 10% and the demand for fresh fruit increases by 4% then the income elasticity is +0.4. Demand is rising less than proportionately to income.

Luxury goods and services have an income elasticity of demand > +1 i.e. demand rises more than proportionate to a change in income—for example an 8% increase in income might lead to a 10% rise in the demand for new kitchens. The income elasticity of demand in this example is +1.25.

(2) *Explain inferior goods.* Inferior goods have a negative income elasticity of demand meaning that demand falls as income rises. Typically, inferior goods or services exist where superior goods are available if the consumer has the money to be able to buy it. Examples include the demand for cigarettes, low–priced own label foods in supermarkets and the demand for council–owned properties.

Conclusion

By the time you reach the end of this course, you'll be quite familiar with the words supply and demand. We take our time on this subject for good reason:

An understanding of supply and demand is the foundation of economic problem solving. You'll be hard-pressed to make wise economic choices without it.

Although markets are not always perfectly competitive, you may be surprised at how accurately many real-world phenomena can be described using the simple rules of supply and demand. In the next chapters we'll use these rules to explain how consumers and producers respond to price changes and government policies.

Supply and demand may be the most common words in economics, but applying these concepts to the real world requires a bit of elaboration. Elasticity is the first of several concepts we will study that will help you to apply the concepts of supply and demand to business and policy questions. In this chapter we saw how elasticity can be used to set prices so as to maximize revenue. In the coming chapters we will use elasticity to predict the effects of government intervention in the market, and we will dig deeper into the consumer and producer choices that drive elasticity.

Key Term

Quantity Demanded	Substitutes	Quantity Supplied
Law of Demand	Complements	Law of Supply
Demand Schedule	Normal Goods	Supply Schedule
Demand Curve	Inferior Goods	Supply Curve
Equilibrium Price	Mid-point Method Perfectly	Total Revenue
Equilibrium Quantity	Elastic Demand	Price Elasticity of Supply
Surplus (Excess Supply)	Perfectly Inelastic Demand	Cross-price Elasticity of
Shortage (Excess Demand)	Elastic	Demand
Elasticity	Inelastic	Income Elasticity of
Price Elasticity of Demand	Unit-elastic	Demand

Review Questions

1. Explain why a demand curve slopes downward.
2. Explain why a supply curve slopes upward.
3. Explain why the equilibrium price is often called the market-clearing price.
4. You are advising a coffee shop manager who wants to estimate how much sales will change if the price of a latte rises. Explain why he should measure

elasticity in percentage terms rather than in terms of dollars and cups.

5. Explain why the coffee shop manager should measure elasticity using the mid–point method in his calculations.

6. Name two related goods you consume which would have a positive cross–price elasticity. What happens to your consumption of the second good if the price of the first good increases?

7. Name two related goods you consume which would have a negative cross–price elasticity. What happens to your consumption of the second good if the price of the first good increases?

8. Consider the following events:

a. The price of cell phones goes down by 25 percent during a sale.

b. You get a 25 percent raise at your job.

Which event represents a shift in the demand curve? Which represents a movement along the curve? What is the difference?

9. Consider the following events:

a. A maggot infestation ruins a large number of apple orchards in Washington state.

b. Demand for apples goes down, causing the price to fall.

10. Which event represents a shift in the supply curve? Which represents a movement along the curve? What is the difference?

11. In each of the following examples, name the fac– tor that affects demand and describe its impact on your demand for a new cell phone.

a. You hear a rumor that a new and improved model of the phone you want is coming out next year.

b. Your grandparents give you $500.

c. A cellular network announces a holiday sale on a text–messaging package that includes the purchase of a new phone.

d. A friend tells you how great his new cellphone is and suggests that you get one, too.

Application

1.Using the demand schedule in table below, draw the daily demand curve for slices of pizza in a college town.

Price（$）	Quantity demanded（slices）
0.00	350
0.50	300
1.00	250
1.50	200
2.00	150
2.50	100
3.00	50
3.50	0

2. Consider the market for cars. Which determinant of supply is affected by each of the following events? Choose from: prices of related goods, technology, prices of inputs, expectations, and the number of sellers in the market.

a. A steel tariff increases the price of steel.

b. Improvements in robotics increase efficiency and reduce costs.

c. Factories close because of an economic downturn.

d. The government announces a plan to offer tax rebates for the purchase of commuter rail tickets.

e. The price of trucks falls, so factories produce more cars.

3.Consider the market for corn. Say whether each of the following events will cause a shift in the supply curve or a movement along the curve. If it will cause a shift, specify the direction.

a. A drought hits corn–growing region.

b. The government announces a new subsidy for biofuels made from corn.

c. A global recession reduces the incomes of consumers in poor countries, who rely on corn as a staple food.

d. A new hybrid variety of corn seed causes a 15 percent increase in the yield of corn per acre.

e. An advertising campaign by the beef producers' association highlights the health benefits of corn–fed beef.

Problems 4 and 5 refer to the demand schedule shown in Table 2P–2. For each price change, say whether demand is elastic, unit–elastic, or inelastic, and say whether total revenue increases, decreases, or stays the same.

4. Price increases from $10 to $20. Demand is _____ and total revenue_____.

5. Price decreases from $70 to $60. Demand is_____ and total revenue_____.

Price ($)	Quantity demanded
80	0
70	50
60	100
50	150
40	200
30	250
20	300
10	350
0	400

Problems 6–9 refer to the figure below.

6. Draw the price effect and the quantity effect for a price change from $60 to $50. Which effect is larger? Does total revenue increase or decrease? No calculation is necessary.

7. Draw the price effect and the quantity effect for a price change from $30 to $20. Which effect is larger? Does total revenue increase or decrease? No calculation is necessary.

8. Draw the price effect and the quantity effect for a price change from $60 to $70. Which effect is larger? Does total revenue increase or decrease? No calculation is necessary.

9. Draw the price effect and the quantity effect for a price change from $10 to $20. Which effect is larger? Does total revenue increase or decrease? No calculation is necessary.

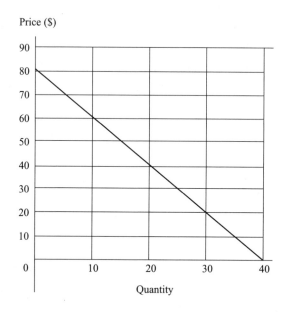

10. In each of the following instances, determine whether the good is normal or inferior, and whether it is income-elastic or income-inelastic.

a. If income increases by 10 percent and thequantity demanded of a good increase by5 percent, the good is and_____.

b. If income increases by 10 percent and the quantity demanded of a good decrease by 20 percent, the good is and_____.

2

Consumer Choice

Everyone is a consumer as we need to make consumption decisions almost every day. One of the most common cases is when you step into a grocery shop to buy food for dinner tonight. Although you are facing with thousands of goods, you are still limited by the cash in your pocket or the amount left in your cards. As we are all rational, or assumed to be rational, we would like to buy the bundle of foods that best suits our needs and desires by taking into account the prices of different kind of foods as well as our financial status. This can be seen as a trade-off between consuming various goods: If you buy more of one good, you must cut the expenditures of other goods. Actually, we may encounter a lot of other trade-offs. If we spend more time relaxing ourselves and choose to work less, we will earn less income and then have less money for consumption. If we decide to consume more in the current period and save less, we have to reduce our future consumption instead.

2.1 Consumer's problem

The consumer's problem can be summarized as a problem faced by a typical consumer that her desires are always limited by her resources. The theory of consumer choice is used to solve this problem how an individual can make her optimal decision within the constraint of income or time. There are three basic steps involved in solving consumer's problem.

（a）Firstly, we must know the desire of the consumer. This desire of what the consumer want to do can be represented by the concept, preference. Unless we know the preferences of a typical consumer, it is hard for us to tell which solution is good from her point of view. In order to compare various preferences in a quantitative way, the utility function will be introduced.

（b）Secondly, the activities a typical consumer can do are also need to be considered after taking her income and prices of different goods she faces into account. In other words, the consumer is constrained by his/her limited budget when making decisions. This is so called budget constraint.

（c）Thirdly, this is the step that put the above two steps together. What the consumer wants to do is limited by what she can do. This gives us a chance to find the optimal choice that maximizes the consumer's welfare.

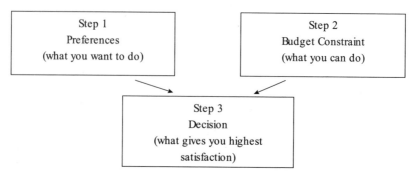

Figure 2-1   A Model of Consumer Choice

This framework makes an important implication that the theory of consumer choice indicates how an individual makes a decision, given her particular preferences. In economics, we cannot judge whether the goals of an individual make sense or not. However, we can only tell whether an individual is trying to achieve his or her goals in a rational fashion or not. For example, the theory only shows how many concerts you should go, given your preferences for concerts and other commodities like movies. But it does not show whether it is rational to put concerts in the first place. Another point needs to be mentioned is the definition of an economic good. Economic goods are much broader than tangible goods that we can easily buy in real world, such as a sandwich, a shirt and so on. An economic good is anything that will increase the level of satisfaction of an individual when consumed. A common example is leisure. Everyone enjoy relaxing instead of working and more leisure will increase your satisfaction, then leisure is a good.

2.2   Preferences

In order to solve the consumer's problem, we must know the consumer's preferences for all goods and services. This is the first step in Figure 2-2. Though there are thousands of goods available, to keep it simple only two goods are assumed to be available. This assumption is to make the problem as simple as possible without losing its generality.

For following illustrations, let us use Grace as an example consumer. Grace is making her weekly dinner decisions and is choosing between prawn sandwiches and beef burgers. To know her tastes, we ask Grace some questions about her preferences among different bundles of sandwiches and burgers. Here, a bundle is just a particular combination of the two commodities. In Figure 2–2, weekly consumption of prawn sandwiches is measured on the horizontal axis, while weekly consumption of beef burgers is measured on the vertical axis. Bundle a consists of 3 pieces of prawn sandwiches and 2 beef burgers, and bundle b is made of 4 pieces of sandwiches and 1 burger. Then we may ask Grace which one she prefers, a or b, or she feels indifferent between these two bundles.

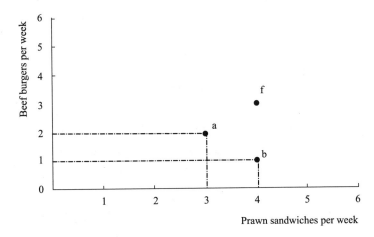

Figure 2–2　Alternative Commodity Bundles

There are three assumptions related to consumer preferences.

(a) Completeness. When the consumer is given with any two bundles, she can specify which one she prefers, or whether she is indifferent between them. This is called completeness.

If an individual cannot tell us which bundle is preferred to another, it is hard for us to predict which bundle she will choose under various circumstances. Hence, if the preferences of a consumer are not complete, the theory of consumer choice is out of use. The preferences of Grace are assumed to be complete. Though she can rank any possible combinations of various goods, there may be some inconsistencies.

(b) Transitivity. Transitivity is an assumption that is used to rule out one certain type of inconsistency. If bundle x is preferred to bundle y, and bundle y is preferred to bundle z, then x must be preferred to z. For example, if spending the evening going to concerts is preferred to watching movies, and watching movies is preferred to reading novels, then going to concerts must be preferred to reading novels. This assumption of transitivity guarantees that consumer preferences will be consistent.

（c）Non-satiation. The third assumption is non-satiation. For all feasible amounts of commodities, the consumer is never satiated. A bundle with more of either commodity is always preferred to a bundle with less. This is referred to non-satiation. Though this assumption is also important, it is less fundamental than the other two assumptions as rational consumers may be satiated with some goods after some point. While you would prefer 3 pieces of sandwiches to 2 pieces of sandwiches, you might be full after having 5 pieces of sandwiches and will be sick if you continue eating. If you stop eating more sandwiches, then the non-satiation assumption of preferences will be violated. However, it is often more convenient to assume that the non-satiation assumption always holds.

For simplicity, if something is good, more is better. It can be illustrated by Figure 2-3. According to the non-satiation assumption, bundle c is preferred to bundle d, because c has more of sandwiches and burgers. Bundle f has more sandwiches the bundle d but the same number of burgers; hence, bundle f is also preferred to bundle d. Indeed, any point to the north-east of bundle d is preferred to bundle d.

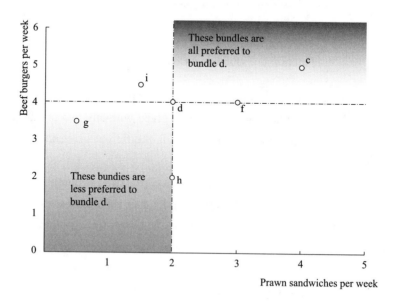

Figure 2-3   Ranking commodity bundles

Compared bundle g with bundle d, bundle g has fewer sandwiches and burger than bundle d. Then, bundle d is preferred to bundle g. Bundle h is less preferred to bundle d as bundle h has fewer burgers though it has the same number of sandwiches. Bundle d is preferred to any point to the south–west of it.

For bundle i, it consists of fewer sandwiches but more burgers than bundle d. It is hard to tell which one is preferred or whether Grace is indifferent between these two bundles. Therefore, a new tool, called indifference curve, needs to be introduced.

2.3 Indifference curve

The preferences of Grace are assumed to be satisfied all three assumptions explained above. We can ask her a series of questions about her preferences among different consumption bundles and then summarizing them in a Table. However, such a Table could be very long, and it is quite hard to compare preferences among different bundles in this long Table. Therefore, we turn to a simple graphic way, rather than the long Table, to describe a consumer's preference.

The assumption of non–satiation allows us to identify some bundles that Grace ranks above or below any arbitrarily selected bundle. If asking Grace more questions, then we can find some bundles that she ranks as being exactly equivalent to the arbitrarily selected bundle. Consider bundle k in Figure 2–4 which consists of 7 pieces of sandwiches and 5 pieces of burgers. For example, we ask Grace the following question: If you were consuming bundle k, and I took away 3 pieces of sandwiches, how many burgers would I need to give you to make you just as satisfied as you were at the beginning? Suppose Grace is rational and honest. She answers that she would require 3 and a half more burgers. Hence, by definition, she is indifferent between the bundle j which consists of 4 pieces of sandwiches and 8.5 pieces of burgers and the initial bundle k.

We could find another bundle that makes Grace to be indifferent between this one and the original one by asking: Starting at point k again, suppose we take away 1 piece of burger this time. How many pieces of sandwiches we have to give you to compensate that 1 piece of burger? If the answer is 1 piece of sandwich, then Grace is also as well off as she were originally with 8 pieces of sandwiches and 4 pieces of burgers. This bundle is denoted as point m in Figure 2–4.

If we go on this process indefinitely, starting at point k, take away different amounts of one commodity, find out the amount of the other commodity required for compensation, and then record the bundles in Figure 2–4. Assuming that fractions of units of the commodities can be consumed, the outcome is summarized in the curve U_1, which contains all bundles among which a consumer is indifferent. Hence, U_1 is referred to as an indifference curve. The indifference curve is quite intuitive in that it actually divides all bundles into three cases: Those that are equivalent to point k (points on the curve) ; those that are better off than point k (points above the curve) ; and those are worse off than point k (points below the curve) . For example, point n is preferred to point k as point n is above U_1. We learn from the assumption of non-satiation that bundle n is preferred to bundle q, because bundle n has more burgers and no fewer piece of sandwiches than bundle q. As bundle q is on the same indifference curve as bundle k, bundle n must be preferred to bundle k as long as it is preferred to bundle q by the assumption of transitivity. Using similar arguments, it is easy to find that any bundle below U_1 is inferior to any bundle that is on U_1.

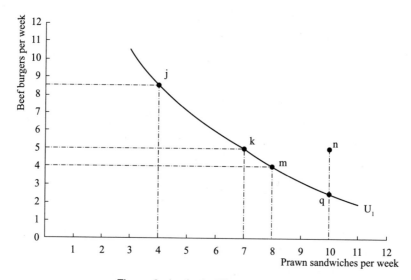

Figure 2-4   An Indifference curve

What is the slope of the indifference curve? The slope of any curve is the change in the value of the variable measured on the vertical axis divided by the change in the variable measured on the horizontal. It is obvious that the slope of U_1 is negative. That is, whenever the number of sandwiches increases, the number of burgers decreases. If the assumption of non-satiation holds, then the indifference curve must be downward-sloping. Suppose there is an upward-sloping indifference curve as shown in Figure 2–5 Two points on this indifference curve are marked m and n. Recall the assumption of non-satiation, n must be preferred to m as bundle n contains more pieces of sandwiches and burgers than bundle m. It is impossible for a person to be indifferent between two bundles and prefer one to the other at the same time. Therefore, an indifference curve must slope downwards as long as the assumption of non-satiation holds.

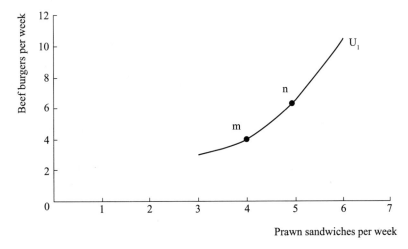

Figure 2–5　With non–satiation, an indifference curve cannot slope upwards

The slope of an indifference curve has an important economic interpretation. Its absolute value is the rate at which the consumer is willing to trade one good for another. For example, around bundle r in Figure 2–5 the slope of the indifference curve is −4. This 4 here is just the number of burgers that Grace is willing to substitute for one piece of sandwich. This is the definition of the marginal rate of substitution, abbreviated MRS. The marginal rate of substitution in above example indicates the rate at which Grace would be willing to substitute beef burgers for on additional piece of prawn sandwiches and still be as happy as she was before.

As drawn in Figure 2–5, the marginal rate of substitution declines as we move down the indifference curve. For example, around point m, MRS=1/2, which is smaller than its value of 4 around point r. Around point r, Grace has a lot of beef burgers relative to prawn sandwiches and is therefore willing to give up quite a few burgers in return for an addition piece of sandwich. This is the reason why the MRS of point r is high. On the other hand, around bundle m, Grace has a lot of sandwiches relative to burgers, so she is not willing to give up many burgers in return for another piece of sandwich. This is the reason why the MRS of point m is lower. The decline of MRS as we move down along an indifference curve is called a diminishing marginal rate of substitution. An indifference curve with a diminishing marginal rate of substitution usually curves inward or is convex to the origin.

When we construct the indifference curve U_1, we chose the arbitrary starting point k. We can start at any other point as well, such as point d and point c in Figure 2-6. If we start from bundle d, we can generate indifference curve U_0. In the same way, we can build indifference curve U_2 if we start from point c. In short, an indifference curve can be drawn through each point in the quadrant. The entire collection of indifference curves is called the indifference curve map or indifference curve family, which tells us everything about the individual's preferences. Figure 2-6 shows that Grace prefers any bundle on U_2 to any point on U_1. Given the assumption of non-satiation, any bundle that lies above indifference curve U_1 is preferred to any point on U_1. Thus, bundle c is preferred to any point on U_1. And by the definition of an indifference curve, all bundles on U_2 are equivalent to c. Hence, all bundles on U_2 are superior to all bundles on U_1. Following the same logic, Grace prefers any point on U_1 to any point on U_0. It can be concluded that if Grace wants to make herself as happy as possible, we need to seek to consume a bundle on the highest indifference curve that she can afford.

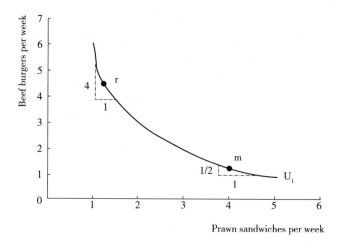

Figure 2-6　Diminishing marginal rate of substitution

Figure 2–7 shows that all three indifference curves seem to be parallel with each other. Given that many indifference curves inhabit the same quadrant, can they intersect? Definitely not. As long as our assumptions about preferences hold, there is no possibility for the indifference curves to intersect. Figure 2–8 demonstrates why they cannot intersect. It shows an indifference curve U_3 intersecting with indifference curve U_2 at point c. Since point a and c are on the same indifference curve, U_3, the consumer should be indifferent between bundle a and c. Similarly, point b and c both lie on the same indifference curve, U_2. Hence, bundle b is viewed as equivalent to bundle c. Provided the assumption of transitivity, Grace should be indifferent between a and b. However, bundle a consists of fewer pieces of sandwiches and burgers than bundle b. According to the assumption of non-satiation, bundle b has to be preferred to bundle a. Thus, a contradiction shows up: Bundle a cannot be worse than or equivalent to bundle b at the same time. Therefore, we reach a conclusion that the indifference curves cannot intersect as long as the preferences assumptions hold.

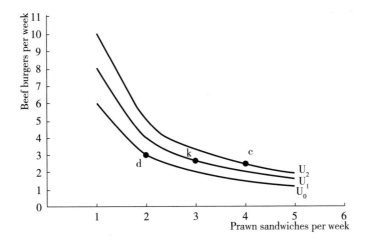

Figure 2–7 An indifference curve family

To sum up, the essential properties of the indifference curves are shown in Figure 2–9.

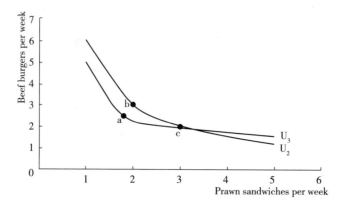

Figure 2-8   Indifference curves cannot cross

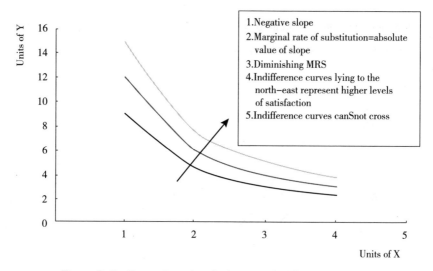

Figure 2-9   Properties of typical convex indifference curves

2.4   Perfect substitutes and perfect complements

In two special cases, indifference curves become straight lines. Substitutes are two goods that have similar qualities and fulfil similar desires. These include tea and coffee, coal and natural gas, or apple and orange. While many goods are general substitutes for each other like these, some are so similar that they can be called perfect substitutes. Coca Cola and Pepsi are a good example of perfect substitutes.

Different brands of milk, tomatoes, potatoes, and many other types of produce are also always perfect substitutes. It is hard for us to tell the difference between any two brands in the store that are roughly the same price.

Since both goods are essentially the same, the rules of diminishing marginal utility simply do not apply to perfect substitutes. If the price is the same, you would always be indifferent to having one brand versus the other, no matter how many amounts you already have of each brand. You are perfectly indifferent between the two. You could spend all of your money on each or split the money half and half between the two, or trade one for the other at any point along the curve and still get the same utility. This represents a marginal rate of substitution of 1 at every point. As a result, the indifference curve for perfect substitutes, shown in Figure 2-10 is always linear. For example, Mengniu and Yili are two brands of milk. Since you are willing to trade one carton for the other, the slope of the indifference curve is 1.

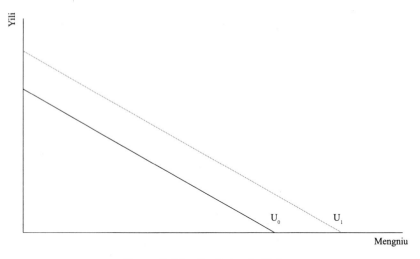

Figure 2-10   Perfect substitutes

The marginal rate of substitution is not always going to be 1, though. Perfect complements, unlike substitutes, are goods that have to be consumed together. Pairs of shoes, socks and gloves are all perfect complements. In each of these cases, having just one of a good without its complement is not useful at all. If you are working in a hotdog restaurant, you would generally like to have enough buns for your hot dogs. Having more buns than hot dogs does not increase your utility, as they are not really good for much besides holding hot dogs, and they just sit around until you get more hot dogs.

The indifference curve for two complements are L–shaped, part horizontal and part vertical. If you already have 5 hot dogs and 5 buns. Now you are given another bun. Since you cannot do anything with the extra bun, you still have the same amount of utility as when you had 5 hot dogs and 5 buns. The same is true whether you have 8 buns or 10. You still only get the same amount of utility as when you had 5 of each. The same is also true for when you get more hot dogs. In most cases, it does not do any good to have more hot dogs without bunds. The L–shaped indifference curve that gives the relationship between perfect complements is shown in Figure 2–11.

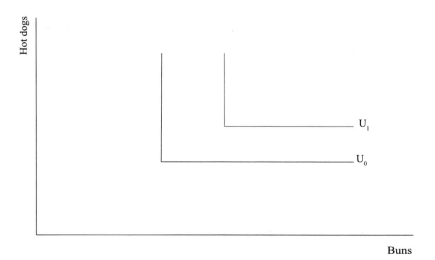

Figure 2–11　Perfect complements

2.5　Utility

When we talk about preferences, we do not give the consumer's satisfaction a numerical measure. All we need is quality information of the type, such as, bundle a is preferred to bundle b. However, it is very convenient if we can score the preferences, especially when coping the problems in which the consumer chooses among a lot of goods. In a two-good case, keeping track of the rankings among all possible bundles is relatively easy in a graphic way. For more than 3 goods, however, it is troublesome to keep track of the rankings of the various bundles using diagrams. A more convenient way to record this information is to assign each bundle a number that indicates the consumer's satisfaction of it. If bundle a has a higher score than bundle b, this implies that the consumer prefers bundle a to bundle b. If bundle a has the same score as bundle c, the consumer is indifferent between bundle a and bundle c. The score associated with each bundle is called its total utility. A utility function is a function that shows the total utility associated with each bundle. Suppose that the individual consumes n goods, x_1, x_2, x_3, $\cdots$, x_n. Then the utility function $U(x_1, x_2, x_3, \cdots, x_n)$ tells us the amounts of total utility associated with various quantities of each goods. Sometimes a bundle's utility score is called its number of utils.

Next, we can use an example to explain the concepts we have learn before in a numerical way. Suppose there are two consumers, Grace and Crystal, and two kind of goods, Pepsi and Coco Cola. Grace prefers Pepsi to Coco Cola while Crystal prefers Coco Cola to Pepsi. That is, Grace likes Pepsi more than Coco Cola and Crystal likes Coco Cola more than Pepsi. In a more specific way, Pepsi gives Grace a utility of 4 and Coco Cola gives her a utility of 3. Similarly, Crystal receives a utility of 4 from Coco Cola and a utility of 3 from Pepsi.

But will Grace keep drinking Pepsi without a stop? The answer is absolutely not. The concept of marginal utility should be introduced. Marginal utility is the amount of utility added which is resulted from consuming one additional unit of a good or service. Let's go back to Pepsi. If Grace drinks a second glass of Pepsi, she may feel that it is less tasty than the very first glass. That is, the marginal utility of the second glass is a little bit lower than the marginal utility of the first glass. How about the third glass? She enjoys less than the first two. A fourth glass? She may feel too much sugar. This is called diminishing marginal utility: The additional utility received from consuming extra unit of a good or service tends to be smaller than the utility received from the previous unit. A negative marginal utility is possible. When Grace is offered a fifth glass of Pepsi, she may feel indifferent between drinking it or not. If she is indifferent between having it or not, the fifth glass add nothing to the total utility and the marginal utility is zero now. When the sixth glass is served, Grace may feel sick after drinking it. In this case, the sixth glass reduces her total utility and the marginal utility becomes negative.

Figure 2–12 illustrates the idea of concave utility curve and the downward sloping marginal utility curve. Panel A plots the total utility that Grace gains from drinking more and more glasses of Pepsi. The curve slopes upward to begin with, flattening out as additional glasses add less and less to her total utility. The fifth glass, her total utility peaks at the point marked A—and the slope of the curve is completely flat. Beyond that point, each extra glass has negative marginal utility and the curve of total utility begins to slope downward. Panel B shows the marginal utility of each glass of Pepsi rather than total utility. The line in this graph is downward sloping, showing that your marginal utility is decreasing with each additional glass. At point A, the marginal utility is zero: Grace get no extra enjoyment from the fifth glass. The marginal utility is negative at the sixth glass. Point A is significant as it is a link between Panel A and Panel B: When the marginal utility of an additional unit of a good is zero, you have already maxed out the total utility you can receive from consuming that good.

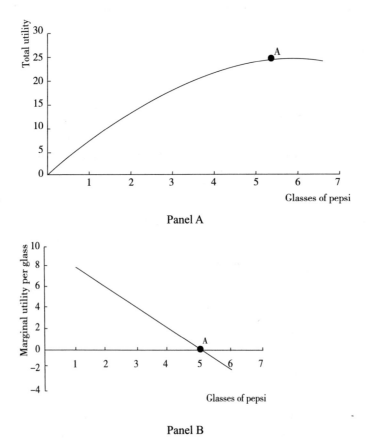

Panel A

Panel B

Figure 2–12　Diminishing marginal utility

If we assume that the amount of goods consumed in a certain period by an individual is Q, then the marginal utility can be expressed as the first derivative of the total utility with respect to the quantity consumed when the change in quantity is extremely small.

$$MU = \frac{\partial U(Q)}{\partial Q}$$

Recall the concept of marginal rate of substitution (MRS) . It is equal to the absolute value of the slope of the indifference curve at any given point. It is also the rate at which the consumer would be willing to trade or substitute between the two goods. If we name the two goods X and Y, respectively, the marginal rate of substitution can also be represented as the ratio of the marginal utilities of the two goods.

$$\text{Absolute value of the slope} = MRS = \frac{MU_X}{MU_Y}$$

Although diminishing marginal utility is a common property of many things, it doesn't mean everything will end up in negative marginal utility. For example, the amount in your bank account will never give you negative marginal utility. If there is no savings in your bank account, the first ¥1000 will give you an extremely high marginal utility. If you have already had ¥1000000 savings, the marginal utility of adding another ¥1000 might be pretty smaller. This marginal utility given by ¥1000 may be smaller and smaller when you have more and more savings in your bank account, but it is almost impossible for you to have negative marginal utility.

For most daily consumption decision, you would never get anywhere near the point of negative marginal utility. Get back to the example of Grace's dinner decisions. Suppose that her utility function for prawn sandwiches (X) and beef burgers (Y) is $=2\sqrt{X}+Y$. This means that a bundle containing 4 pieces of prawn sandwiches and 9 pieces of beef burgers is associated with a utility of 13 ($=2\sqrt{4}+9$) utils. A bundle that consists of 9 pieces of sandwiches and 7 pieces of burgers also has 13 ($=2\sqrt{9}+7$) utils, and thus, Grace is indifferent between it and a bundle with X = 4 and Y = 9. On the other hand, a bundle with X = 16 and Y = 7 is preferred to either of these two bundles as its utility is 15 ($=2\sqrt{16}+7$) .

How can utility be related to indifference curves? Consider points m and n in Figure 2-13, which lie on the same indifference curve, U_1. Suppose that the utility of bundle n is 80. Then, given the definition of indifference curve, every bundle on U_1 produces a utility of 80. It is reasonable to associate indifference curve U_1 with the number of 80. Indifference curves to the north–east of U_1 are preferred to U_1 and must have higher utility levels than 80. For example, indifference curve U_2 is to the north–east of U_1 and then might have a utility index of 800. Bundles on indifference curves below U_1 are given lower levels of utility, such as U_0, which might have a utility of 8.

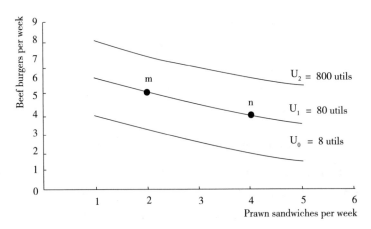

Figure 2–13   Ordinal utility numbers

Be careful, the fact that U_2 has a score of 800 utils and U_1 has a score of 80 utils does not mean that bundles on U_2 are 10 times as good as bundles on U_1. These numbers tell us only that U_2 is better than U_1, but not by how much. For example, when you were told that Runner 1 was first in a 400m race and Runner 2 was second, all this information provides is that Runner 2 is slower than Runner 1. It does not tell you that Runner 2 took twice as long as Runner 1. In the same way, utility scores only tell you the order of various bundles, that is, these utility measurements are relative rather than absolute. Numbers such as first, second, and third, which provide only information on orderings, are referred to as ordinal numbers. Hence, the utility function that gives us the indifference curves in Figure 2–13 is referred to as an ordinal utility function. The certain numbers of utils with different bundles have no meanings except an order of something the person likes more or less.

Can ordinal utility numbers be used to compare the happiness of two different individuals? The answer might be yes. You can simply compare the utility levels of these two people. If Grace has more utils than Crystal, then Grace is happier than Crystal.

Unfortunately, this reasoning is totally incorrect. Since Grace's utility numbers are ordinal, this means we can choose any number we like, as long as we keep the ordering of the indifference curves intact. For example, we could say that utility at U_0 is 10 utils; at U_1 950 utils, and at U_2 5213 utils. However, if we can arbitrarily characterize Grace's utility level as 15 utils or 59 trillion utils, when comparing this number to the level of utility gained by Crystal, does it make any sense?

Intuitively, there is no scientific way to compare the amounts of happiness that different people attain from consuming various commodities. Therefore, the theory of consumer choice does not give us chance to make interpersonal comparisons of utility.

However, if we make different assumptions on the nature of the utility function, then such comparisons can be possible. Specifically, if we assume that a bundle that creates 30 utils is not only better than a bundle with 10 utils, it is also three times as good as 10 utils. Generally speaking, the utility numbers assigned to bundles tell you exactly how much happier one bundle makes the consumer than another bundle. As opposed to first, second and third, numbers like one, two and three show that three is exactly three times the size of one, and the absolute difference between them is two. These numbers are referred to as cardinal numbers. Then the utility functions whose values tell us exactly how much better some bundles are than other bundles are called cardinal utility functions. People's utilities can be compared if utility functions are cardinal and if people have the same utility function.

Although cardinal utility functions make interpersonal comparisons possible, there is no way to establish whether individuals derive the same amount of satisfaction from consuming the same bundle of commodities. Our discussion of consumer choice theory will therefore assume that utility functions are ordinal.

2.6 Budget constraints

The indifference map or utility function provides a platform for modelling tastes as they represent what the consumer wants to do in the sense of comparable preferences. However, the consumer cannot do whatever she wants as she is always limited by what she can do. This limitation is the so-called budget constraint.

Let's return to Grace, a consumer of prawn sandwiches and beef burgers.

Suppose Grace has a weekly food budget of ¥120, all of which she spends on sandwiches and burgers. Suppose further the price of a beef burger is ¥30 and the price of a sandwich is ¥15, and Grace's purchases of sandwiches and burgers will not cause their price to change. A consumer in this situation is seen as a price taker– the consumer has no control over the prices she faces, in the sense that the price of each unit is not affected by the number of units she purchases.

Provided these assumption, Grace's expenditures on sandwiches and burgers must sum to exactly ¥120. Letting X denotes the number of prawn sandwiches Grace has, her sandwiches expenditure is ¥15X. Similarly, if Y denotes the number of beef burgers, her expenditure on burgers is ¥30Y. Since Grace's total expenditure is ¥120, if she spends her entire income, her purchases must satisfy the equation.

$$15X + 30Y = 120 \qquad (2\text{–}1)$$

Thus, for example, if Grace buys 2 burgers, from Equation 2–1, she can only buy 4 pieces of sandwiches: $(15 \times 4) + (30 \times 2) = 120$. Alternatively, if her sandwich consumption is 2 pieces, then her consumption on burgers can only be 3: $(15 \times 2) + (30 \times 3) = 120$.

To represent Grace's choice in a graphic way, we must plot several points that satisfy Equation 2–1. In Figure 2–14, point r represents 3 beef burgers and 2 prawn sandwiches, and point s represents 4 prawn sandwiches and 2 beef burgers. Hence, the line associated with Equation 2–1 is BC_1, which pass through both point r and point s. Any combination of sandwiches and burgers that lies along BC_1, by construction, satisfies Equation 2–1. Line BC_1 is then referred to as the budget constraint because it shows hoe the consumer's choices are constrained by her income and prices she faces. Any bundle on or below BC_1 (the shaded area) can be affordable as it involves an expenditure less than or equal to income. The collection of bundles that can be bought is known as the feasible set. Any point above BC_1 is not affordable by the consumer because it involves an expenditure greater than income.

We can go deep into the budget constraint BC_1.

First, the vertical and horizontal intercepts represent bundles that only contain one of the commodities. The vertical intercept is the point associated with X=0. At this point, Grace will spend all he income on beef burgers, buying 4 of them. Similarly, at the horizontal intercept, Grace has no beef burgers, but can consume 8 pieces of prawn sandwiches.

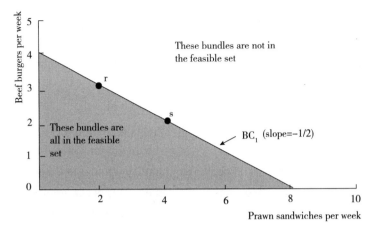

Figure 2–14　Linear budget constraint

Second, the slope of the budget line has its economic interpretation. Note that the rise is 1 and the run is 2, so the slope is −1/2. Note also that 1/2 is the ratio of the price per sandwiches to the price per burgers. This is not a coincidence. The negative slope of the budget constraint implies the rate at which the market permits an individual to substitute one commodity for the other. Since the price of sandwiches is half of the price of burgers, the consumer can trade two pieces of sandwiches for each piece of burger. In other words, the slope of the budget constraint shows the opportunity cost of one good in terms of the other, that is, the amount of one good that the consumer gives up when she consumes an additional unit of another good. The negative of the slope of the budget constraint is 1/2 shows that the opportunity cost of 2 pieces of sandwiches is 1 piece of burger.

Suppose that the price per unit of X is P_X, the price per unit of Y is P_Y and the total income is I. Then, the budget constraint can be written as

$$P_X \times X + P_Y \times Y = I$$

If X is measured on the horizontal axis and Y on the vertical axis, the vertical intercept is total income divided by the price of Y, or I/P_Y. Similarly, the horizontal intercept is I/P_X. Dividing the rise, I/P_Y, by the run, I/P_X, the slope of the budget constraint is $-P_X/P_Y$. Here, P_X/P_Y is the price of X in terms of Y. If P_X goes up, the price of X in terms of Y must go up, but only if P_X is the numerator.

2.7　Changes in prices and income

Given current income and prices, all feasible consumption bundles are on the budget constraint. What if any of these changes? Recall the example above that $P_X = 15$, $P_Y = 30$ and $I = 120$. The associated budget constraint line, $15X+30Y = 120$, is drawn as BC_1 in Figure 2–15. What if the income falls to ¥60? Then the new budget constraint is described by $15X+30Y=60$. The vertical intercept of this line is 2 and the horizontal intercept is 4. With these two points, we find that the new budget line is BC_0. The slope of these two lines is the same, $-1/2$, because an income change does not affect P_X /P_Y, the opportunity cost of sandwiches in terms of burgers. Because BC_0 and BC_1 have the same slope, they by definition are parallel.

To sum up, when income changes but relative prices do not, a parallel shift in the budget constraint is induced. If income decreases, the constraint shifts inwards; if income increases, it shifts outwards.

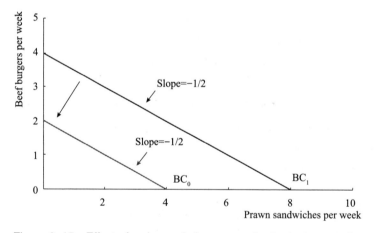

Figure 2–15　Effect of a change in income on the budget constraint

Next suppose the price of a piece of prawn sandwich increases to ¥30, but everything else stays the same. Consider again the original constraint, $15X+30Y=120$, which is reproduced in Figure 2–16 as BC_1. The new budget constraint with new price of sandwiches is then $30X+30Y=120$. This new budget constraint has a vertical intercept of 4, which is the same as that of BC_1. Since the price of burgers has stayed the same, if Grace spends all of her money on burgers, she can buy just as many as she did before. The horizontal intercept, however, is now changed to 4 pieces of sandwiches. With these two intercepts, we find that the new budget constraint is BC_3, whose slope is -1. This value reflects the fact that the market now allows consumers to trade 1 burger for each piece of sandwich.

In general, when the price of one commodity changes and other things stay the same, the budget constraint moves along the axis of the good whose price changes. If the price goes up, the line pivots in; if the price goes down, the line pivots out.

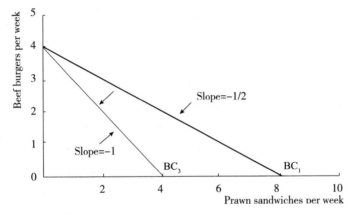

Figure 2-16   Effect of a change in relative prices on the budget constraint

Whenever consumers are price takers, their budget constraints are straight lines. The properties of linear budget constraints are listed in Figure 2–17.

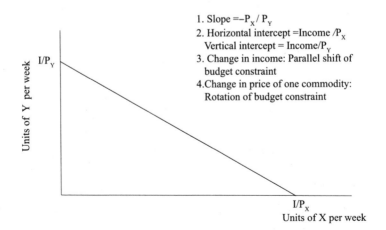

Figure 2-17   Properties of linear budget constraint

2.8 The consumer's equilibrium

The indifference map shows us what a consumer wants to do; the budget constraint shows us what a consumer can do. Then, we can put these two tools together to find out what the consumer actually does. Here, we assume that the consumers are always rational that they will definitely choose the optimal bundle that maximizes their utility given their budget.

2.8.1 Interior solutions

Let's return to Grace's choice between sandwiches and burgers again. Recall that her indifference curves have the conventional shape depicted in Figure 2−17, and her budget constraint is the straight line BC_1 from Figure 2−16.

In Figure 2−18, we superimpose Grace's indifference map upon her budget constraint. The problem is to fins Grace's most preferred combination of sandwiches and burgers subject to her budget constraint that her expenditures cannot exceed her income. This is the bundle we expect her to consume.

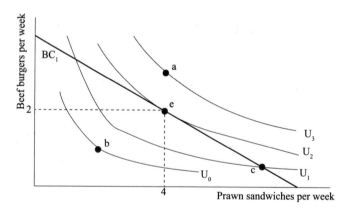

Figure 2−18　Consumer equilibrium

Consider first bundle a on indifference curve U_3. This point is rule out as it lies above the budget line BC_1. Grace might like to be on indifference curve U_3, but she simply cannot afford any bundle on it. Next consider bundle b. This bundle is obviously in the feasible set because it lies below the budget constraint. But it cannot be optimal since Grace is not spending her whole income. She is just throwing away her income that could have been spent on sandwiches and/or burgers if we assume that she cannot save her income.

What about bundle c? Since it lies on the budget constraint, the bundle is feasible, and Grace is not throwing away any income. However, she can still do better by putting herself on a higher indifference curve. Finally, Grace will reach bundle e, where she consumes 4 pieces of prawn sandwiches and 2 pieces of beef burgers. This bundle lies on budget constraint BC_1. It is affordable. Moreover, it is more desirable than bundle c, because e lies on U_2, which is above U_1. Indeed, no point on budget line BC_1 touches an indifference curve that is higher than U_2. Therefore, bundle e maximizes Grace's welfare, subject to budget constraint BC_1. In other words, there is no way for Grace to reallocate her income between prawn sandwiches and beef burgers that would make her better off than she is at bundle e. Grace's consumption of bundle e is referred to as an equilibrium. This is a situation that will persist because the rational individual has no incentive to change his or her behavior. Observe that bundle e contains at least some amount of each commodity, it is interior to the quadrant. This kind of equilibrium is called an interior solution.

Note that at the equilibrium, indifference curve U_2 barely touches the budget constraint. This occurs because the consumer is trying to attain the very highest indifference curve she can while still keeping on the budget constraint. Technically, line BC_1 is tangent to curve U_2 at point e. This means that at point e, the slope of the indifference curve U_2 is equal to the slope of budget constraint BC_1. The absolute value of the slope of the indifference curve is the marginal rate of substitution of burgers for sandwiches, MRS. Moreover, the absolute value of the slope of the budget line is P_X/P_Y. Hence, at the equilibrium, the absolute values of these two slopes are equal, or

$$MRS = P_X/P_Y \qquad (2-2)$$

If a particular bundle makes the utility of a consumer as high as possible, then it must satisfy Equation 2–2. That is, if the consumer's marginal rate of substitution is not equal to the relative price, then she could be better off by reallocating her income between the two commodities. In short, the marginal rate of substitution shows the rate at which the consumer is willing to trade one good for the other; the slope of the budget constraint is the rate at which she is able to trade one good for the other. In equilibrium, these must be equal. Equation 2–2 is the relationship between the marginal rate of substitution and the price ratio that is crucial to determining whether individuals are rational. Different people can satisfy this equality even if their equilibrium bundles are not the same.

2.8.2 Corner solutions

The equilibriums described so far are the combinations of both commodities, that is interior solutions. However, because thousands of commodities are available, one cannot expect a consumer to purchase some of everything. You may do not purchase a particular commodity. But this does not necessarily imply that you dislike it. You may like it if you are given it for free and it would increase your welfare. Given your income and the prices you face, it is not worthwhile for you to purchase it.

Figure 2–19 shows the situation of Crystal, who faces the same price for sandwiches and burgers as Grace. According to the figure, point e is on the highest indifference curve that can be reached subject to the budget constraint. She devotes all her income to burgers and no sandwich. Such an equilibrium that occurs at the corner formed by the budget constraint and the axis is referred to as a corner solution. Contrary to Equation 2, MRS $\neq$ P_X/P_Y. Rather, the indifference curve is flatter than the budget constraint; that is, P_X/P_Y exceeds MRS Thus, Crystal would like to purchase fewer pieces of sandwiches and use the money to purchase additional burgers. Why would we conclude that she is in equilibrium? Because Crystal is already consuming as few pieces of sandwiches as possible: None at all. Consequently, no reallocation of Crystal's income can increase her utility. Hence, e is her equilibrium consumption bundle.

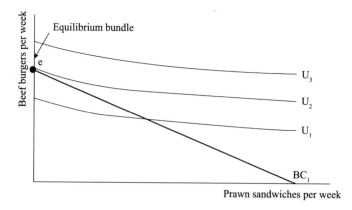

Figure 2–19   Corner solution

In summary, for a corner solution involving zero sandwich, the condition for an equilibrium is characterized not simply by an equality, but by the inequality in Equation 2–3.

$$MRS \leqslant P_X/P_Y \qquad (2-3)$$

This inequality allows for the possibility that, at the corner, the slope of the budget constraint just happens to equal the slope of indifference curve.

Similarly, at the other corner, where the consumption of burger is zero, the inequality goes the other way.

2.9 The theory of utility maximization

Recall that the highest possible indifference curve has the highest possible level of utility. The consumer's problem can be described as the problem to maximize the value of her utility function subject to her budget constraint.

From the previous section, we have learned that the marginal rate of substitution equals the ratio of marginal utilities everywhere along an indifference curve. As long as there is an interior solution, in equilibrium, the marginal rate of substitution also equals the relative price of the two commodities. Therefore, in equilibrium.

$$\frac{MU_X}{MU_Y} = \frac{P_X}{P_Y} \qquad (2-4)$$

If we slightly rearrange Equation 2–4, we will get

$$\frac{MU_X}{P_X} = \frac{MU_Y}{P_Y} \qquad (2-5)$$

The marginal utility of a commodity divided by its price is just the marginal utility per Chinese yuan spent on the good. Hence, Equation 2–5 says that a bundle maximizes total utility only if the marginal utility of the last Chinese yuan spent on each good is the same. To see why, suppose that Grace had chosen a commodity bundle in which $\frac{MU_Y}{P_Y}$ is less than $\frac{MU_X}{P_X}$. By spending a Chinese yuan less on burgers and a Chinese yuan more on sandwiches, utility would rise, even though the total expenditures of Grace would stay the same. Therefore, the original bundle could not have been an equilibrium. Similarly, if Grace were at a point where $\frac{MU_Y}{P_Y}$

is greater than $\dfrac{MU_X}{P_X}$, she could increase her utility without spending more money simply by switching one Chinese yuan from sandwiches to burgers. In order for the consumer to maximize utility, he must choose a commodity bundle such that

$$\frac{MU_X}{P_X} = \frac{MU_Y}{P_Y}$$

In short, when the marginal utility of the last Chinese yuan is the same for each commodity, there is no way that income can be reallocated between commodities so as to increase total utility.

How consumer respond to change

Recall that an increase in income shifts the budget constraint out, and a decrease in income has the opposite effect. As long as both goods are normal, an increase in income leads to more consumption. Here, we will add indifference curves to analyze that a consumer would buy more when she receives more income.

Suppose that the income of Grace has increased to ¥240. The increase in her income means that she has access to higher indifference curves that contain more burgers and sandwiches than before. As is the case with any optimization, the goal is to find the indifference curve that is tangent to the new budget constraint. This process is shown in Figure 2-20. When her income increases to ¥240, he ends up buying 8 sandwiches and 4 burgers.

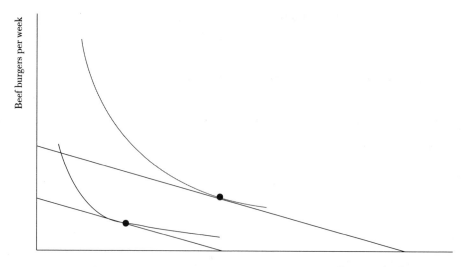

Figure 2-20　Increases in income with normal goods

Recall again that a change in price rotates the budget constraint. When the price of a good increases, you cannot afford the same amount of goods as before. The effect is the same as if you had lost some income. Suppose that the burger restaurant has a seasonal discount that decreases the price of burgers to ¥20, and the budget constraint rotates outward. The collection of goods that was optimal before the price change is no longer available. Figure 2–21 show this effect: Grace moves from indifference curve U_1 to U_2. The process of optimization is still the same, even as the budget constraint changes. All we need to do is to find the indifference curve that is tangent to new budget constraint.

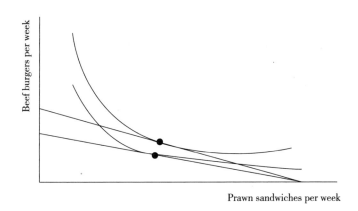

Figure 2–21   Overall effect of a price decrease

The effect of a price change can be broken into two parts, the income effects and the substitution effects. Depending on the type of good, the income and substitution effects ill have different impacts on the optimal consumption bundle of the consumer when prices change. For normal goods, a price increase will lead to a smaller change in the income effect versus substitution effect, and so a consumer will consume less. Figure 2–22 shows the overall response to the price change with indifference curves, in two steps. One corresponds to the substitution effect, and the other to the income effect.

Panel A shows the first step, in which consumption responds to the changes in relative prices (substitution effect) by moving along the original indifference curve to the point where the marginal rate of substitution is equal to the new slope of the budget constraint shown by the dashed line, which is parallel to the original budget constraint. Panel B shows the second step, when consumption shifts up to the highest indifference curve that is now accessible due to the increase in purchasing power (income effect) . This new consumption bundle is at point e_3.

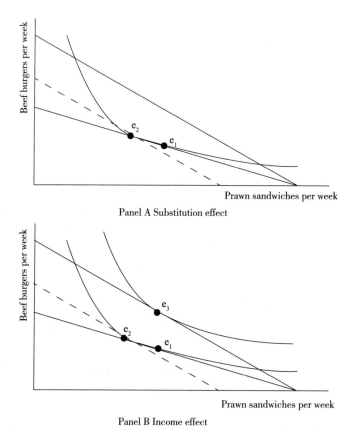

Panel A Substitution effect

Panel B Income effect

Figure 2–22   Overall response to the price change with indifference curves

Conclusion

The ideas in this chapter are at the very heart of economic analysis. Everything in the following chapters (and for that matter, the preceding chapters) is in some way based on the assumption that people attempt to maximize their utility within the limitations of the resources available to them.

We'll enrich this picture in the coming chapters, seeing that individuals have to answer a lot of tough questions when making even commonplace decisions. When will the costs arrive relative to the benefits? What are the risks? Am I fully informed about the situation? Are others competing with me for the same goal?

The idea of utility maximization is remarkably flexible. We'll see that people often have preferences that extend far beyond a narrow definition of their own benefit. Sometimes theypursue their goals in unexpected or not entirely rational ways. Nonetheless, the essentialidea of individuals pursuing the things they want in the face of scarcity drives economicanalysis from A to Z.

Key Term

Utility	Bundle	Budget Constraint
Revealed Preference	Marginal Utility	Income Effect
Utility Function	Diminishing Marginalutility	Substitution Effect

Review Questions

1. Which of the following activities give you positiveutility?
a. Playing sports
b. Receiving a prestigious scholarship
c. Buying a new TV
d. Eating brussels sprouts
e. All of the above

2. Your gym offers two classes at the same time:Weightlifting and yoga. Both classes are included in your membership and have space available.Your friend tells you he wants to work on his strength and take the weightlifting class, but you always see him in yoga class. Which class giveshim more utility? How do you know this?

3. What happens to the marginal rate of substitution as you move along a convex indifference curve?A linear indifference curve?

4. Explain why an MRS between two goods must equal the ratio of the price of the goods for the consumer to achieve maximum satisfaction.

5. Describe the indifference curves associated with two goods that are perfect substitutes.What if they are perfect complements?

6. What is the difference between ordinal utility and cardinal utility?Explain why the assumption of cardinal utility is not needed in order to rank consumer choices.

Applications

1. Draw indifference curves that represent the following individuals' preferences for hamburgers and soft drinks. Indicate the direction in which the individuals' satisfaction(or utility)is increasing.

a. Joe has convex indifference curves and dislikes both hamburgers and soft drinks.

b. Jane loves hamburgers and dislikes soft drinks. If she is served a soft drink, she will pour it down the drain rather than drink it.

c. Bob loves hamburgers and dislikes soft drinks. If heis served a soft drink, he will drink it to be polite.

d. Molly loves hamburgers and soft drinks, but insists on consuming exactly one soft drink for every two hamburgers that she eats.

e. Bill likes hamburgers, but neither likes nor dislikes soft drinks.

f. Mary always gets twice as much satisfaction from an extra hamburger as she does from an extra soft drink.

2. If Jane is currently willing to trade 4 movie tickets for 1 basketball ticket, then she must like basketball better than movies. True or false? Explain.

3. Janelle and Brian each plan to spend ¥20000 on the styling and gas mileage features of a new car. They can each choose all styling, all gas mileage, or somecombination of the two. Janelle does not care at all about styling and wants the best gas mileage possible. Brian likes both equally and wants to spend an equal amount on each. Using indifference curves and budget lines, illustrate the choice that each person will make.

3

Production Function

We have spoken of inputs like land and labor and outputs like wheat and toothpaste. But if you have a fixed amount of inputs, how much output can you get? On any day, given the available technical knowledge, land, machinery, and so on, only a certain quantity of tractors or toothpaste can be obtained from a given amount oflabor. The relationship between the amount of input required and the amount of output that can be obtained is called the production function.

3.1 Theory of production and marginal products

A modern economy has an enormously varied set of productive activities. A farm takes fertilizer, seed, land, andlabor and turns them into wheat or corn. Modern factories take inputs such as energy, raw materials, computerized machinery, and labor and use them to produce tractors, DVDs, or tubes of toothpaste. An airline takes airplanes, fuel, labor, and computerized reservation systems and provides passengers with the ability to travel quickly through its network of routes.

3.1.1 The production function

We have spoken of inputs like land and labor and outputs like wheat and toothpaste. But if you have a fixed amount of inputs, how much output can you get? On any day, given the available technical knowledge, land, machinery, and so on, only a certain quantity of tractors or toothpaste can be obtained from a given amount of labor. The relationship between the amount of input required and the amount of output that can be obtained is called the production function.

The production function specifies the maximum output that can be produced with a given quantity of inputs. It is defined for a given state of engineering and technical knowledge. There are literally millions of different production functions–one for each and every product or service. Most of them are not written down but are in people's minds. In areas of the economy where technology is changing rapidly, like computer software and biotechnology, production functions may become obsolete soon after they are used. And some, like the blueprints of a medical laboratory or cliff house, are specially designed for a specific location and purpose and would be useless anywhere else. Nevertheless, the concept of a production function is a useful way of describing the productive capabilities of a firm. Mathematically, we may write this as follows:

Equation 3-1

$$X = f(a_1, a_2, \ldots, a_n)$$

This equation tells us the quantity of the product X which can be produced by the given quantities of inputs (landslabor, capital) that are used in the process of production. Here it may be noted that production function shows only the maximum amount of output which can be produced from given inputs. It is because production function includes only efficient production process.

Equation 3-2

$$Q = f(L, K)$$

Here, "Q" represents the output, whereas "L" and "K" are the inputs, representing labor and capital (such as machinery) respectively. Note that there may be many other factors as well but we have assumed two-factor inputs here.

3.1.2 Total, average, and marginal product

Starting with a firm's production function, we can calculate three important production concepts: Total, average, and marginal product. We begin by computing the total physical product, or total product, which designates the total amount of output produced, in physical units such as bushels of wheat or number of sneakers. Figure 3-1 (a) and column (2) of Table 3-1 illustrate the concept of total product. For this example, they show how total product responds as the amount oflabor applied is increased. The total product starts at zero for zerolabor and then increases as additional units oflabor are applied, reaching a maximum of 3900 units when 5 units oflabor are used. Once we know the total product, it is easy to derive an equally important concept, the marginal product. Recall that the term "marginal" means "extra."

The marginal product illustrates the increase in the number of pizzas that can be produced by hiring an additional employee is called the marginal product of that employee. In general, the marginal product of any input into the production process is the increase in output that is generated by an additional unit of input.

For example, assume that we are holding land, machinery, and all other inputs constant. Thenlabor's marginal product is the extra output obtained by adding 1 unit oflabor. The third column of Table 3-1 calculates the marginal product. The marginal product of labor starts at 2000 for the first unit of labor and then falls to only 100 units for the fifth unit. Marginal product calculations such as this are crucial for understanding how wages and other factor prices are determined.

The final concept is the average product, which equals total output divided by total units of input. The fourth column of Table 3−1 shows the average product of labor as 2000 units per worker with one worker, 1500 units per worker with two workers, and so forth. In this example, average product falls through the entire range of increasinglabor input.

Figure 3−1 plots the total and marginal products from Table 3−1. Study this figure to make sure you understand that the blocks of marginal products in (b) are related to the changes in the total product curve in (a) .

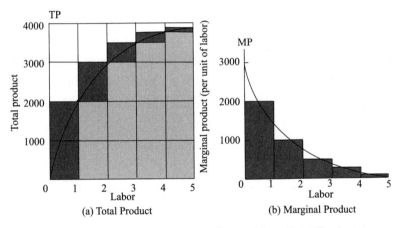

(a) Total Product   (b) Marginal Product

Figure 3−1   Marginal Product Is Derived from Total Product

Table 3−1   Total, Marginal and Average Product

(1) Units of labor input	(2) Total product	(3) Marginal product	(4) Average product
0	0		
		2000	2000
1	2000		
		1000	
2	3000		1500
		500	
3	3500		1167
		300	
4	3800		950
		100	
5	3900		780

The Table shows the total product that can be produced for different inputs oflabor when other inputs (capital, land, etc.) and the state of technical knowledge are unchanged. From total product, we can derive important concepts of marginal and average products.

Time period

The production function is differently defined in the short run and in the long run. This distinction is extremely relevant in microeconomics. The distinction is based on the nature of factor inputs.

Those inputs that vary directly with the output are called *variable factors*. These are the factors that can be changed. Variable factors exist in both, the short run and the long run. Examples of variable factors include daily-wage labor, raw materials, etc.

On the other hand, those factors that cannot be varied or changed as the output changes are called *fixed factors*. These factors are normally characteristic of the short run or short period of time only. Fixed factors do not exist in the long run.

Consequently, we can define two production functions: short-run and long-run. The ***short-run production function*** defines the relationship between one variable factor (keeping all other factors fixed) and the output. *The law of returns* to a factor explains such a production function.

For example, consider that a firm has 20 units of labor and 6 acres of land and it initially uses one unit of labor only (variable factor) on its land (fixed factor) . So, the land-labor ratio is 6:1. Now, if the firm chooses to employ 2 units of labor, then the land-labor ratio becomes 3:1 (6:2) .

It measures by how much proportion the output changes when inputs are changed proportionately.

3.2 The short-run production function

The firm may change only the quantities of the variable inputs in the short run when the quantities of the fixed inputs remain unchanged.

That is, in the short run, the output quantity can be increased (or decreased) by increasing (or decreasing) the quantities used of only the variable inputs. This functional relationship (of dependence) between the variable input quantities and the output quantity is called ***the short run production function***.

We have to remember here, of course, that in the short-run, the firm uses a particular combination of fixed inputs, and its short–run production function is obtained in respect of that combination.

In the long run, however, all the inputs used by the firm, the variable inputs and the so–called fixed inputs, all are variable quantities and the firm's production is a function of all these inputs. This functional relation of dependence between all the inputs used by the firm and the quantity of its output is called the long run production function of the firm.

We may illustrate the difference between the short–run and the long run production functions in the following way. Let us suppose that the firm uses only two inputs X and Y to produce its output of one commodity, Q, and of these two inputs X is a variable input and Y is a fixed input.

Therefore, in this case, the firm's short–run production function may be written as:

Equation 3-3

$$q = f(x, \bar{y})$$

where $\bar{y}$ is the fixed quantity of the fixed input y. The firm's long run production function in this example would be:

Equation 3-4

$$q = f(x, y)$$

where x and y are the variable quantities of the inputs X and Y.

We may write the firm's short–run production function (8.5) in the following form also:

Equation 3-5

$$q = h(x)$$

For, in our example, in the short–run, the change in the firm's output depends on the change in the quantity used of the input X only.

3.3 The long–run production function

The long–run production function is different in concept from the short run production function. ***Definition of Long Run Production Function.*** Long run production function refers to that time period in which all the inputs of the firm are variable. It can operate at various activity levels because the firm can change and adjust all the factors of production and level of output produced according to the business environment. Here, all factors are varied in the same proportion. The law that is used to explain this is called *the law of returns to scale*.

The relationships between changing input and output is studied in the laws of returns to scale, which is based on production function and isoquant curve. The term isoquant has been derived from a Greek work iso, which means equal.

Mathematically, we may write this as follows:

Equation 3-6

$$Q = f(X_1, X_2, \cdots, X_n)$$

In production theory, in order to make a brief analysis, we usually use the production function of two factors of production to study the long–term production problem. If the producer uses two variable factors of production, labor and capital, to produce a product, the long–term production function of the two variable factors of production can be written as:

Equation 3-7

$$Q = f(L, K)$$

Here, "Q" represents the output, whereas "L" and "K" are the inputs, representing labor and capital (such as machinery) respectively. Note that there may be many other factors as well but we have assumed two–factor inputs here.

3.3.1　Isoquant curve

Isoquant curve *is the locus of points showing different combinations of capital and labor, which can be employed to produce same output.* When the constant Q is used to express the given production level, the production function corresponding to the equal production curve is obtained.

Equation 3-8

$$Q= f(L, K)=Q^d$$

It is also known as equal product curve or production indifference curve. Isoquant curve is almost similar to indifference curve. However, there are two dissimilarities between isoquant curve and indifference curve. Firstly, in the graphical representation, indifference curve takes into account two consumer goods, while isoquant curve uses two producer goods. Secondly, indifference curve measures the level of satisfaction, while isoquant curve measures output.

Following are the assumptions of isoquant curve:

i. Assumes that there are only two inputs, labor and capital, to produce a product

ii. Assumes that capital, labor, and good are divisible in nature

iii. Assumes that capital andlabor are able to substitute each other at diminishing rates because they are not perfect substitutes

iv. Assumes that technology of production is known

On the basis of these assumptions, isoquant curve can be drawn with the help of different combinations of capital andlabor. The combinations are made such that it does not affect the output.

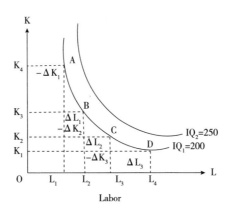

Figure 3–2   Isoquant Curve

Figure 3–2 represents an isoquant curve for four combinations of capital and labor:

In Figure 3–2, IQ_1 is the output for four combinations of capital and labor. Figure 3–2 shows that all along the curve for IQ_1 the quantity of output is same that is 200 with the changing combinations of capital and labor. The four combinations on the IQ_1 curve are represented by points A, B, C, and D.

Table 3–2 shows the relationship between input and output for IQ_1 curve:

Table 3–2   Relationship between Input and Output in Isoquant Curve

Points	Input combinations	Output
	K+L	
A	OK_4+OL_1	200
B	OK_3+OL_2	200
C	OK_2+OL_3	200
D	OK_1+OL_4	200

In Table 3-2, as we move from A to D, capital starts decreasing with the increase in labor. This shows that capital is substituted bylabor, while keeping the output unaffected.

As discussed earlier, isoquant curve is almost similar to indifference curve. The properties of isoquant curve can be explained in terms of input and output.

Some of the properties of the isoquant curve are as follows:

i. Negative Slope: Implies that the slope of isoquant curve is negative. This is because when capital (K) is increased, the quantity of labor (L) is reduced or vice versa, to keep the same level of output. As shown in Table 3-2, when the quantity of labor is increased from one unit to two units, the quantity of capital is decreased from four to three, to keep the level of output constant, which is 200.

ii. Convex to Origin: Shows the substitution of inputs and diminishing marginal rate of technical substitution (which is discussed later) in economic region. This implies that marginal significance of one input (capital) in terms of another input (labor) diminishes along with the isoquant curve. For example, in Table 3-2, it can be seen when more and more units of capital are used to produce 200 units of output, less or less units of labor are used.

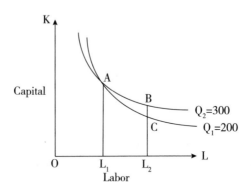

Figure 3-3   Intersecting isoquant curves

iii. Non-intersecting and Non-tangential: Implies that two isoquant curves (as shown in Figure 3-2) cannot cut each other.

In Figure 3-3, the two isoquant curves intersect at point A. The point B on isoquant having $Q_2=300$ and point C on isoquant curve having $Q_1=200$ with the same amount of labor that is OL_2. However, the capital is different that is BL_2 in case of point B and CL_2 in case of point C. A is the common point of isoquant for B and C points.

Now, according to isoquant definition, the output produced at A is the same as produced on B and C points. On isoquant curve Q_1, the output produced at A and C is 200 while on Q_2 curve the output priced at A and B is 300.

To make the input at point B and C equal, the following formula is used:
Equation 3-9

$$OL_2 + BL_2 = OL_2 + CL_2$$
$$BL_2 = CL_2$$

However according to Figure 3–3, $BL_2 > CL_2$ but the intersection of two isoquants implies that BL_2 and CL_2 are equal with respect to their output, which is not possible. Therefore, it is stated that isoquant curves cannot intersect; otherwise the law of production would not be applicable.

iv. Upper isoquant have high output: Implies that upper curve of the isoquant curve produces more output than the curve beneath. This is because of the larger combination of input result in a larger output as compared to the curve that s beneath it. For example, in Figure 3–3 the value of capital at point B is greater than the capital at point C. Therefore, the output of curve Q_2 is greater than the output of Q_1.

Marginal rate of technical substitution

Marginal Rate of Technical Substitution (MRTS) is the quantity of one input (capital) that is reduced to increase the quantity of the other input (L), so that the output remains constant.

Table 3–3 shows the marginal rate of technical substitution:

Table 3–3　MRTS of L for K

Combination	Input L	Input K	Output	MRTS of L for K
P	1	15	150	
Q	2	11	150	4 : 1
R	3	8	150	3 : 1
S	4	6	150	2 : 1
T	5	5	150	1 : 1

Table 3–3 shows that how muchlabor is required to replace one unit of capital while keeping the output same for all combinations of capital and labor, which is 150.In such a case, MRTS can be calculated with the help of the following formula:

Equation 3-10

$$MRTS = \Delta K / \Delta L$$

Where, ΔK = Change in Capital, ΔL= Change in labor

For example, in Table 3–3 at point Q MRTS can be calculated as follows:

$$\Delta K = \text{new capital} - \text{old capital}$$

$$\Delta K = 15 - 11$$

$$\Delta K = 4$$

$$\Delta L = 2 - 1$$

$$\Delta L = 1$$

Therefore, MRTS at point Q would be:

$$MRTS = \Delta K / \Delta L$$

$$MRTS = 4/1 \text{ or } 4:1$$

Similarly, we can calculate MRTS at different points, which are R, S, and T.

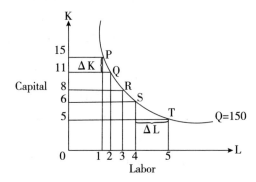

Figure 3–4　Curve of MRTS

Forms of isoquants

The shape of an isoquant depends on the degree to which one input can be substituted by the other. Convex isoquant represents that there is a continuous substitution of one input variable by the other input variable at a diminishing rate.

However, in economics, there are other forms of isoquants, which are as follows:

i. Linear Isoquant: Refers to a straight–line isoquant. Linear isoquant represents a perfect substitutability between the inputs, capital andlabor, of the production function. It implies that a product can be produced by using either capital or labor or using both, if capital andlabor are perfect substitutes of each other. Therefore, in a linear isoquant,

MRTS between inputs remains constant, and thus line isoquant is also called *production function with fixed substitution ratio.*

The algebraic form of production function in case of linear isoquant is as follows:

Equation 3-11

$$Q = \alpha K + \beta L$$

Here, Q is the weighted sum of K and L.

Slope of curve can be calculated with the help of following formula:

$$MPK = \Delta Q / \Delta K = \alpha$$

$$MPL = \Delta Q / \Delta L = \beta$$

$$MRTS = MPL / MPK$$

$$MRTS = -\beta / \alpha$$

However, linear isoquant does not have existence in the real world.

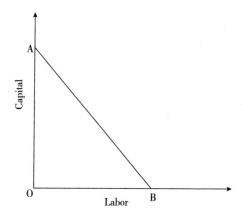

Figure 3–5   Linear isoquant

ii. L–shaped Isoquant: Refers to an isoquant in which the combination between capital and labor are in a fixed proportion. The graphical representation of fixed factor proportion isoquant is L in shape. The L–shaped isoquant represents that there is no substitution between labor and capital and they are assumed to be complementary goods.

It represents that only one combination of labor and capital is possible to produce a product with affixed proportion of inputs. For increasing the production, an organization needs to increase both inputs proportionately.

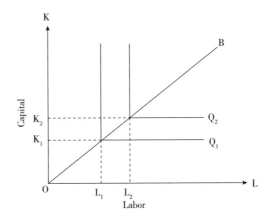

Figure 3-6   L-shaped isoquant

In Figure 3-6, it can be seen OK_1 units of capital and OL_1 units of labor are required for the production of Q_1. On the other hand, to increase the production from Q_1 to Q_2, an organization needs to increase inputs from K_1 to K_2 and L_1 to L_2 both.

This relationship between capital and labor can be expressed as follows:

Equation 3-12

$$Q = f(K, L) = \min(\alpha K, \beta L)$$

Where, min=Q equals to lower of the two terms, αK and βL.

For example, in case $\alpha K > \beta L$, then $Q = \beta L$ and in case $\alpha K < \beta L$ then, $Q = \alpha K$.

L-shaped isoquant is applied in many production activities and techniques where labor and capital are in fixed proportion. For example, in the process of driving a car, only one machine and one labor is required, which is a fixed combination.

iii. Kinked Isoquant: Kinked isoquant refers to an isoquant that represents different combinations of labor and capital. These combinations can be used in different processes of production, but in fixed proportion. According to L-shaped isoquant, there would be only one combination between capital and labor in a fixed proportion. However, in real life, there can be several ways to perform production with different combinations of capital and labor.

For example, there are two machines in which one is large in size and can perform all the processes involved in production, while the other machine is small in size and can perform only one function of production process. In both the machines, combination of capital employed and labor used is different.

Let us understand kinked isoquant with the help of another example. For example, to produce 100 units of product X, an organization has used four different techniques of production with fixed-factor proportion.

The combination between inputs and their ratio is provided in Table 3-4:

Table 3-4   Production techniques used for producing product X

No.	Technique	Capital+Labor	Capital/labor
1	OA	10+2	10 : 2
2	OB	6+3	6 : 3
3	OC	4+6	4 : 6
4	OD	3+10	3 : 10

In Table 3-4, OA, OB, OC, and OD represent the four production techniques. The fixed capital-labor ratio for OA technique is 10:2, for OB it is 6:3, for OC 4:6, and for OD is 3:10. Therefore, different production techniques use different fixed combinations of capital and labor.

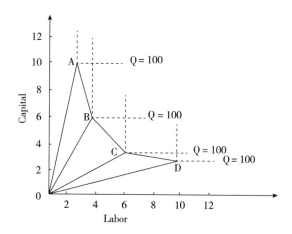

Figure 3-7   Techniques for fixed proportion of production

Elasticity of factor substitution

We have studied that **MRTS** *is associated with the slope of an isoquant and represents ratio of marginal changes in inputs.* MRTS does not represent the substitutability between the two inputs, capital and labor, with different combinations of inputs.

However, it is important to measure the degree of substitutability between the two inputs. Therefore, economists have developed a formula for estimating the extent of substitutability between the two inputs, capital andlabor, which is known as elasticity of factor substitution.

Elasticity of factor substitution (a) refers to the ratio of percentage change in capital–labor ratio to the percentage change in MRTS.

It is mathematically represented as follows:

Equation 3-13

σ = percentage change in capital labor ratio/percentage change in MRTS

Or,

$$\sigma = [(AK/AL)/AMRTS] \times [MRTS/(K/L)]$$

If change produced in capital–labor ratio by change in MRTS–is equal and in opposite direction, then $\sigma =1$. If the change produced in capital–labor ratio is greater than the change in MRTS, then $\sigma >1$. In case the change in capital–labor ratio is greater than the change in MRTS, then $\sigma <1$. High elasticity of substitution between factors implies that the factors can easily substituted to each other, while a low elasticity represents that substitution of factors is possible to a certain extent.

The degree of elasticity depends on the shape of isoquant curve. If the shape of isoquant curve is linear and factors are perfect substitutes, then the substitution elasticity would be infinite. In case the factors are complementary to each other and isoquants are L–shaped, then the substitution elasticity is zero. The elasticity of substitution is negative between factors due to the inverse relation of factor–ratio and MRTS. The elasticity of substitution would be less as the convexity of the isoquant curve increases.

Table 3–5　Comparison Chart

BASIS for COMPARION	SHORT–RUN PRODUCTION FUNCTION	LONG–RUN PRODUCTION FUNCTION
Meaning	Short run production function alludes to the time period, in which at least one factor of production is fixed	Long run production function connotes the time period, in which all the factors of production are variable
Law	Law of variable proportion	Law of returns to scale
Scale of production	No change in scale of production	Change in scale of production
Factor–ratio	Changes	Does not change
Entry and Exit	There are barriers to entry and the firms can shut down but cannot fully exit	Firms are free to enter and exit

To sum up, the production function is nothing but a mathematical presentation of technological input–output relationship.

For any production function, short run simply means a shorter time period than the long run. So, for different processes, the definition of the long run and short run varies, and so one cannot indicate the two time periods in days, months or years. These can only be understood by looking whether all the inputs are variable or not.

3.3.2 The law of diminishing returns

Using production functions, we can understand one of the most famous laws in all economics, the law of diminishing returns:

*Under the **law of diminishing returns,** a firm will get less and less extra output when it adds additional units of an input while holding other inputs fixed. In other words, the marginal product of each unit of input will decline as the amount of that input increases, holding all other inputs constant.*

The law of diminishing returns expresses a very basic relationship. As more of an input such as labor is added to a fixed amount of land, machinery, and other inputs, thelabor has less and less of the other factors to work with. The land gets more crowded, the machinery is overworked, and the marginal product oflabor declines.

Diminishing returns are a key factor in explaining why many countries in Asia are so poor. The law of diminishing returns i a widely observed empirical regularity rather than a universal truth like the law of gravity. It has been found in numerous empirical studies, but exceptions have also been uncovered. Moreover, diminishing returns might not hold for all levels of production. The very first inputs oflabor might actually show increasing marginal products, since a minimum amount of labor may be needed just to walk to the field and pick up a shovel. Notwithstanding these reservations, diminishing returns will prevail in most situations.

Constant returns to scale denote a case where a change in all inputs leads to a proportional change in output. For example, if labor, land, capital, and other inputs are doubled, then under constant returns to scale output would also double. Many handicraft industries (such as hair – cutting in America or handloom operation in a developing country) show constant returns.

Increasing returns to scale (also called economies of scale) arise when an increase in all inputs leads to a more–than–proportional increase in the level of output. For example, an engineer planning a small–scale chemical plant will generally find that increasing the inputs of labor, capital, and materials by 10 percent will increase the total output by more than 10 percent. Engineering studies have determined that many manufacturing processes enjoy modestly increasing returns to scale for plants up to the largest size used today.

Decreasing returns to scale occur when a balanced increase of all inputs leads to a less–than– proportional increase in total output. In many processes, scaling up may eventually reach a point beyond which inefficiencies set in. These might arise because the costs of management or control become large. One case has occurred in electricity generation, where firms found that when plants grew too large, risks of plant failure grew too large. Many productive activities involving natural resources, such as growing wine grapes or providing clean drinking water to a city, show decreasing returns to scale.

Production shows increasing, decreasing, or constant returns to scale when a balanced increase in all inputs leads to a more–than–proportional, less–than–proportional, or just–proportional increase in output.

Conclusion

In this chapter, we've explored the costs that all firms face when they produce goods or services. Understanding the relationship between inputs, outputs. To attain economic efficiency,a price–taking firm chooses an input combination such that the marginal physical products of the inputs are proportional to their input prices. Changes in factor prices, technology, and the nature of output can affect the total cost of producing a given output level.

Key Term

Economic Profit	Diminishing Marginal Product
Production Function	Diminishing Return
Marginal Product	Marginal Technology Substitution Rate
Isoquant Line	

Review Questions

1. What is a production function? How does a long–runproduction function differ from a short–run production function?

2. Why is the marginal product of labor likely to increase initially in the short run as more of the variable input is hired?

3. Why does production eventually experience diminishing marginal returns to labor in the short run?

4. You are an employer seeking to fill a vacant position on an assembly line. Are you more concerned with theaverage product of labor or the marginal product of labor for the last person hired? If you observe that your average product is just beginning to decline, should you hire any more workers? What does this situation implyabout the marginal product of your last worker hired?

5. What is the difference between a production function and an isoquant?

6. Faced with constantly changing conditions, why would a firm ever keep any factors fixed? What criteria determine whether a factor is fixed or variable?

7. Explain the term "marginal rate of technical substitution." What does a MRTS=4 mean?

8. Explain why the marginal rate of technical substitution is likely to diminish as more and more labor is substituted for capital.

Application

1. Suppose a desk manufacturer is producing in the short run (with its existing plant and equipment) . The manufacturer has observed the following levels of production corresponding to different numbers of workers:

Number of workers	Number of desks
1	10
2	18
3	24
4	28
5	30

Continuation Table

Number of workers	Number of desks
6	28
7	25

a. Calculate the marginal and average product of labor for this production function.

b. Does this production function exhibit diminishing returns to labor? Explain.

c. Explain intuitively what might cause the marginal product of labor to become negative.

2. For each of the following examples, draw a representative isoquant. What can you say about the marginal rate of technical substitution in each case?

a. A firm can hire only full–time employees to produce its output, or it can hire some combination of full–time and part–time employees. For each full–time worker let go, the firm must hire an increasing number of temporary employees to maintain the same level of output.

b. A firm finds that it can always trade two units of labor for one unit of capital and still keep output constant.

c. A firm requires exactly two full–time workers to operate each piece of machinery in the factory.

3. The marginal product of labor in the production of computer chips is 50 chips per hour. The marginal rate of technical substitution of hours of labor for hours of machine capital is 1/4. What is the marginal product of capital?

4

Cost of Production

Learning Objectives

LO 4.1   Recognize how to consider costs in the short and long term.

LO 4.2   Distinguish between fixed and variable costs.

LO 4.3   Explain the nature of short–term cost including marginal cost and marginal factor cost.

LO 4.4   Draw an isocost line to represent the output level of equal cost.

LO 4.5   Derive the long–term cost function.

4.1 Basic insights of costs

4.1.1 Total revenue, total cost, and profit

To define profit, we have to start with two other economic concepts that may be familiar: Revenue and cost. The amount that a firm receives from the sale of goods and services is its total *revenue*. (As discussed in Chapter 3, total revenue is calculated as the quantity sold multiplied by the price paid for each unit.) The amount that a firm pays for all of the inputs that go into producing goods and services is its *total cost*. Total cost includes one-time expenses like buying a machine as well as ongoing expenses like rent, employee salaries, raw materials, and advertising. In other words, total cost is anything and everything that the company expends to make its products.

Together, revenue and cost determine how much profit a firm makes. In the simplest terms, profit is the difference between total revenue and total cost, as shown in Equation 4-1.

Equation 4-1
$$\text{Profit} = \text{Total revenue} - \text{Total cost}$$

Unfortunately, measuring profit for a real firm is rarely so simple. To see the complexity, let's break things down into the two parts, revenue and cost. Revenue is relatively straightforward to measure. As Equation 4-2 shows, it's equal to the quantity of each product the firm sells, multiplied by the price at which it's sold.

Equation 4-2
$$\text{Revenue} = \text{Quantity} \times \text{Price}$$

Of course, very few companies sell only one product. When multiple products are involved, revenue equals quantity times price for all of the products a firm sells, as Equation 4-2a shows:

Equation 4-2a
$$\text{Revenue} = \text{Quantity} \times \text{Price}$$
$$\text{Revenue} = (Q_1 \times P_1) + (Q_2 \times P_2) + \cdots + (Q_n \times P_n)$$

Revenue calculations are generally quite simple. Cost is the tricky factor when thinking about profits. We'll see in the next few sections of the chapter that measuring different types of costs–particularly opportunity costs–is complicated, but makes a big difference for important decisions about production.

4.1.2 Measuring costs: which costs matter

For a firm to minimize costs, we must clarify what is meant by costs and how to measure them.

（1）*Opportunity cost.* A benefit, profit, or value of something that must be given up to acquire or achieve something else. Since every resource (land, money, time, etc.) can be put to alternative uses, every action, choice, or decision has an associated opportunity cost. *Opportunity costs* are fundamental costs in economics, and are used in computing cost benefit analysis of a project. Such costs, however, are not recorded in the account books but are recognized in decision making by computing the cash outlays and their resulting profit or loss.

（2）*Fixed cost and variable cost.* The first complicating factor in calculating costs is the distinction between fixed costs that do not depend on the quantity of output produced and variable costs that depend on the quantity of output produced. Fixed costs are those that don't depend on the quantity of output produced. For Pfizer, running a research and development department is a fixed cost; it would be incurred whether any given drug sells well or not. Sometimes a fixed cost is a one-time, upfront payment that has to be made before production can even begin. If you are opening a take–out pizza place, for example, you will have to incur the one-time, upfront fixed cost of buying an oven before you can produce your first pizza. Fixed costs can also be ongoing: If you lease a corner shop for your business, you have to pay the cost of the lease every month, however many pizzas you produce and sell.

Variable costs, on the other hand, depend on the quantity of output produced. These costs include the raw materials that go into production, as well as many types oflabor costs. A drug company's variable costs would include the chemicals that go into pills, packaging materials, and wages of employees in the factories that make and package the pills. A pizza firm's variable costs would include pizza dough and toppings, card- board take–away containers, and the wages of employees. In order to produce more pills or more pizzas, these firms would have to buy more raw materials and hire more employees, adding to their total variable costs.

A firm's total cost is the combination of all of its fixed and variable costs. If a firm produces nothing–if it stops production–then its variable cost is zero. If a pizza firm decides to stop making pizzas, it no longer has to pay employees or buy ingredients. But it will still be obliged to pay for its space until the lease expires. A cost function is a mathematical formula used to chart how production expenses will change at different output levels. In other words, it estimates the total cost of production given a specific quantity produced.

Understanding a firm's cost function is helpful in the budgeting process because it helps management understand the cost behavior of a product. This is vital to anticipate costs that will be incurred in the next operating period at the planned activity level. Also, this allows management to evaluate how efficiently the production process was at the end of the management uses this model to run different production scenarios and help predict what the total cost would be to produce a product at different levels of output. The cost function equation is expressed as.

Equation 4-3

$$C(x) = FC + V(x)$$

where C equals total production cost, FC is total fixed costs, V is variable cost and x is the number of units.

(3) *Explicit and implicit costs.* We can distinguish between two types of cost: Explicit and implicit. *Explicit costs are out–of–pocket costs, that is, payments that are actually made.* Wages that a firm pays its employees or rent that a firm pays for its office are explicit costs. Implicit costs are more subtle, but just as important. An *implicit cost* is any cost that has already occurred but not necessarily shown or reported as a separate expense. They represent the opportunity cost of using resources already owned by the firm. Often for small businesses, they are resources contributed by the owners; for example, working in the business while not getting a formal salary, or using the ground floor of a home as a retail store. Implicit costs also allow for depreciation of goods, materials, and equipment that are necessary for a company to operate.

These two definitions of cost are important for distinguishing between two conceptions of *profit, accounting profit and economic profit*. Accounting profit is a cash concept. It means total revenue minus explicit costs–the difference between dollars brought in and dollars paid out. Economic profit is total revenue minus total cost, including both explicit and implicit costs. The difference is important because even though a business pays income taxes based on its accounting profit, whether or not it is economically successful depends on its economic profit. You need to subtract both the explicit and implicit costs to determine the true economic profit. The equation is:

Equation 4-4

Economic Profit = Total Revenues – Explicit Costs – Implicit Costs

4.2 Isocost lines

4.2.1 Isocost lines

An isoquant shows what a firm is desirous of producing. But, the desire to produce a commodity is not enough. The producer must have sufficient capacity to buy necessary factor inputs to be able to reach its desired production level. The capacity of the producer is shown by his monetary resources, i.e., his cost outlay (or how much money he is capable of spending) on capital and labor, the prices of which are taken as constant, i.e.', given in the market place.

So, like the consumer the producer has also to operate under a budget (resource) constraint. This is picturized by his budget line called *isocost line.* In economics an isocost line shows *all combinations of inputs which cost the same total amount.* Although similar to the budget constraint in consumer theory, the use of the isocost line pertains to cost–minimization in production, as opposed to utility–maximization. For the two production inputs labor and capital, with fixed unit costs of the inputs, the equation of the isocost line is where ω represents the wage rate of labor, γ represents the rental rate of capital, K is the amount of capital used, L is the amount of labor used, and C is the total cost of acquiring those quantities of the two inputs. The cost function equation is expressed as.

Equation 4-5

$$C = \omega L + \gamma K$$

The absolute value of the slope of the isocost line, with capital plotted vertically and labor plotted horizontally, equals the ratio of unit costs of labor and capital. The slope is: The isocost line is combined with the isoquant map to determine the optimal production point at any given level of output. Specifically, the point of tangency between any isoquant and an isocost line gives the lowest–cost combination of inputs that can produce the level of output associated with that isoquant. Equivalently, it gives the maximum level of output that can be produced for a given total cost of inputs. A line joining tangency points of isoquants and isocosts is called the expansion path.

An isocost line is a locus of points showing the alternative combinations of factors that can be purchased with a fixed amount of money. In fact, every point on a given isocost line represents the same total cost. To construct isocost lines we need information about the market prices of the two factors. For example, suppose, the price of labor is Re. 1 per unit and the price of capital is Rs. 4 per unit.

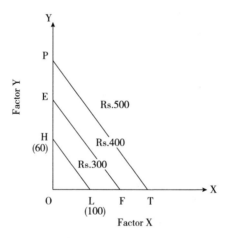

Figure 4–1　Iso-cost line

Table 4–1　Alternative methods of producing six units of output

Method	Units of K	Units of L
a	18	2
b	12	3
c	9	4
d	6	6
e	4	9
f	3	12
g	2	18

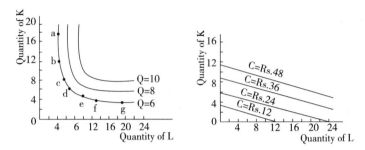

Figure 4–2   Isoquants and isocost lines

Then an outlay of Rs. 36 could buy 9K + 0L, 36L + 0K, or other combinations such as 5K+16L. All these and other various combinations by isocost line C= Rs. 36. Isocost lines C=Rs. 12, C=Rs. 24 and C=Rs. 48 show the alternative combinations of capital and labor that can be purchased or hired by spending Rs. 12, Rs. 24 and Rs. 48, respectively.

These lines are straight lines because factor prices are constant and they have a negative slope equal to the factor–price ratio, i.e., the ratio of labor price to capital price (i.e., the wage ratio and the rate of interest) .

4.2.2   Cost minimization

Here, the firm seeks to minimize its cost of producing a given level of output. To find the least–cost combination of factors for fixed level of output we combine Figure 4–2 in Figure 4–5. Suppose, the producer wants to produce six units of output. He could do so using the combination represented by points A, B or C in Figure 4–3.

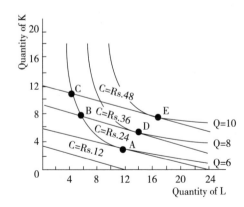

Figure 4–3   Cost minimization

For example, the cost would be Rs. 48 at C, Rs. 36 at B and Rs. 24 at A. The cheapest method is at A, where the iso-quant for output of six (Q=6) is tangent to an isocost line (C=Rs. 24) . In Figure 4-5 the firm tries to find out the least expensive factor combination along its isoquant. It looks for that factor combination that is on the lowest of the isocost lines. Where the isoquant touches (but does not cross) the lowest isocost line is the least cost position.

The tangency point shows that optimization in production is reached when factor prices and marginal product are proportional, with equalized marginal product per rupee. The minimum-cost points are A, D and E. Each such point shows the equilibrium factor combination for maximizing output subject to cost constraint, i.e., subject to fixed factor prices and fixed outlay (on resources) .

We may now speak a few words about the slopes of isoquant and an isocost line. The slope of an isoquant gives the **marginal rate of technical substitution (MKTS)** defined as *the increase in the quantity of one factor that is required to replace a unit decrease in another factor, when output is held constant along any isoquant.* It is also known as the **desired rate of factor substitution**, i.e., the rate at which the producer wants to substitute one factor by the other.

MKTS is, in fact, *the ratio of the marginal products of the factors.* To see this, consider an example. Assume that output is such that the MPL and the MPK are both equal to 2 (units of output) , i.e., MPK=MPL. If the firm is to maintain the same level of output while reducing capital by one unit, it needs to replace one unit of capital by one unit of labor. If at another point on the same isoquant, the MPL=2, while the MPK=1, the firm needs to replace a unit of capital with only half unit of labor.

An isocost line shows the alternative quantities of two factors viz., capital and labor that can be purchased or hired with a fixed sum of money. Its slope is given by the ratio of the prices of the two factors. It is known as the actual rate of factor substitution, the rate at which the firm can substitute labor by capital in the market place.

Thus, in Figure 4-5, given the prices of labor and capital at Re. 1 and Rs. 4 per unit, respectively, the slope of C = Rs. 12 is determined by drawing the line joining points 3K + 0L (which represents outlay of Rs. 12 entirely on capital) and 12L + OK (Rs. 12 spent entirely on labor) . All the isocost lines in the diagram have the same slope because the relative prices of labor and capital are the same. If labor were relatively more expensive, the isocost lines would be steeper in Figure 4-4.

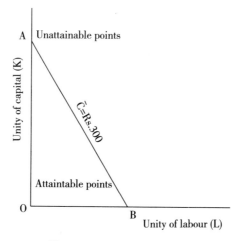

Figure 4–4   An isocost line

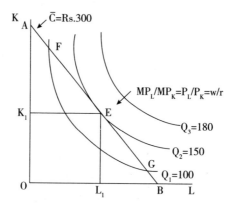

Figure 4–5   Production of maximum output with a fixed outlay

Cost minimization occurs when an isoquant is just tangent to (but does not cross) an isocost line. When this happens the ratio of the prices of factors is the same as the ratio of their marginal products. Symbolically,

Equation 4-6

$$MP_L/MP_K = P_L/P_K$$

4.3   Short–run cost

i. Short-Run Total Cost

A typical short–run total cost curve (STC) is shown in Figure 4–6. This curve indicates the firm's total cost of production for each level of output when the usage of one or more of the firm's resources remains fixed.

When output is zero, cost is positive because fixed cost has to be incurred regardless of output. Examples of such costs are rent of land, depreciation charges, license fee, interest on loan, etc. They are called unavoidable contractual costs. Such costs remain contractually fixed and so cannot be avoided in the short run.

The only way to avoid such costs is by going into liquidation. The total fixed cost (TFC) curve is a horizontal straight line. Total variable is the difference between total cost and fixed cost. The total variable cost curve (TVC) starts from the origin, because such cost varies with the level of output and hence are avoidable. Examples are electricity tariff, wages and compensation of casual workers, cost of raw materials etc.

In Figure 4-6. the total cost (OC) of producing Q units of output is total fixed cost of plus total variable cost (FC) .

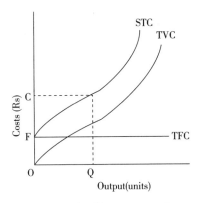

Figure 4-6   Short-run costs

Clearly, variable cost and, therefore, total cost must increase with an increase in output. We also see that variable cost first increase at a decreasing rate (the slope of STC decreases) then increase at an increasing rate (the slope of STC increases) . This cost structure is accounted for by the law of Variable Proportions.

ii. Average and Marginal Cost

One can gain a better insight into the firm's cost structure by analyzing the behavior of short-run average and marginal costs. We may first consider average fixed cost (AFC) .

Average fixed cost is total fixed cost divided by output.

Equation 4-7

$$i.e., AFC = TFC /Q$$

Since total fixed cost does not vary with output average fixed cost is a constant amount divided by output. Average fixed cost is relatively high at very low output levels. However, with gradual increase in output, AFC continues to fall as output increases, approaching zero as output becomes very large. In Figure 4–7, we observe that the AFC curve takes the shape of a rectangular hyperbola.

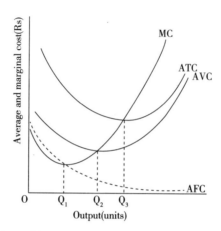

Figure 4–7   Short–run average and marginal cost curves

We now consider average variable cost (AVC) which is arrived at by dividing total variable cost by output.

Equation 4-8

$$i.e., AVC= - TVC/Q$$

In Figure 4–7, AVC is a typical average variable cost curve. Average variable cost first falls, reaches a minimum point(at output level Q_2)and subsequently increases.

The next important concept is one of average total cost (ATC) .

It is calculated by dividing total cost by output.

Equation 4-9

$$i.e., \ ATC = \frac{TC}{Q}$$

$$Alternatively, \ TC = TFC + TVC$$

$$and \ ATC = \frac{TFC}{Q} + \frac{TVC}{Q}$$

$$=AFC+AVC$$

It is, therefore, the sum of average fixed cost and average variable cost.

Equation 4-10

$$ATC = AFC + AVC$$

We know that and that average fixed cost continuously falls over the whole range of output. Thus, ATC declines at first because both AFC and AVC are falling. Even when AVC begins to rise after Q_2, the decrease in AFC continues to drive down ATC as output increases. However, an output of Q_3 is finally reached, at which the increase in AVC overcomes the decrease in AFC, and ATC starts rising.

Since ATC = AFC + AVC, the vertical distance between average total cost and average variable cost measures average fixed cost. Since AFC declines over the entire range of output. AVC becomes closer and closer to ATC as output increases.

We may finally consider short–run marginal cost (SMC) . Marginal cost is the change in short–run total cost attributable to an extra unit of output: or

The ATC curve, illustrated, is U–shaped in Figure 4–7 because the AVC cost curve is U–shaped. This is accounted for by the Law of Variable Proportions. It first declines, reaches a minimum (at Q_3 units of output) and subsequently rises. The minimum point on ATC is reached at a larger output than at which AVC attains its minimum. This point can easily be proved.

$$SWC = \frac{\Delta STC}{\Delta Q}$$

However, since $STC = TFC + TVC$

$$SMC = \frac{\Delta TFC}{\Delta Q} + \frac{\Delta TVC}{\Delta Q}$$

$$= 0 + \frac{\Delta TVC}{\Delta Q}$$

$$= \frac{\Delta TVC}{\Delta Q}$$

Short–run marginal cost refers to the change in cost that results from a change in output when the usage of the variable factor changes. As Figure 4–7 shows, marginal cost first declines, reaches a minimum at Q_X (note that minimum marginal cost is attained at a level of output less than that at which AVC and ATC attain their minimum) and rises there-after.

The marginal cost curve intersects AVC and ATC at their respective minimum points. This result follows from the definitions of the cost curves. If marginal cost curve lies below average variable cost curve the implication is clear: each additional unit of output adds less to total cost than the average variable cost.

Thus, average variable cost has to fall. So long as MC is above AVC, each additional unit of output adds more to total cost than AVC. Thus, in this case, AVC must rise.

Thus, when MC is less than AVC, average variable cost is falling. When MC is greater than AVC, average variable cost is rising. Thus, MC must equal AVC at the minimum point of AVC. Exactly the same reasoning would apply to show MC crosses ATC at the minimum point of the latter curve.

4.3.1　Short-run cost functions

Summary of the Main Points All the important short-run cost relations may now be summed up:

The total cost function may be expressed as:

Equation 4-11

$$TC = k + f(Q)$$

where k is total fixed cost which is a constant, and $f(Q)$ is total variable cost which is a function of output.

Equation 4-12

$$ATC = k/Q + f(Q)/Q = AFC + AVC$$

Since k is a constant and Q gradually increases, the ratio k/Q falls. Hence the AFC curve is a rectangular hyperbola.

Here,

Equation 4-13

$$MC = \frac{d(TC)}{dQ} = \frac{d}{dQ}(k) + \frac{d}{dQ}[f(Q)] = 0 + f'(Q)$$

where $f'(Q)$ is the change in TVC and may be called marginal variable cost (MVC). Thus, it is clear that MC refers to MVC and has no relation to fixed cost. Since business decisions are largely governed by marginal cost, and marginal costs have no relation to fixed cost, it logically follows costs do not affect business decisions.

4.3.2   Relation between MC and AC

There is a close relation between MC and AC. When AC is falling, MC is less than AC. This can be proved as follows:

When AC is falling,

$$\frac{d}{dQ}\left(\frac{TC}{Q}\right) < 0, \quad or, \quad \frac{Q \times \frac{dTC}{dQ} - TC < 0}{Q^2}$$

$$or, \quad \frac{dTC}{dQ} - TC < 0$$

$$or, \quad \frac{dTC}{dQ} - \frac{TC}{Q} < 0$$

$$or, \quad \frac{dTC}{dQ} < \frac{TC}{Q}$$

$$or, \quad MC < AC$$

4.3.3   Cost elasticity

On the basis of the relation between MC and AC we can develop a new concept, viz., the con cept of cost elasticity. It measures the responsiveness of total cost to a small change in the level of output.

It can be expressed as:

Equation 4-14

$$E_C = \frac{\% \ change \ in \ TC}{\% \ change \ in \ Q} = \frac{\Delta TC / TC}{\Delta Q / Q}$$

$$= \frac{\Delta TC}{\Delta Q} \div \frac{TC}{Q} = MC \div AC$$

So, it is the ratio of MC to AC.

The properties of the average and marginal cost curves and their relationship to each other. From the diagram the following relationships can be discovered.

(1) AFC declines continuously, approaching both axes asymptomatically (as shown by the decreasing distance between ATC and AVC) and is a rectangular hyperbola.

（2）AVC first declines, reaches a minimum at Q_2 and rises thereafter. When AVC is at its minimum, MC equals AVC.

（3）ATC first declines, reaches a minimum at Q_3, and rises thereafter. When ATC is at its minimum, MC equals ATC.

（4）MC first declines, reaches a minimum at Q_1, and rises thereafter. MC equals both AVC and ATC when these curves are at their minimum values.

The lowest point of the AVC curve is called the shut（close）–down point and that of the ATC curve the break–even point. These two concepts will be discussed in the context of market structure and pricing. Finally, we see that MC lies below both AVC and ATC over the range in which these curves decline; contrarily, MC lies above them when they are rising.

Table 4-2 numerically illustrates the characteristics of all the cost curves. Column（5）shows that average fixed cost decreases over the entire range of output. Columns（6）and（7）depict that both average variable and average total cost first decrease, then increase, with average variable cost attaining a minimum at a lower output than that at which average total cost reaches its minimum. Column（8）shows that marginal cost per 100 units is the incremental increase in total cost and variable cost.

Table 4-2 short-run cost schedules of a hypothetical firm

（1）Output	（2）Total cost	（3）Fixed cost	（4）Variable cost	（5）Average fixed cost	（6）Average variable cost	（7）Average total cost	（8）Marginal cost（per unit）
Rs.	Rs.	Rs.	Rs.	Rs.	Rs.	Rs.	Rs.
100	6000	4000	2000	40.00	20.00	60.00	20.00
200	7000	4000	3000	20.00	15.00	35.00	10.00
300	7500	4000	3500	13.33	11.67	25.00	5.00
400	9000	4000	5000	10.00	12.50	22.50	15.00
500	11000	4000	7000	8.00	14.00	22.00	20.00
600	14000	4000	10000	6.67	16.67	23.33	30.00
700	18000	4000	14000	5.71	20.00	25.71	40.00
800	24000	4000	20000	5.00	25.00	30.00	60.00
900	34000	4000	30000	4.44	33.33	37.77	100.00
1000	50000	4000	46000	4.00	46.00	50.00	160.00

If we compare columns (6) and (8) we see that marginal cost (per unit) is below average variable and average total cost when each is falling and is greater than each when AVC and ATC are rising.

4.4 Long-run cost

4.4.1 Long run total costs

Long run total cost refers to the minimum cost of production. It is the least cost of producing a given level of output. Thus, it can be less than or equal to the short run average costs at different levels of output but never greater.

In graphically deriving the LTC curve, the minimum points of the STC curves at different levels of output are joined. The locus of all these points gives us the LTC curve. The LTC curve is shown in Figure 4-8:

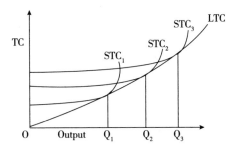

Figure 4-8   LTC Curve

As shown in Figure 4-8, short run total costs curves; STC_1, STC_2, and STC_3 are shown depicting different plant sizes. The LTC curve is made by joining the minimum points of short run total cost curves. Therefore, LTC envelopes the STC curves.

4.4.2 Long run average cost curve

Long run average cost (LAC) can be defined as the average of the LTC curve or the cost per unit of output in the long run. It can be calculated by the division of LTC by the quantity of output. Graphically, LAC can be derived from the Short run

Average Cost (SAC) curves.

While the SAC curves correspond to a particular plant since the *plant is fixed in the short–run*, the LAC curve depicts the scope for expansion of plant by minimizing cost.

4.4.3 Derivation of the LAC curve

Note in the figure, that each SAC curve corresponds to a particular plant size. This size is fixed but what can vary is the variable input in the short–run. In the long run, the firm will select that plant size which can minimize costs for a given level of output.

You can see that till the OM_1 level of output it is logical for the firm to operate at the plat size represented by SAC_2. If the firm operates at the cost represented by SAC_2 when producing an output level OM_2, the cost would be more.

So, in the long run, the firm will produce till OM_1 on SAC_2. However, till an output level represented by OM_3, the firm can produce at SAC_2, after which it is profitable to produce at SAC_3 if the firm wishes to minimize costs.

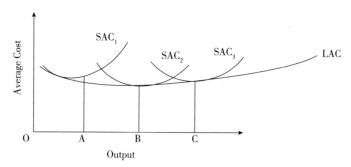

Figure 4–9   Derivation of LAC Curve

Thus, the choice, in the long run, is to produce at that plant size that can minimize costs. Graphically, this gives us a LAC curve that joins the minimum points of all possible SAC curves, as shown in the figure. Thus, the LAC curve is also called an **envelope curve** or **planning curve**. The curve first falls, reaches a minimum and then rises, giving it a U–shape.

We can use returns to scale to explain the shape of the LAC curve. Returns to scale depict the change in output with respect to a change in inputs. During Increasing Returns to Scale (IRS) , the output doubles by using less than double inputs. As a result, LTC increases less than the rise in output and LAC will fall.

● In Constant Returns to Scale （CRS）, the output doubles by doubling the inputs and the LTC increases proportionately with the rise in output. Thus, LAC remains constant.

● In Decreasing Returns to Scale （DRS）, the output doubles by using more than double the inputs so the LTC increases more than proportionately to the rise in output. Thus, LAC also rises. This gives LAC its U-shape.

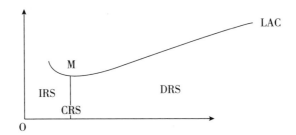

Figure 4-10   Derivation of LAC Curve under Returns to scale

4.4.4   Long run marginal cost

Long run marginal cost is defined at the additional cost of producing an extra unit of the output in the long-run i.e. when all inputs are variable. The LMC curve is derived by the points of tangency between LAC and SAC.

LMC curve can be learned through Figure 4-11.

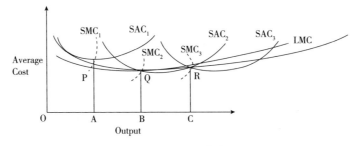

Figure 4-11   LMC Curve

If perpendiculars are drawn from point A, B, and C, respectively; then they would intersect SMC curves at P, Q, and R respectively. By joining P, Q, and R, the LMC curve would be drawn. It should be noted that LMC equals to SMC, when

LMC is tangent to the LAC.

In Figure 4–11 OB is the output at which:

Equation 4-15

$$SAC_2 = SMC_2 = LAC = LMC$$

When LMC < LAC, LAC falls

When LMC = LAC, LAC is constant

When LMC > LAC, LAC rises

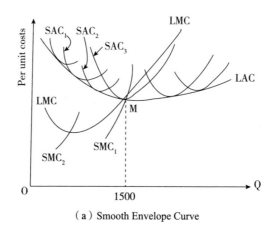

（a）Smooth Envelope Curve

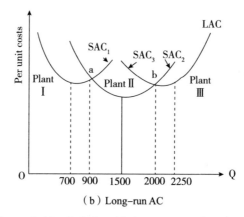

（b）Long-run AC

Figure 4–12   Relationship between LMC and LAC

Conclusion

A firm's cost structure is crucial to understanding the firm's behavior. The present chapter shows that once we know the factor prices and technological opportunities available to the firm, we can derive all of the firm's cost curves.And costs is crucial becausecosts, along with the firm's revenues, determine profits. The pursuit of profits, of course,drives every firm's decision–making process, including how much to produce and whetherto stay in business.

Over the next few chapters, we'll continue to dig into the details of firm behavior that determine the market supply curve. Hold onto your understanding of production functions, different types of costs, and ways of calculating profits. We'll build on them as we continue to describe firm choices and market structures.

Key Term

Total Revenue	Profit	Implicit Costs
Economic Profit	Fixed Costs	Average Variable Cost
Average Cost	Variable Costs	Accounting Profit
Total Cost	Explicit Costs	
Marginal Cost	Average Fixed Cost	

Review Questions

1.A firm pays its accountant an annual retainer of ¥10,000. Is this an economic cost?

2. The owner of a small retail store does her own accounting work. How would you measure the opportunity cost of her work?

3. Please explain whether the following statements are true or false.

a. If the owner of a business pays himself no salary, then the accounting cost is zero, but the economic cost is positive.

b.A firm that has positive accounting profit does not necessarily have positive economic profit.

c. If a firm hires a currently unemployed worker, theopportunity cost of utilizing the worker's services is zero.

4.If the firm's average cost curves are U–shaped, why does its average variable cost curve achieve its minimum at a lower level of output than the average total cost curve?

5. If a firm enjoys economies of scale up to a certain output level, and cost then increases proportionately with output, what can you say about the shape of the long-run average cost curve?

6. How does a change in the price of one input change the firm's long-run expansion path?

7. Distinguish between economies of scale and economies of scope. Why can one be present without the other?

8. Is the firm's expansion path always a straight line?

9. What is the difference between economies of scale and returns to scale?

Application

1. Suppose the economy takes a downturn, and that labor costs fall by 50 percent and are expected to stayat that level for a long time. Show graphically how this change in the relative price of labor and capital affects the firm's expansion path.

2. Suppose a firm must pay an annual tax, which is a fixed sum, independent of whether it produces any output.

a. How does this tax affect the firm's fixed, marginal, and average costs?

b. Now suppose the firm is charged a tax that is proportional to the number of items it produces. Again, how does this tax affect the firm's fixed, marginal, and average costs?

3. The short-run cost function of a company is given by the equation TC=200+55g,where TC is the total cost and q is the total quantity of output, both measured in thousands.

a. What is the company's fixed cost?

b. If the company produced 100000 units of goods, what would be its average variable cost?

c. What would be its marginal cost of production?

d. What would be its average fixed cost?

e. Suppose the company borrows money and expands its factory. Its fixed cost rises by ¥50000, but its variable cost falls to ¥45000 per 1000 units. The cost of interest（i）also enters into the equation. Each1-point increase in the interest rate raises costs by ¥3000. Write the new cost equation.

5

Perfect Competition

Learning Objectives

LO 5.1   Describe the characteristics of a perfectly competitive market.

LO 5.2   Calculate average, marginal, and total revenue.

LO 5.3   Find a firm's optimal quantity of output.

LO 5.4   Describe a firm's decision to shut down and when to exit the market, and explain the difference between these choices.

LO 5.5   Draw a short–run supply curve for a competitive market with identical firms.

LO 5.6   Draw a long–run supply curve for a competitive market with identical firms, and describe its implications for profit–seeking firms.

LO 5.7   Explain why a long–run supply curve might slope upward.

LO 5.8   Calculate the effect of a shift in demand on a market in long–run equilibrium.

We have assuming an economic ideal and that economic ideal is perfect competition. *Market economy* refers to an economy in which private individuals, rather than a centralized planning authority, make the decisions. What do we mean by a market? The word might make you think of a physical location where buyers and sellers come together face–to–face like a farmers' market or a mall. But people do not have to be physically near each other to make an exchange. For example, think of online retailers like Tmall.com or of fruit that is grown in South America but sold all over the world. The term *market* actually refers to the buyers and sellers who trade a particular good or service, not to a physical location.

Making simplifying assumptions can help us zero in on important ideas. In this chapter, we will make a big simplifying assumption—that markets are competitive. *A competitive market* is one in which fully informed, price–taking buyers and sellers easily trade a standardized good or service. Let's unpack this multipart definition: Imagine you're driving up to an intersection where there is a gas station on each corner. This scenario demonstrates the four important characteristics of a perfectly competitive market.

5.1   Characteristics of a competitive market

Competitive market. A market with many buyers and sellers trading identical products so that each buyer and seller is a *price taker*. A competitive market, sometimes called a perfectly competitive market, has four characteristics:

A.The goods offered by the various sellers are largely the same.

As a result of these conditions, the actions of any single buyer or seller in the market have a negligible impact on the market price. Each buyer and seller take the market price as given.

An example is the market for milk. No single buyer of milk can influence the price of milk because each buyer purchases a small amount relative to the size of the market. Similarly, each seller of milk has limited control over the price because many other sellers are offering milk that is essentially identical. Because each seller can sell all he wants at the going price, he has little reason to charge less, and if he charges more, buyers will go elsewhere. Buyers and sellers in competitive markets must accept the price the market determines and, therefore, are said to be *price takers.Individuals can't affect the going price.* The opposite of being a price taker is having *market power,* or the ability to noticeably affect market prices.

B. Goods and services are standardized.

The second essential characteristic of a perfectly competitive market is that the goods and services being traded are standardized. Each enterprise not only produces a product of the same quality, but also has no difference in the quality, performance, shape, packaging and other aspects of the product. As a result, no enterprise can influence the price and form a monopoly through the particularity of its own product and other products, so as to enjoy the monopoly benefits. For consumers, no matter which enterprise's products they buy, they are homogeneous and undifferentiated products, so that many consumers can't form preferences according to the differences of products, and buyers don't care about manufacturers and brands when they buy goods in the market. That is to say, when all kinds of goods have complete substitutability with each other, it is easy to approach the completely competitive market.

C. Firms can freely enter or exit the market.

It means that any manufacturer can enter or exit a market completely freely and without any difficulty. That is to say, access to or exit from the market is completely decided by the producers themselves, and is not limited by any social laws and other social forces. As there are no social barriers to enter and exit the market, when there is net profit in an industry market, many new producers will be attracted to enter the industry market, resulting in the decline of profit and the gradual disappearance of profit. When there are losses in the industry market, many producers will withdraw from the market, which will cause the emergence and growth of the industry market profits. In this way, in a long period of time, producers can only obtain normal profits, but not monopoly interests.

D. Complete information.

That is to say, every buyer and seller of market has all the information ports related to their own economic decisions. Thus, every consumer and every manufacturer can make their own optimal economic decisions according to the complete information they have, so as to obtain the maximum economic benefits. Moreover, since every buyer and seller know the established market price, they trade according to the established market price, which also excludes the situation that a market may trade according to different prices at the same time due to the blocked information.

5.2   Demand curve in competitive market

For the whole industry, the demand curve is a downward sloping curve and the supply curve is an upward sloping curve. The price of products in the whole industry is determined by such demand and supply. As shown in Figure 5−1 (a).

Demand curve of fully competitive manufacturers

The demand curve of a complete competitive firm is a horizontal line starting from a given market price level. As shown in Figure5−1 (b).

Income curve of fully competitive manufacturers

Totalyield curve: A straight line with constant slope from the origin.

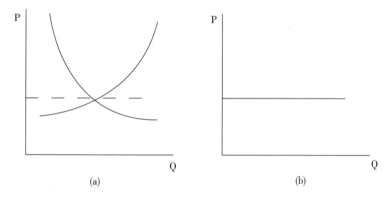

Figure 5 –1   Demand curve of perfectly competitive market and firm

5.3   Revenues in a perfectly competitive market

A firm in a competitive market, like most other firms in the economy, tries to maximize profit, which equals total revenue minus total cost. To see how it does this, we first consider the revenue of a competitive firm. To keep matters concrete, let's consider a certain firm. What can we say about your firm's revenue? we talked about **total revenue:** The price that a firm receives for each good, multiplied by the quantity of that good it sells. In this case, the firm sells only one good. Its total revenue is therefore equal to the price times the quantity it sells, or $P \times Q$. For instance, if the price is 1 per goods, and the firm produces 100 pieces, its total revenue will be 100.

Total revenue from the sale of output is equal to price times quantity.

Equation 5-1

Total Revenue=Price × Quantity

TR=P×Q

Table 5-1 shows revenue for a firm in a competitive market. The third column in the Table shows total revenue at various quantities. Price remains the same regardless of the quantity that the firm produces, because the firm is a price taker in a competitive market. So, if the quantity produced triples, from 100 to 300 pieces, revenue also triples from 100 francs to 300.

We also need to consider two other measures of revenue: average revenue and marginal revenue. *Average revenue* is total revenue divided by the quantity sold. *Total revenue* is P × Q. So average revenue is (P × Q) divided by Q, or simply P. In other words, for any firm selling one product, average revenue is equal to the price of the good.

（1）Definition of average revenue: Total revenue divided by the quantity sold.

Equation 5-2

Average Revenue=total Revenue/Quantity

AR=TR/Q

Marginal revenue is the revenue generated by selling an additional unit of a good. In our example, this is simply the market price, because one unit of the good always generates revenue of 1 × P =P. For a firm in a competitive market, marginal revenue is equal to the price of the good. (If the market were not competitive, however, producing an additional unit of a good might affect the market price.)

（2）Definition of marginal revenue: The change in total revenue from an additional unit sold.

Equation 5-3

Marginal Revenue =change in Total Revenue/ change in Quantity

MR= ΔTR/ΔQ

We can check these rules in Table 5-1 by calculating average and marginal revenue directly from quantity and price. Average revenue, shown in column 4, is equal to the value in column 3 (total revenue) divided by the value in column 1 (quantity). Marginal revenue, shown in column 5, is calculated by subtracting total revenue in one row from total revenue in the next row, as quantity increases. We can confirm that at any quantity, average and marginal revenue are both equal to price for this price–taking firm in a competitive market.

Table 5-1　Revenue for a certain competitive firm

Quantity (Q)	Price (P)	Total revenue (TR=P×Q)	Average revenue (AR=TR/Q)	Marginal revenue (MR=ΔTR/ΔQ)
100	1	100	1	1
200	1	200	1	1
300	1	300	1	1
400	1	400	1	1
500	1	500	1	1

Revenue curve

As we can see from Figure 5-2, the curve of competitive firm

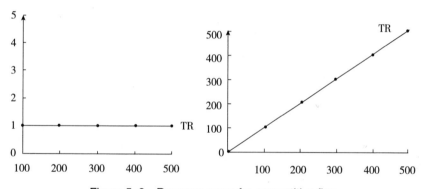

Figure 5-2　Revenue curve for competitive firm

The equilibrium point of intersection of market demand curve D and supply curve S determines that the market equilibrium price is P. Because of the large number of sellers and buyers in the fully competitive market, no one can manipulate the market price. Therefore, the manufacturer is the passive receiver of the given market price. The level line starting from the given price level P_0 is the demand curve of the fully competitive enterprise. The enterprise will not and does not need to change this price level. In other words, if the manufacturer's price is higher than P_0, the consumer will not buy any products of the enterprise and transfer to other manufacturers for purchase. As long as the manufacturer is willing to accept the price, it can sell as much as it wants. However, this does not mean that the transaction volume will be enlarged accordingly, so how many products manufacturers produce depends on their cost structure. Therefore, the demand curve of the fully competitive firm is a horizontal line starting from the established market price.

Therefore, the demand level line of a fully competitive enterprise indicates that no matter how the sales volume changes, the sales price of the enterprise is fixed in the short term. Therefore, the revenue increment of each additional product sales is always equal to the unit price. Curve of average and marginal revenue: AR curve, MR curve and D curve of demand overlap and equal to the established market price P. That is $AR = MR = P$.

The cost curves

We have already stated that the market supply curve is a normal looking upward sloping supply curve. But what about the firms' supply curve? The following diagrams will attempt to explain that each firm's supply curve is their marginal cost curve.

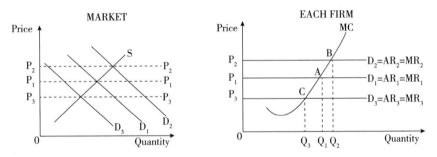

Figure 5–3   Frommarginal cost curve to supply curve

Assume that initially, D_1 is the market demand curve, S the market supply curve, and so the given market price is P_1. This means that each firm in the market has an individual demand curve of D_1. This also represents their average revenue curve (AR) and their marginal revenue curve (MR).

One of the key assumptions we made earlier was that each firm tries to maximize profits. This occurs at the level of output where marginal cost=marginal revenue (MC=MR).

Looking at the diagram for the firm, when the price is P_1, the condition MC = MR occurs at point A, giving an output of Q_1. If there is a shift to the right of the demand curve in the market (due to increased real incomes, for example), the given price will rise to P_2, and each firm will have an individual demand curve of D_2. This time, MC = MR occurs at point B, giving output Q_2. For a shift to the left in market demand, the given price is P_3, MC = MR occurs at C and output for each firm is Q_3.

From the analysis above, you can see that, effectively, if a firm wants to find out how much he should supply at any given price, he simply reads this amount off the marginal cost curve. The marginal cost curve is doing the job of a supply curve; it tells the firm its supply for any given price. Hence, the marginal cost curve is the firm's supply curve.

5.4   The shut–down point

So, a perfectly competitive firm's marginal cost curve is its supply curve. But as you will see, its supply curve is not the whole of the marginal cost curve.

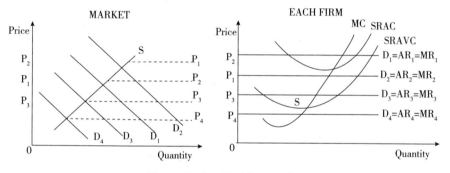

Figure 5 –4   Shutdown point

The two diagrams above are very similar to the two previous diagrams except I've added the firm's average cost and average variable cost curves (both are short run curves).

Let's assume that the given market price is P_1. Does each firm make profit or loss? Well, given the information we have, it is probably best to compare average revenue and average cost (we don't have TR and TC).

At P_1, AR > AC, so the firm is making **super normal profit.**

At P_2, AR = AC, so each firm is making **normal profit,** or, in other words, breaking even.

At P_3, AR < AC, so each firm is making a **loss.** But, AR > AVC. This means that the revenue each firm receives, on average, is still higher than their variable costs. They can "cover" their variable costs. They can still pay wages, pay for raw materials and pay for the power to run the machines. They can exist! The costs they can't cover are some of the fixed costs. Imagine this as being behind on the rent! A problem but not the end of the world. The point is that the firm can keep operating.

Below point S, the **shutdown point,** the firm has to shut down even in the short run. For instance, at the given price P_4, AR < AVC. The firm cannot even cover its variable costs of production. If a firm cannot even afford the raw materials or the labor to make enough of the product to minimize their losses, then they are in real trouble! They must shut down.

The implication of all this is that, although the firm's supply curve is the marginal cost curve, in the short run it is only that part of the MC curve that is above point S. The supply curve for a perfectly competitive firm in the short run is the part of the marginal cost curve above the average variable cost curve.

5.5   Profit maximization

The goal of a competitive firm is to maximize profit, which equals total revenue minus total cost. We have just discussed the firm's revenue, and in the last chapter we discussed the firm's costs. We are now ready to examine how the firm maximizes profit and how that decision leads to its supply curve.

Profit maximization requires the firm to manage its internal operations efficiently (prevent waste, encourage worker morale, choose efficient production processes, and so forth) and to make sound decisions in the marketplace (buy the correct quantity of inputs at least cost and choose the optimal level of output). Because profits involve both costs and revenues, the firm must have a good grasp of its cost structure. We will exam the production equilibrium point for maximizing profit in Figure 5-5.

a. If marginal revenue is greater than the marginal cost, the firm should increase its output.

b. If marginal cost is greater than marginal revenue, the firm should decrease its output.

c. At the profit-maximizing level of output, marginal revenue and marginal cost are exactly equal.

d. These rules apply not only to competitive firms, but to firms with market power as well.

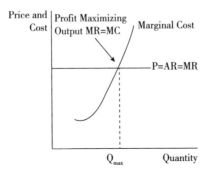

Figure 5-5   Profit maximization

The reason underlying this proposition is that the competitive firm can always make additional profit as long as the price is greater than the marginal cost of the last unit. Total profit reaches its peak—is maximized—when there is no longer any extra profit to be earned by selling extra output. At the maximum–profit point, the last unit produced brings in an amount of revenue exactly equal to that unit's cost. What is that extra revenue? It is the price per unit. What is that extra cost? It is the marginal cost.

The general rule then is: *A profit-maximizing firm will set its output at that level where marginal cost equals price. Diagrammatically, this means that a firm's marginal cost curve is also its supply curve.*

5.6   Short–term equilibrium and short–run supply curve

5.6.1   Short–term equilibrium

First of all, we need to look at the possible situations in which firms may find themselves in the short run.

With each of the three diagrams above, the situation for the firm is only drawn. The "market" diagram, from which the given price is derived, is the same every time, so I've missed it out. The main thing is that you understand that the prices P_1, P_2 and P_3 are determined by market demand and market supply. Also note that in all three

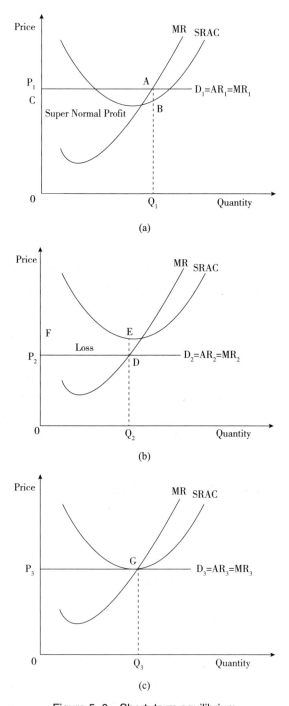

Figure 5–6   Short–term equilibrium

diagrams, the MC curve cuts the AC curve at its lowest point. Look back at the "Costs and revenues" topic if you don't remember why.

The three diagrams show the three situations in which a firm could find itself in the short run.

In the top diagram, the given price is P_1. The firm wants to maximize profits, so it produces at the level of output where MC = MR. This occurs at point A. Drop a vertical line to find the firm's output (Q_1). At Q_1, AR > AC and the difference between average revenue and average cost is the distance AB. This is the profit per unit. To find the total super normal profit, we must multiply the profit per unit per the number of units. In the diagram, this is the area $ABCP_1$ (the red box).

In the middle diagram, the given price is P_2. In this case, it is clear that the firm will not be making a profit. The AC curve is above the AR curve at all levels of output. The firm will still want to minimize its losses, though. This can be done, again, with the trusty old formula, MC = MR. This occurs at point D giving output Q_2. At Q_2, AR < AC and the difference between average revenue and average cost is the distance DE. This is the loss per unit. To find the total losses, we must multiply the loss per unit per the number of units. In the diagram, this is the area $DEFP_2$ (the red box).

In the final diagram, at the bottom, the given price is P_3. Again, the firm will produce the level of output for which MC = MR. This occurs at point G, giving a level of output of Q_3. Notice that at this point, AR = AC, so the firm is making normal profit.

So, in the short run, a perfectly competitive firm could be making super normal profit, or a loss, or just normal profit, depending on the given market price. Note that if the firm's losses get too big in the short run (i.e. AR < AVC) then it will have to shut down (see the section above).

5.6.2   Short–run supply curve of competitive firm

Under perfect competition, a firm produces an output at which marginal cost equals price. If the price is higher than the marginal cost, it will pay the firm to expand its output so as to equal its price. If, on the other hand, the price is less than the marginal cost, it is incurring a loss, and it will reduce its output till the marginal cost and the price are made equal. Hence, the marginal cost curve of the firm is the supply curve of the perfectly competitive firm in the short-run.

But, even in the short-run, a firm will not supply at a price below its minimum average variable cost. That is, in the short-run, a firm must try to cover its' Variable cost at least. Hence, the short-run supply curve of a firm coincides with that portion of the short-run marginal cost curve which lies above the minimum point of the short-run average variable cost (SAVC) curve.

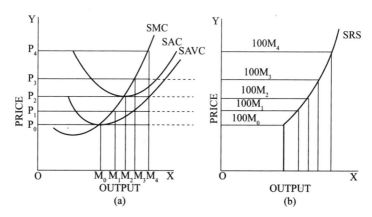

Figure 5-7   Deriving short-run supply Curve of industry

In this diagram, Figure 5-7(a) relates to a firm and 5-7(b) gives the supply curve of the industry. First look at the Figure 5-7(a), which relates to a single firm. Along the axis OX are represented the output supplied and along OY the prices. SMC curve is the short-run marginal cost curve, and, as mentioned above, it is the short-run supply curve of the firm. But only that portion of SMC curve which lies above the short-run average variable cost (SAVC), which means the thick portion above the dotted portion.

Thus, at the price OP_0, OM_0 output will be supplied, at OP_1 price, OM_1, quantity will be supplied at OP_2 price, OM_2 will be supplied, and so on. Nothing will be supplied below the price OP, because prices below OP_0 correspond to the dotted portion of the SMC which is below the minimum point of the SAVC (short-run average variable cost) curve.

5.6.3   Derivation of short-run supply curve of industry

Now from the supply curve of a firm, let us derive the supply curve of the "entire" industry of which all the firms are a constituent part. The supply curve SRS of the industry is derived by the lateral summation (i.e., adding up sideways) of that part of all the firms' marginal cost curves which lies above the minimum point on their average friable cost curves. This industry is supposed to consist of 100 identical firms like the firm represented by the Figure 5–7(a). We see that the short–run supply curve SRC of the industry rises upwards, because the short–run marginal curve SMC rises upwards.

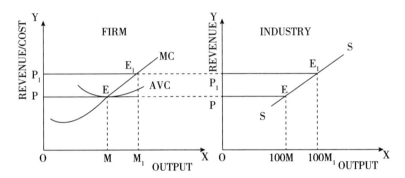

Figure 5–8   Short–run supply curve of competitive industry

5.7   The long run equilibrium of firm

The two sets of diagrams below will help to show that in the long run, all firms in a perfectly competitive market earn only normal profit.

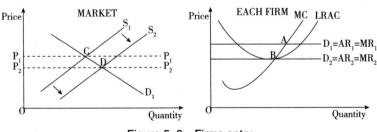

Figure 5–9   Firms entry

In the diagrams above, the initial price is P_1, due to the fact that the initial demand and supply curves, D_1 and S_1, cross at point C. This given price means that each firm's demand curve is D_1. MC = MR occurs at point A. AR > AC, so each firm

133

is making super normal profits. But what will happen as we move towards the long run? Remember that there are no barriers to entry or exit in a perfectly competitive market. This means that new firms will be attracted, in quite large numbers, into the market. This will increase market supply, shifting the supply curve to the right. This will keep happening until the given price is such that all firms in the market earn only normal profit. All of the super normal profit will have been competed away. Once the supply curve has shifted all the way to S_2, with a given price of P_2, then every firm in the industry will be earning normal profit and there will be no incentive for any firm to enter or leave the industry. This is, therefore, the long run equilibrium.

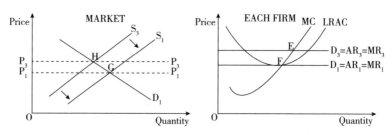

Figure 5-10   Firms exit

In the second set of diagrams above, each firm is making a loss at the initial price P_1. MC = MR occurs at point F, where AR < AC. As we said earlier, firms can take a reasonable sized loss in the short run, but this is not sustainable as we move into the long run. Again, there are no barriers to exit, so some firms will leave the industry, causing the market supply curve to shift to the left. This will keep happening until the given price is such that all firms in the market earn only normal profit. Once the supply curve has shifted all the way to S_3, with a given price of P_3, then every firm in the industry will be earning normal profit and there will be no incentive for any firm to enter or leave the industry. This is, therefore, the long run equilibrium.

Notice that I haven't drawn a set of "long run" diagrams for the situation where firms earn normal profit in the short run. This is because nothing happens. If firms are earning normal profit in the short run, there is no incentive for any firms to leave or enter the industry. The diagram stays the same so that the long run equilibrium looks the same as the short run equilibrium.

It is also important to note that, in the long run, all firms in a perfectly competitive market are both allocatively efficient (because price = MC) and productively efficient (because at the equilibrium output, MC = AC). In the topic on "Market failure", the fact that a market has not failed if it is efficient in both these ways was discussed.

Summing up

Condition for Long Run Equilibrium of a Firm

For a firm to achieve long run equilibrium, the marginal cost must be equal to the price and the long run average cost. That is, LMC = LAC = P. The firm adjusts the size of its plant to produce a level of output at which the LAC is minimum. Now, we know that at equilibrium:

Short–run marginal cost = Long–run marginal cost

Short–run average cost = Long–run average cost

Therefore, in the long–run, we have: SMC = LMC = SAC = LAC = P = MR

Hence, at the minimum point of the LAC, the plant works at its optimal capacity and the minima of the LAC and SAC coincide. Also, the LMC cuts the LAC at the minimum point and the SMC cuts the SAC at the minimum point. Therefore, at the minimum point of the LAC, the equality mentioned above is achieved.

5.7.1   Long–run supply curve of industry

The long–run is supposed to be a period sufficiently long to allow changes to be made both in the size of the plant and in the number of firms in the industry. Whereas in the short period, an increase in demand is met by over–using the existing plant, in the long–run, it will be met not only by the expansion of the plants of the existing firms but also by the entry into the industry of new firms.

Moreover, we have seen that, in the short–run, a firm produces that output at which its marginal cost is equal to the price. But, in the long–run, the price must be equal to both the–marginal cost and the average cost. The reason is that an industry will be in equilibrium when all firms in the industry are making normal profits, and they will be making normal profits only if the price, i.e., average revenue (AR) is equal to average cost AC.

The shape of supply curve, in the long run, will depend on whether the industry is subject to the law of constant return (i.e., constant costs), or to diminishing returns (i.e., increasing costs) or to increasing returns (i.e., diminishing costs). We show these curves below.

5.7.2　Supply curve of constant cost industry

In the Figure 5−11(a) which relates to a firm, LMC is the long−run marginal cost curve, and LAC is the long−run average cost curve. They intersect at R which means that at the point R, the marginal cost is equal to the average cost. Here they are also equal to price OP. The output at this point is OM. Thus, at the output OM, MC = AC = Price.

Now look at the Figure 5−11(b). Corresponding to OP price, the long−run supply curve is LSC, which is a horizontal straight line parallel to the X−axis. This means that whatever the output along the X−axis, price is the same OP where the marginal cost and average cost are equal. The cost remains the same, because it is a constant cost industry.

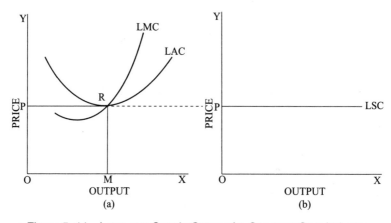

Figure 5−11　Long−run Supply Curve of a Constant Cost Industry

It is an industry in which, even if the output is increased (or decreased), the economies and diseconomies cancel out so that the cost of production does not change. Also, when new firms enter the industry to meet the increased demand, they do not raise or lower the cost per unit.

Thus, the industry is able to supply any amount of the commodity at the price OP which is equal to the minimum long−run average cost which ensures normal profit to all the firms engaged in the industry. That is, every firm will be in the long−run equilibrium where Price = MC = AC. All firms have identical cost conditions.

Hence, in the case of a constant cost industry, the long–run supply curve LSC is a horizontal straight line (i.e., perfectly elastic) at the price OP, which is equal to the minimum average cost. This means that whatever the output supplied; the price would remain the same.

5.7.3 Supply curve of a decreasing cost industry

In the case of an increasing cost industry, the cost of production increases as the existing firms expand or the new firms enter into the industry to meet an increase in demand. The external diseconomies outweigh the external economies. The increased demand for the productive resources required to produce larger output to meet increased demand for the product raises their prices resulting in higher cost of production.

The rise in costs will shift both the average and marginal cost curves upward and the minimum average cost will rise. This means that the additional supplies of the product will be forthcoming at higher prices, whether the additional supplies come from the expansion of the existing firms or from the new firms which may have entered the industry. All this is shown in the following diagram (Figure 5–12).

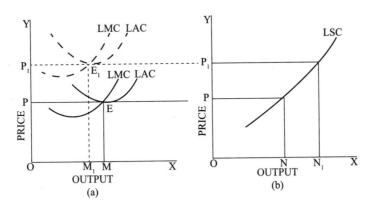

Figure 5–12   Long-run Supply curve of Increasing Cost Industry

The Figure 5–12(a) shows the position of individual firms. The position of the dotted LMC and LAC curves shows that they have been shifted upwards where each firm achieves a long–run equilibrium so that the price OP, =MC = AC. But, in the Figure 5–12(b) which relates to the industry, we find that at the price OP i larger amount ON, is supplied than at the price OP (i.e., ON).

This means that the long–run supply curve LSC slopes upwards to the right as the output supplied increases. That is, more will be supplied at higher prices. This is probably typical of the actual competitive world, because higher prices have to be paid for the scarce productive resources to attract them from other uses so that production in this particular industry may be increased. Thus, we see that in the case of an increasing cost industry, the long–run supply curve slopes upward to the right.

5.7.4   Long–run supply curve of a decreasing cost idustry

The Figure 5–13(a) shows how the new, i.e., dotted LMC and LAC curves have been shifted downwards from their original position, when the LMC and LAC curves intersect at E where every firm was the equilibrium and was producing OM. The new curves intersect at E_1 which means that, at this point, the firms in the industry have achieved the long–run equilibrium, each producing OM, output, so–that the price OP =MC = AC. But looking at the Figure 5–13(b), we find that, at OP_1 price, ON is supplied which is more than ON supplied at the original price OP.

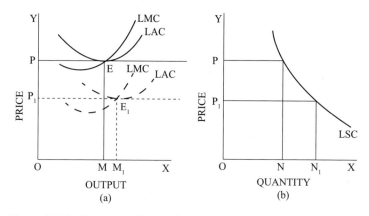

Figure 5–13   Long–run Supply Curve of a Decreasing Cost Industry

The LSC slopes downwards to the right which means that the additional supplies of the output are forthcoming at lower prices, since both the marginal cost and average cost have fallen owing to cheaper supplies of the productive resources.

Summing up

Thus, we find that, while the short–run supply curve of the industry always slopes upwards to the right, the long–run supply curve may be a horizontal straight line, sloping upwards or sloping downwards depending upon the fact whether the industry in question is a constant cost industry, increasing cost industry or decreasing cost industry. But the long–run upward sloping curve is more typical of the actual world.

Conclusion

In this chapter, we dug into the wants and constraints that drive firm behavior in competitive markets. Firms will choose to produce a quantity that maximizes their profits. In the short run, they will shut down if their revenues don't cover their variable costs of production. In the long run, they will exit the market if their revenues don't cover their total costs of production.

This analysis leads to some surprising conclusions about long–run supply in competitive markets: Firms earn zero economic profit; they operate at their efficient scale; and long–run supply is, in theory, perfectly elastic. Firms are able to enter and exit the market freely to adjust the quantity supplied at a given price.

These choices by firms benefit consumers by keeping prices low and ensuring that supply is responsive to needs. As we have noted, however, real–world markets are not guaranteed to be perfectly competitive. Firms may wield market power, or offer products that are not perfectly standardized. There may be barriers that prevent firms from freely entering or exiting the market. Understanding what perfect competition looks like, we can now spend the next few chapters looking at how firms behave when we relax the assumptions of perfect competition.

Key Term

Competitive Market	Average Revenue
Price Taker	Marginal Revenue
Market Power	

Review Questions

1. Why would a firm that incurs losses choose to produce rather than shut down?

2. Explain why the industry supply curve is not the long-run industry marginal cost curve.

3. In long-run equilibrium, all firms in the industry earn zero economic profit. Why is this true?

4. What is the difference between economic profit and producer surplus?

5. Why do firms enter an industry when they know that in the long run economic profit will be zero?

6. At the beginning of the twentieth century, there were many small American automobile manufacturers. At the end of the century, there were only three large ones. Suppose that this situation is not the result of lax federal enforcement of antimonopoly laws. How do you explain the decrease in the number of manufacturers? (Hint: What is the inherent cost structure of the automobile industry?)

7. Because industry X is characterized by perfect com-petition, every firm in the industry is earning zero economic profit. If the product price falls, no firm can survive. Do you agree or disagree? Discuss.

8. An increase in the demand for movies also increases the salaries of actors and actresses. Is the long-run supply curve for films likely to be horizontal or upward sloping? Explain.

Application

1. Suppose a firm is operating in a competitive market and is maximizing profit by producing at the point where marginal revenue=marginal cost.Now suppose that consumer wealth decreases in this market(and the good is a normal good). What might you expect to happen to the profit-maximizing output quantity for the firm?

2. Suppose you are the manager of a watchmaking firm operating in a competitive market. Your cost of production is given by $C=200+2q^2$, where q is the level of output and C is total cost.(The marginal cost of production is 4q; the fixed cost is ¥200.)

a. If the price of watches is ¥100, how many watches should you produce to maximize profit?

b. What will the profit level be?

c. At what minimum price will the firm produce a positive output?

3. Suppose that a competitive firm's marginal cost of producing output g is given by MC(q)=3+2q. Assume that the market price of the firm's product is ¥9.

a. What level of output will the firm produce?

b. What is the firm's producer surplus?

c. Suppose that the average variable cost of the firm is given by AVC(q)=3+q. Suppose that the firm's fixed costs are known to be ¥3. Will the firm be earning a positive, negative, or zero profit in the short run?

4. Suppose the same firm's cost function is C(q)=4q²+16.

a. Find variable cost, fixed cost, average cost, average variable cost, and average fixed cost.(Hint: Marginal cost is given by MC=8q.)

b. Show the average cost, marginal cost, and average variable cost curves on a graph.

c. Find the output that minimizes average cost.

d. At what range of prices will the firm produce a positive output?

e. At what range of prices will the firm earn a negative profit?

f. At what range of prices will the firm earn a positive profit?

6

Imperfect Competition

In this chapter we'll see how monopolists such as De Beers calculate the optimal quantity and price to maximize their profits. We'll also see that a monopolist profit from its control of the market, but consumers lose—and, in general, total surplus decreases. For these reasons, governments usually try to limit monopoly power, using a range of policies that we'll discuss. Even the mighty De Beers has been unable to resist these pressures. It now controls only about 40 percent of the world diamond market—still a huge share, but a far cry from its heyday.

This look at monopolies takes us away from the model of perfect competition. In looking beyond markets with lots of firms competing against each other, we start to see the range and diversity of markets that make up the economy.

Natural monopoly a market in which a single firm can produce, at a lower cost than multiple firms, the entire quantity of output demanded.

6.1 Definition of imperfect competition

If a firm can affect the market price of its output, the firm is classified as an imperfect competitor.

Imperfect competition prevails in an industry whenever individual sellers can affect the price of their output. The major kinds of imperfect competition are monopoly, oligopoly, and monopolistic competition.

Graphical Depiction. Figure 6−1 shows graphically the difference between the demand curves faced by perfectly and imperfectly competitive firms. Figure 6−1(a) reminds us that a perfect competitor faces a horizontal demand curve, indicating that it can sell all it wants at the going market price. An imperfect competitor, in contrast, faces a downward−sloping demand curve. Figure 6−1(b) shows that if an imperfectly competitive firm increases its sales, it will definitely depress the market price of its output as it moves down its dd demand curve.

Another way of seeing the difference between perfect and imperfect competition is by considering the price elasticity of demand. For a perfect competitor, demand is perfectly elastic; for an imperfect competitor, demand has a finite elasticity. As an exercise in use of the elasticity formulas, calculate the elasticities for the perfect competitor in Figure 6−1(a) and the imperfect competitor at point B in Figure 6−1(b).

The fact that the demand curves of imperfect competitors slope down has an important implication: Imperfect competitors are price−makers not price−takers.

They must decide on the price of their product, while perfect competitors take the price as given.

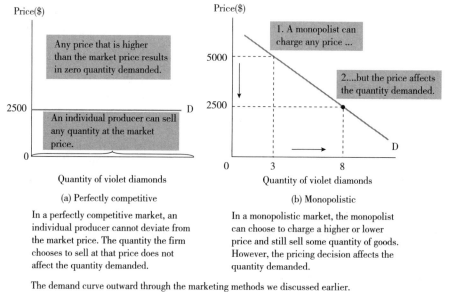

Figure 6–1   Competitive versus monopolistic demand curves

6.2   Patterns of imperfect competition

A modern industrial economy like the United States is a jungle populated with many species of imperfect competition. The dynamics of the personal computer industry, driven by rapid improvements in technology, are different from the patterns of competition in the not–so–lively funeral industry. Nevertheless, much can be learned about an industry by paying careful attention to its market structure, particularly the number and size of sellers and how much of the market the largest sellers control. Economists classify imperfectly competitive markets into three different market structures.

Monopoly

At one pole of the competitive spectrum is the perfect competitor, which is one firm among a vast multitude of firms. At the other pole is the monopoly, which is a single seller with complete control over an industry. (The word comes from the Greek words mono for "one" and polist for "seller.") A monopolist is the only firm producing in its industry, and there is no industry producing a close substitute. Moreover, for now we assume that the monopolist must sell everything at the same price—there is no price discrimination.

True monopolies are rare today. Most monopolies persist because of some form of government regulation or protection. For example, a pharmaceutical company that discovers a new wonder drug may be granted a patent, which gives it monopoly control over that drug for a number of years. Another important example of monopoly is a franchised local utility, such as the firm that provides your household water. In such cases there is truly a single seller of a service with no close substitutes. One of the few examples of a monopoly without government license is Microsoft Windows, which has succeeded in maintaining its monopoly through large investments in research and development, rapid innovation, network economies, and tough (and sometimes illegal) tactics against its competitors.

But even monopolists must always be looking over their shoulders for potential competitors. The pharmaceutical company will find that a rival will produce a similar drug; telephone companies that were monopolists a decade ago now must reckon with cellular telephones; Bill Gates worries that some small firm is waiting in the wings to unseat Microsoft's monopolistic position. In the long run, no monopoly is completely secure from attack by competitors.

Oligopoly

The term oligopoly means "few sellers." Few, in this context, can be a number as small as 2 or as large as 10 or 15 firms. The important feature of oligopoly is that each individual firm can affect the market price. In the airline industry, the decision of a single airline to lower fares can set off a price war which brings down the fares charged by all its competitors.

Oligopolistic industries are common in the U.S. economy, especially in the manufacturing, transportation, and communications sectors. For example, there are only a few car makers, even though the automobile industry sells many different models. The same is true in the market for household appliances: Stores are filled with many different models of refrigerators and dishwashers, all made by a handful of companies. You might be surprised to know that the breakfast cereal industry is an oligopoly dominated by a few firms even though there seem to be endless varieties of cereals.

Monopolistic competition

The final category we examine is **monopolistic competition**. In this situation, a large number of sellers produce differentiated products. This market structure resembles perfect competition in that there are many sellers, none of whom has a large share of the market. It differs from perfect competition in that the products sold by different firms are not identical. Differentiated products are ones whose important characteristics vary. Personal computers, for example, have differing characteristics such as speed, memory, hard disk, modem, size, and weight. Because computers are differentiated, they can sell at slightly different prices.

The classic case of monopolistic competition is the retail gasoline market. You may go to the local Shell station, even though it charges slightly more, because it is on your way to work. But if the price at Shell rises more than a few pennies above the competition, you might switch to the Merit station a short distance away.

Table 6–1 Alternative Market Structures

Types of Market Structures				
Structure	Number of producers and degree of product differentiation	Part of economy where prevalent	Firm's degree of control over price	Methods of marketing
Perfect competition	Many producers;identical products	Financial markets and agricultural products	None	Market exchange or auction
Imperfect competition				
Monopolistic competition	Many producers; many real or perceived. differences in product	Retail trade (pizzas, beer...), personal computers	Some	Advertising and quality rivalry; administered prices
Oligopoly	Few producers; little or no difference in product . Few producers;products are differentiated	Steel, chemicals.... Cars, word–processing software...		
Monopoly	Single producer; product without close substitutes	Franchise monopolies (electricity, water); Microsoft Windows; patented drugs	Considerable	Advertising

6.3   Why do imperfect competition exist

Barriers to Entry. Although cost differences are the most important factor behind market structures, barriers to entry can also prevent effective competition. Barriers to entry are factors that make it hard for new firms to enter an industry. When barriers are high, an industry may have few firms and limited pressure to compete. Economies of scale act as one common type of barrier to entry, but there are others, including legal restrictions, high cost of entry, advertising, and product differentiation.

Legal Restrictions. Governments sometimes restrict competition in certain industries. Important legal restrictions include patents, entry restrictions, and foreign–trade tariffs and quotas. A patent is granted to an inventor to allow temporary exclusive use (or monopoly) of the product or process that is patented.

For example, pharmaceutical companies are often granted valuablepatents on new drugs in which they have invested hundreds of millions of research– and–development dollars. Patents are one of the few forms of government–granted monopolies that are generally approved of by economists. Governments grant patent monopolies to encourage inventive activity. Without the prospect of monopoly patent protection, a company or a sole inventor might be unwilling to devote time and resources to research and development. The temporarily high monopoly price and the resulting inefficiency is the price society pays for the invention.

Governments also impose entry restrictions on many industries. Typically, utilities, such as telephone, electricity distribution, and water, are given franchise monopolies to serve an area. In these cases, the firm gets an exclusive right to provide a service, and in return the firm agrees to limit its prices and provide universal service in its region even when some customers might be unprofitable.

Free trade is often controversial, as we will see in the chapter on that subject. But one factor that will surprise most people is how important international trade is to promoting vigorous competition.

We can see the effect of restricting foreign competition in terms of Figure 6–2. Suppose a small country like Belgium or Benin decides that only its national airlines should provide airline service in the country. It is unlikely that such tiny airlines could have an efficient fleet of airplanes, reservation and repair systems, and Internet support. Service to Belgium and Benin would be poor, and prices would be high.

What has happened is that the protectionist policy has changed the industry structure from Figure 6-2(b) to Figure 6-2(c).

When markets are broadened by abolishing tariffs in a large free-trade area, vigorous and effective competition is encouraged and monopolies tend to lose their power. One of the most dramatic examples.

High Cost of Entry. In addition to legally imposed barriers to entry, there are economic barriers as well. In some industries the price of entry simply may be very high. Take the commercial-aircraft industry, for example. The high cost of designing and testing new airplanes serves to discourage potential entrants into the market. It is likely that only two companies— Boeing and Airbus—can afford the ¥10 to ¥20 billion that the next generation of aircraft will cost to develop.

In addition, companies build up intangible forms of investment, and such investments might be very expensive for any potential new entrant to match. Consider the software industry. Once a spreadsheet program (like Excel) or a word-processing program (like Microsoft Word) has achieved wide acceptability, potential competitors find it difficult to make inroads into the market. Users, having learned one program, are reluctant to switch to another. Consequently, in order to get people to try a new program, any potential entrant will need to run a big promotional campaign, which would be expensive and may still result in failure to produce a profitable product. (Recall our discussion of network effects in Chapter 6.)

6.4 Monopoly

A firm is a **monopoly** if it is the sole seller of its product and if its product does not have close substitutes. Charging different prices for similar goods is not pure price discrimination. Product differentiation gives a supplier greater control over price and the potential to charge consumers a premium price arising from differences in the quality or performance of a product. The fundamental cause of monopoly is **barriers to entry**:

Scarce resources. The most straightforward cause of barriers to entry is scarcity in some key resource or input into the production process. Though not an especially common source of monopoly power, it was the case, at first, in the diamond market. Diamonds come out of the ground in only a limited number of places, after all. If a firm owns all the diamond mines (as De Beers effectively did in the 1870s), it has control of the production process. A new firm cannot simply enter the market without somehow gaining control of a mine.

Economies of scale. In last chapter, we discussed the idea of economies of scale–instances when, as a firm produces more output, its average costs go down. In some industries, economies of scale are so powerful that competition between two or more firms simply doesn't make much sense; in these cases, the required infrastructure is too costly to replicate.

The government gives a single firm the exclusive right to produce some good or service.

Government intervention. Governments may create or sustain monopolies where they would not otherwise exist. In many U.S. states, for example, the government has created a monopoly on the sale of alcoholic beverages. In Iran, an elite branch of the army called the Revolutionary Guard Corps controls the construction industry as well as the oil and gas industries. Governments usually say they are creating monopolies in the public interest. In some cases, though, critics wonder if the real reason is to use monopoly power to benefit insiders.

The costs of production make a single producer more efficient than a large number of producers.

6.4.1 Monopoly resources

The simplest way for a monopoly to arise is for a single firm to own a key resource.

(1) *Government-created monopoly.* In many cases, monopolies arise because the government has given one person or firm the exclusive right to sell some good or service. Sometimes the monopoly arises from the sheer political clout of the would–be monopolist. Kings, for example, once granted exclusive business licenses to their friends and allies. At other times, the government grants a monopoly because doing so is viewed to be in the public interest. For instance, our government has given a monopoly to a company called China telecom, which maintained the database of tele–communication.

(2) *Natural monopoly. Natural monopoly refers a monopoly that arises because a single firm can supply a good or service to an entire market at a smaller cost than could two or more firms.* A natural monopoly arises when there are economies of scale over the relevant range of output. Figure 6–2 shows the average total costs of a firm with economies of scale. In this case, a single firm can produce any amount of output at least cost. That is, for any given amount of output, a larger number of firms leads to less output per firm and higher average total cost.

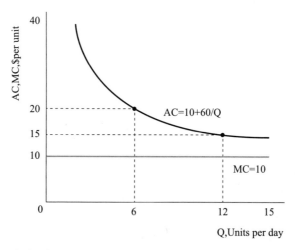

Figure 6–2　Average total costs of a firm with economies of scale

6.4.2　Demand curve and revenue cure

Demand curve

The key difference between a competitive firm and a monopoly is the monopoly's ability to influence the price of its output. A competitive firm is small relative to the market in which it operates and, therefore, takes the price of its output as given by market conditions. By contrast, because a monopoly is the sole producer in its market, it can alter the price of its good by adjusting the quantity it supplies to the market.

One way to view this difference between a competitive firm and a monopoly is to consider the demand curve that each firm faces. When we analyzed profit maximization by competitive firms in last chapter, we drew the market price as a horizontal line. Because a competitive firm can sell as much or as little as it wants at this price, the competitive firm faces a horizontal demand curve, as in panel (a) of Figure 6–3. In effect, because the competitive firm sells a product with many perfect substitutes (the products of all the other firms in its market), the demand curve that any one firm face is perfectly elastic.

By contrast, because a monopoly is the sole producer in its market, its de–

mand curve is the market demand curve. Thus, the monopolist's demand curve slopes downward for all the usual reasons, as in panel (b) of Figure 6–3. If the monopolist raises the price of its good, consumers buy less of it. Looked at another way, if the monopolist reduces the quantity of output it sells, the price of its output increases.

What point on the demand curve will the monopolist choose? As with competitive firms, we assume that the monopolist's goal is to maximize profit. Because the firm's profit is total revenue minus total costs, our next task in explaining monopoly behavior is to examine a monopolist's revenue.

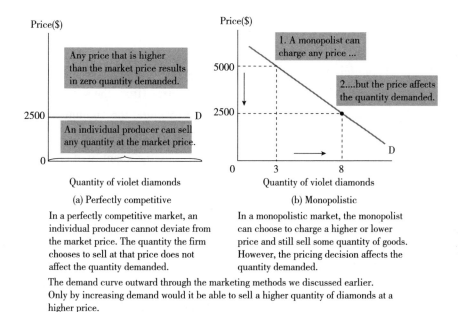

In a perfectly competitive market, an individual producer cannot deviate from the market price. The quantity the firm chooses to sell at that price does not affect the quantity demanded.

In a monopolistic market, the monopolist can choose to charge a higher or lower price and still sell some quantity of goods. However, the pricing decision affects the quantity demanded.

The demand curve outward through the marketing methods we discussed earlier. Only by increasing demand would it be able to sell a higher quantity of diamonds at a higher price.

Figure 6–3   Competitive versus monopolistic demand curves

A monopoly's revenue

Suppose that a town with a single producer of water. Table 6–2 shows how the monopoly's revenue might depend on the amount of water produced. The first two columns show the monopolist's demand schedule. If the monopolist produces 1 gallon of water, it can sell that gallon for ¥8. If it produces 2 gallons, it must lower the price to ¥7 in order to sell both gallons. And if it produces 3 gallons, it must lower the price to ¥6. And so on. If you graphed these two columns of numbers, you would get a typical downward–sloping demand curve.

Table 6-2   The monopoly's revenue

Quantity (q)	Price P	Total revenue TR	Average revenue (AR=TR/Q)	Marginal revenue (MR=ΔTR/ΔQ)
0 gallons	¥9	¥0		
1 gallons	¥8	¥8	¥8	¥8
2 gallons	¥7	¥14	¥7	¥6
3 gallons	¥6	¥18	¥6	¥4
4 gallons	¥5	¥20	¥5	¥2
5 gallons	¥4	¥20	¥4	0
6 gallons	¥3	¥18	¥3	−2

The third column of the Table presents the monopolist's total revenue. It equals the quantity sold (from the first column) times the price (from the second column). The fourth column computes the firm's average revenue, the amount of revenue the firm receives per unit sold. We compute average revenue by taking the number for total revenue in the third column and dividing it by the quantity of output in the first column. Average revenue always equals the price of the good. This is true for monopolists as well as for competitive firms.

The last column of Table 6-2 computes the firm's marginal revenue, the amount of revenue that the firm receives for each additional unit of output. We compute marginal revenue by taking the change in total revenue when output increases by 1 unit. For example, when the firm is producing 3 gallons of water, it receives total revenue of ¥18. Raising production to 4 gallons increases total revenue to ¥20. Thus, marginal revenue is ¥20 minus ¥18, or ¥2.

Table 6-2 shows a result that is important for understanding monopoly behavior. A monopolist's marginal revenue is always less than the price of its good. For example, if the firm raises production of water from 3 to 4 gallons, it will increase total revenue by only ¥2, even though it will be able to sell each gallon for ¥5. For a monopoly, marginal revenue is lower than price because a monopoly faces a downward-sloping demand curve. To increase the amount sold, a monopoly firm must lower the price of its good. Hence, to sell the fourth gallon of water, the monopolist must get less revenue for each of the first three gallons.

Marginal revenue is very different for monopolies from what it is for competitive firms. When a monopoly increases the amount it sells, it has two effects on total revenue (P × Q):

N   **The output effect:** More output is sold, so Q is higher.

N   **The price effect:** The price falls, so P is lower.

Because a competitive firm can sell all it wants at the market price, there is no price effect. When it increases production by 1 unit, it receives the market price for that unit, and it does not receive any less for the amount it was already selling. That is, because the competitive firm is a price taker, its marginal revenue equals the price of its good. By contrast, when a monopoly increases production by 1 unit, it must reduce the price it charges for every unit it sells, and this cut in price reduces revenue on the units it was already selling. As a result, a monopoly's marginal revenue is less than its price.

Figure 6–4 graphs the demand curve and the marginal–revenue curve for a monopoly firm. (Because the firm's price equals its average revenue, the demand curve is also the average–revenue curve.) These two curves always start at the same point on the vertical axis because the marginal revenue of the first unit sold equals the price of the good. But, for the reason we just discussed, the monopolist's marginal revenue is less than the price of the good. Thus, a monopoly's marginal–revenue curve lies below its demand curve.

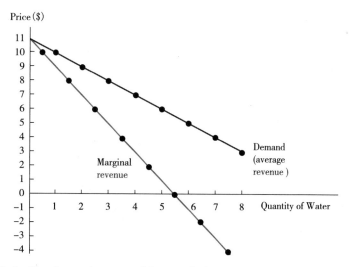

Figure 6–4   The demand curve and the marginal–revenue curve for a monopoly firm

You can see in the figure (as well as in Table 6–2) that marginal revenue can even become negative. Marginal revenue is negative when the price effect on revenue is greater than the output effect. In this case, when the firm produces an extra unit of output, the price falls by enough to cause the firm's total revenue to decline, even though the firm is selling more units.

6.4.3 Short-term equilibrium

Even though the ultimate aim of the monopolist is to make maximum profit, the monopolist cannot determine both the market price and the quantity he decides to sell. The monopolist can produce output for which the price accepted by the customers. Or the monopolist can fix price, but it may not demand by the market. Short run equilibrium of monopolist can be represented as in the Figure I. At equilibrium, the following two conditions must satisfy.

（1）Marginal Cost (MC) curve must cut Marginal Revenue (MR) from below.

（2）Marginal Cost (MC) must be equal to Marginal Revenue (MR).

Further "R" is the point demand curve tangent. And "P" is the price of the commodity. Here the monopolist can earn an excess profit equals to the shaded area "PQRS", because Average Total Cost (ATC) passes through the point "S" and price is above that point. So, the monopolist can earn excess profit.

In pure competition the firm is a price–taker, so that its only decision is output determination. The monopolist is faced by two decisions: setting his price and his output. However, given the downward–sloping demand curve, the two decisions are interdependent.

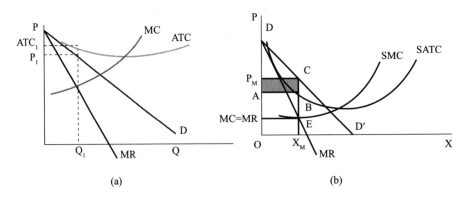

(a) (b)

Figure 6-5 Short-term equilibrium

The monopolist will either set his price and sell the amount that the market will take at it, or he will produce the output defined by the intersection of MC and MR, which will be sold at the corresponding price, P. The monopolist cannot decide independently both the quantity and the price at which he wants to sell it. The crucial condition for the maximization of the monopolist's profit is the equality of his MC and the MR, provided that the MC cuts the MR from below.

6.4.4   Long–term equilibrium of monopolist

What difference does it make that the firm is a monopolist rather than a perfect competitor?

Since producers are profit maximizers, they will produce the quantity where MC=MR (same procedure as for the short–run equilibrium). In a monopolistically competitive market, there are low barriers to entry so it is easy for other firms to come in and steal economic profit from the firms currently in the market (Theory of Contestable Markets). To counteract this, producers in the market will produce at a quantity that yields zero economic profit, because why would you join this market if there's no supernormal profit? This means the quantity the firm produces will be both where MC=MR and Price (the Demand curve) intersects the Average Total Cost curve. If you draw a vertical line up from the market quantity, it will go through both of these points. The price is again found by drawing a horizontal line to the y–axis.

Recall from our look at firm behavior in Chapter 7 that any profit–maximizing firm follows two rules in choosing its output level:

The Marginal Output Rule: If the firm does not shut down, it should produce output at a level where marginal revenue is equal to marginal cost.

The Shutdown Rule: If for every choice of output level, the firm's average revenue is less than its average economic cost, then the firm should shut down.

A monopolist is no exception to these two rules. To apply them, we need to know the monopolist's cost and revenue functions. A monopolist's cost function is found the same way as any other firm's cost function–follow the process discussed Later. The difference between monopoly and competition comes on the revenue side, so we will focus our attention there.

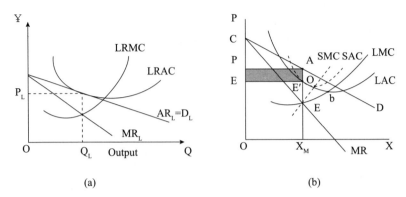

Figure 6–6　Monopolist with suboptimal plant and excess capacity

6.4.5　Price discrimination

Perfect price discrimination. Dividing its customers into just three categories—tudents, business owners, and others—is a blunt way of discriminating among them.

In reality, there are not just three types of customer–there are millions, all with their own individual willingness to pay. What if Microsoft was able to price discriminate more accurately by charging every individual customer a price exactly equal to her willingness to pay?

6.4.5.1　Conditions necessary for profitable price discrimination

（1）*The firm must be a price maker.* To see why this condition is necessary suppose that the supplier was a price taker. In this case, all consumers of the supplier's product would be willing to pay the same price for a unit of the good. The best that the firm could do would be to charge everybody their common willingness to pay for the good, and the ability to charge different customers different prices would be of no value to the firm. In contrast, a price maker faces a downward–sloping demand curve so it can profit from charging higher prices to those consumers who are willing to pay more for its output.

（2）*The firm must be able to identify which consumer is which.* Suppose that you own a restaurant and you are sure that some diners are willing to pay more for the meals than others. If you could, you would like to price discriminate. But you face a difficult problem: it is impossible to tell how much any particular person is willing to pay. If you. cannot identify an individual consumer's willingness to pay, then you cannot practice price discrimination. This is one reason that most restaurants charge everyone the same prices. Sometimes, partial identification of consumers' willingness to pay is possible. For instance, even though bar owners cannot tell how much any specific customer is willing to pay for a drink, they know that women are typically willing to pay less than men. While the identification of willingness to pay is not perfect, the monopolist may be able to benefit from being able to. divide customers into groups with different demand curves—in this case, men and women.

(3) *Consumers must not be able to engage in arbitrage.* Concern with consumer arbitrage explains why the bar staff on "ladies' nights" are instructed to watch that women do not order drinks for the men sitting with them. It also explains why Mercedes–Benz and other European car manufacturers have sought US government action to stop car consumers from going to Europe, buying European models at low prices and shipping them back for resale in America.It also explains why some agents focus on ferring goofs in low price from Hongkong and other countries to mainland China.

6.4.5.2　Third–degree price discrimination

(1) *First-degree price discrimination. First-degree price discrimination* is also called **Price discrimination**, sometimes known as **optimal pricing,** which refers to the practice ofcharging customers different prices for the same good. It involves "discriminating" between customers on the basis of their willingness to pay. Examples of price discrimination are all around us. This type of discrimination clearly entails setting prices that differ across consumers. When a single consumer buys more than one unit of a good, perfect price discrimination also entails selling different units to the **same consumer** at different prices. If Mary is willing to pay ¥3.00 for her first tea egg of the day, but only ¥2.00 for the second, then a perfectly price–discriminating would charge her ¥3.00 for the first egg and ¥2.00 for the second.

If successful, the firm can extract the **entire consumer surplus** that lies underneath the demand curve and turn it into **extra revenue or producer surplus.** This is hard to achieve unless a business has full information on every consumer's individual preferences and willingness to pay. The transactions costs involved in finding out through market research what each buyer is prepared to pay is the main barrier to a business's engaging in this form of price discrimination.

If the monopolist can perfectly segment the market, then the average revenue curve becomes the marginal revenue curve. A monopolist will continue to sell extra units as long as the extra revenue exceeds the marginal cost of production.

In reality, most suppliers and consumers prefer to work with **price lists** and **menus** from which trade can take place rather than having to negotiate a price for each unit bought and sold.

（2）*Second-degree price discrimination.* In reality, no firm can observe every individual buyer's willingness to pay for its product. There may, however, be something about the buyer that the seller can observe that reveals information about the consumer's willingness to pay. We will see how a monopolist can use the consumer's own actions as a basis of discrimination. This practice is known as second–degree price discrimination.

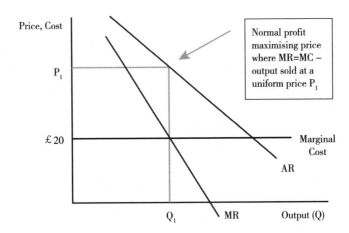

Figure 6-7　First-Degree Price Discrimination

Examples of this can be found in the hotel industry where spare rooms are sold on a last–minute standby basis.In these types of industry, the **fixed costs** of production are high. At the same time the **marginal or variable costs** are low and predictable. If there are unsold rooms or flight tickets, it is in the hotel's best interest to offload spare capacity at a discount prices, providing that the extra revenue at least covers the marginal cost of each unit.

There is nearly always some **supplementary profit** to be made. Firms may be quite happy to accept a smaller profit margin if it means that they manage to steal an advantage on their rival firms.

（3）*Third-degree price discrimination.* This type of discrimination, in which the supplier is able to identify separate groups of buyers and charge them different prices, is known as third–degree price discrimination. Unlike first–degree price discrimination, third–degree price discrimination is an important real–world phenomenon. While suppliers typically can not.

Examples of this can be found in the flight industry. Customers booking early with airline carriers such as EasyJet or RyanAir will normally find lower prices if they are prepared to book early. This gives the airline the advantage of knowing how full their flights are likely to be and is a source of cash flow prior to the flight taking off.

Closer to the time of the scheduled service the price rises, on the justification that consumer's demand for a flight becomes inelastic. People who book late often regard travel to their intended destination as a necessity and they are likely to be willing and able to pay a much higher price.

Peak and off-peak pricing

Peak and off–peak pricing and is common in the telecommunications industry, leisure retailing and in the travel sector. For example, telephone and electricity companies separate markets by time: There are three rates for telephone calls: A daytime peak rate, and an off–peak evening rate and a cheaper weekend rate. Electricity suppliers also offer cheaper off–peak electricity during the night.

At **off–peak times,** there is plenty of spare capacity and marginal costs of production are low (the supply curve is elastic).

At **peak times** when demand is high, short run supply becomes relatively inelastic as the supplier reaches capacity constraints. A combination of higher demand and rising costs forces up the profit maximizing price.

6.5 Monopolistic competition

In this chapter we examine markets that have some features of competition and some features of monopoly. This market structure is called monopolistic competition. **Monopolistic competition** describes a market structure in which many firms sell products that are similar but not identical. Monopolistic competition describes a market with the following attributes:

N **Many sellers:** There are many firms competing for the same group of customers.

N **Product differentiation:** Each firm produces a product that is at least slightly different from those of other firms. Thus, rather than being a price taker, each firm faces a downward–sloping demand curve.

N **Free entry:** Firms can enter (or exit) the market without restriction. Thus, the number of firms in the market adjusts until economic profits are driven to zero.

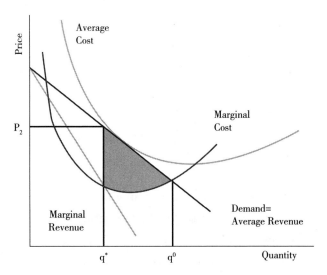

Figure 6–8　The model of monopolist competition

Product differentiation

The goods produced by firms operating in a monopolistically competitive market are subject to product differentiation. The goods are essentially the same, but they have slight differences.

Product differentiation is usually achieved in one of three ways: ① physical differences, ② perceived differences, ③ support services.

Physical Differences: In some cases, the product of one firm is physically different form the product of other firms. One good is chocolate, the other is vanilla. One good uses plastic, the other aluminum.

Perceived Differences: In other cases, goods are only perceived to be different by the buyers, even though no physical differences exist. Such differences are often created by brand names, where the only difference is the packaging.

Support Services: In still other cases, products that are physically identical and perceived to be identical are differentiated by support services. Even though the products purchased are identical, one retail store might offer "service with a smile," while another provides express checkout.

6.5.1　Demand curve for monopolist

The four characteristics of monopolistic competition mean that a monopolistically competitive firm faces a relatively elastic, but not perfectly elastic, demand curve, such as the one displayed in the exhibit to the right. Each firm in a monopolistically competitive market can sell a wide range of output within a relatively narrow range of prices.

Demand is relatively elastic in monopolistic competition because there are more close substitutes than a pure monopolist. There are no perfect substitutes (as is the case with perfect competition). Elasticity depends on number of rivals and degree of product differentiation.

6.5.2　Short-term equilibrium for monopolist

Monopolistically competitive industries look like monopolies in the short-run, as is shown in the graph below. The firm has a downward sloping demand curve because of product differentiation. Profit can be positive (as shown below), negative or equal to zero dependent upon market conditions. The firm produces where marginal revenue equals marginal cost. Price is given by the demand curve at profit maximizing output and profit equals (p–ATC) Q.

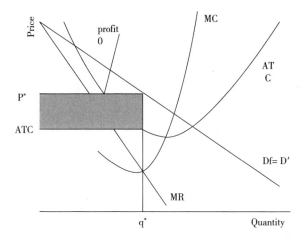

Figure 6-9　Short-term equilibrium for monopolist

The only difference between monopolistic completion and monopoly in the short-run is that discussed in the previous section—firm demand is smaller and more elastic than market demand for monopolistic competition whereas for monopoly firm demand equals market demand.

Similar to both monopoly and perfect completion,firms in monopolistic competition may decide to shutdown.The decision is the same for all firms in the short-run:

If P>ATC=>profit>0=>produce

If P=ATC=>profit=0=>produce

If P<ATC=>profit<0=>decision to produce or shutdown depends on:

If P < AVC => shutdown

If P ⩾ AVC => produce

6.5.3　Long-term equilibrium for monopolist

Monopolistically competitive industries act like perfectly competitive industries in the long-run. This is because, like perfect competition, firms can freely enter and exit the industry. That is, no entry barriers exist to keep out competition. As a result, similar to perfect competition, profit serves as a signal to firms to either enter or exit the industry in the long-run.

If profit > 0 => entry occurs driving down prices and profit.

With entry and more competition market demand is split between more competing firms. Hence, market demand falls and becomes more elastic.

If profit < 0 => exit occurs driving up prices and profit.

With exit and less competition market demand is split between fewer competing firms. Hence, market demand rises and becomes less elastic.

Therefore, profit moves to profit = 0 where there exists no entry or exit => profit = 0 is the long-run equilibrium in the market, just as it is in perfect completion.

The graph below shows a monopolistically competitive firm in long-run equilibrium with zero profit.

Use the graph above and compare to long-run equilibriums in perfect competition and monopoly. The graph will also be used to evaluate monopolistic competition with respect to technological and allocative efficiency. From the graph we can see that the following is true:

（1）P=ATC.

(2) MC = MR.

(3) P > MC.

Efficiency requires:

Technological Efficiency

Firm Technological Efficiency

Recall that for firm technological efficiency we ask the question: Does the firm produce on its cost curves? Clearly, as is true with perfect competition, the firm must produce on its cost curves. Competition requires it do so because if it does not profit becomes negative and the firm is driven out of business. Hence, monopolistically competitive firms will be efficient in this manner.

Industry Technological Efficiency

Recall that for industry technological efficiency we ask the question: Does the firm produce at the minimum point of the average total cost curve in the long–run? In other words, we are asking whether the firm takes advantage of all economies of scale.

Clearly, the answer here is no. Zero profit requires a tangency between the downward sloping demand curve and the long–run average total cost curve. But that tangency ensures that the firm will be producing with long–run costs too high, inefficiency results.

Allocative Efficiency

Recall that for allocative efficiency we ask the question: Is price (or marginal social benefit) equal to marginal (social) cost? Clearly, from the graph above price exceeds marginal cost resulting in allocative inefficiency. Similar to a monopoly, a monopolistically competitive firm produces too little at too high a price.

The above discussion seems to imply that monopolistically competitive firms are just as inefficient as monopoly firms but this is not correct. In monopolistic competition entry and exit ensure that price falls so that profit equals zero, which is lower than for monopolies. The lower price is monopolistic completion means that they are more efficient than monopolies but less efficient than perfectly competitive firms.

How could monopolistically competitive firms be made more efficient?

The source of the inefficiency in monopolistic competition is product differentiation. Thus, wouldn't getting rid of product differentiation make the market more efficient? The answer to this question turns out to be not as clear as it might seem.

For example, no product differentiation means that all consumers would only be consuming exactly the same product. For example, everyone would drink only Fresca, drive only a dodge Dakota, eat only beef, etc. These are my preferences for soft drinks, a car, and food but may not be your preferences. Consumers actually get value from having choices because preferences varybetween different consumers. That is, product differentiation is valuable in and of itself. Of course, this is only true for actual and not imaginary product differentiation.

6.5.4 The so-called excess capacity theorem

A persistent view in the popular culture is that the market produces too many varieties of different products. Consider these lyrics from the song "It's All Too Much":

Do market economies generally have too many kinds of chocolate chip biscuits (and other commodities)? To think about this question, recall that under long-run equilibrium, each monopolistic competitor produces output at a level at which its average cost curve is tangent to its average revenue curve. Since the firm's average revenue curve slopes downwards, the firm's average cost curve must also be downward sloping at the long-run equilibrium output level. From this fact, some economists incorrectly concluded that there are too many firms in the market under the long-run, monopolistically competitive equilibrium.

This incorrect conclusion became known as the excess capacity theorem and was based on the following line of argument. Because average costs are decreasing at the equilibrium per firm output level, industry-wide average costs would be lower if the given industry output level were produced by fewer firms, each of which produced more output per firm.

This theorem missed a crucial point: variety is valuable. While having fewer firms may lower the average costs of a given amount of total output (somehow measured), it would also reduce the amount of variety. Suppose, for example, that the number of petrol stations in Germany were cut in half. The petrol stations that remained would indeed have lower average costs as they increased their volumes and took advantage of economies of scale. But consumers would have to drive further to reach the nearest petrol station. Once we consider the added inconvenience, the true cost of obtaining petrol might well be higher with fewer stations. In short, by itself, a falling average cost curve tells us nothing more than that variety is costly. It does not tell us how these costs compare with the benefits of variety.

Non–price competition

Non–price competition refers to the efforts on the part of a monopolistic competitive firm to increase its sales and profits through product variation and selling expenses instead of a cut in the price of its product. The monopolistic competitor can always change his product either by varying its physical attributes or by changing the promotional programmers.

Product variation and selling expenses make the firm's demand curve less elastic and increase the costs of production. Consequently, the amount of profits which the firm can earn by producing the quantity of the product that equates its MR with MC will also be changed.

6.6　Oligopoly

An **oligopoly** is a market with only a few sellers, each offering a product similar or identical to the others. The word is derived from the Greek for few (entities with the right to) sell. Because there are few participants in this type of market, each oligopolist is aware of the actions of the others. The decisions of one firm influence, and are influenced by the decisions of other firms. Strategic planning by oligopolists always involves taking into account the likely responses of the other market participants. This causes oligopolistic markets and industries to be at the highest risk for collusion. One example is the market for tennis balls. Another is the world market for crude oil: A few countries in the Middle East control much of the world's oil reserves.

The oligopoly form of market is characterized by
—a few large dominant firms, with many small ones,
—a product either standardized or differentiated,
—power of dominant firms over price, but fear of retaliation,
—technological or economic barriers to become a dominant firm,
—extensive use of nonprice competition because of the fear of price wars.
The above characteristics imply that there are two kinds of oligopolies:
Pure oligopoly — have a homogenous product. Pure because the only source

of market power is lack of competition. An example of a pure oligopoly would be the steel industry, which has only a few producers but who produce exactly the same product.

Impure oligopoly — have a differentiated product. Impure because have both lack of competition and product differentiation as sources of market power. An example of an impure oligopoly is the automobile industry, which has only a few producers who produce a differentiated product.

All "big" business is in the oligopoly form of market. Being a major corporation almost automatically implies that the company has means of controlling its market.

Some of the major models are:

(i) The Cournot (duopoly) Model,

(ii) The Edge–worth (duopoly) Model,

(iii) The Chamberlin (duopoly) Model,

(iv) Sweezy's Kinked Demand Curve Model,

(v) The Centralised Cartel Model (a Perfect Collusion Model),

(vi) The Market Sharing Cartel Model, and

(vii) Price–leadership Model.

(a) Price leadership is "the form of imperfect collusion in which the firms in an oligopolistic industry tacitly (i.e., without formal agreement) decide to set the same price as the leader for the industry". The price–leader may be the lowest cost firm, or which is more likely, the dominant or largest firm in the industry. In the latter case, the dominant firm sets the price, allows the other firms belonging to the industry to sell all they want at that price, and then the dominant firm enters the market to meet the residual element.

(b) Sweezy Model:

Paul Sweezy has developed his model on the basis of the kinked demand curve. This model tries to explain the price–rigidity often observed in oligopolistic markets.

6.6.1 Cournot's duopoly model

Cournot duopoly, also called **Cournot competition**, is a model of imperfect competition in which two firms with identical cost functions compete with homogeneous products in a static setting. It was developed by Antoine A. Cournot in his "Researches into the Mathematical principles of the Theory of Wealth",

1838. Cournot's duopoly represented the creation of the study of oligopolies, more particularly duopolies, and expanded the analysis of market structures which, until then, had concentrated on the extremes: Perfect competition and monopolies.

Let us first state the assumptions which are made by Cournot in his analysis of price and output under duopoly. First, Cournot takes the case of two identical mineral springs operated by two owners who are selling the mineral water in the same market. Their waters are identical. Therefore, his model relates to the duopoly with homogeneous products. Secondly, it is assumed by Cournot, for the sake of simplicity, that the owners operate mineral springs and sell water without incurring any cost of production. Thus, in Cournot's model, cost of production is taken as zero; only the demand side of the market is analyzed.

It may be noted that the assumption of zero cost of production is made only to simplify the analysis. His model can be presented when cost of production is positive. Thirdly, the duopolists fully know the market demand for the mineral water; they can see every point on the demand curve. Moreover, the market demand for the product is assumed to be linear, that is, market demand curve facing the two producers is a straight line. Lastly, Cournot assumes that each duopolist believes that regardless of his actions and their effect upon market price of the product, the rival firm will keep its output constant, that is, it will go on producing the same amount of output which it is presently producing.

In other words, the duopolist will decide about the amount of output which is most profitable for him to produce in the light of his rival's present output and assumes that it will remain constant. In other words, for determining the output to be produced, he will not take into account reactions of his rival in response to his variation in output and thus decides its level of output independently.

Now, we may suppose, on the other hand, that the company alone reduces its price. In that case a much larger increase in its demand may be expected. Thus, where no one else raises its price the firm is likely to have a relatively elastic demand curve like dd'.

Here point C represents the oligopolist's current price–quantity combination.

Cournot's Approach to Equilibrium of the Duopolists:

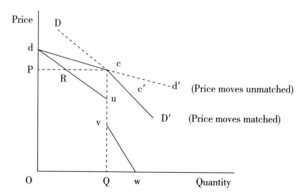

Figure 6–10　Inflexible (rigid) oligopoly price

Suppose the demand curve confronting the two producers of the mineral water is the straight–line MD as shown in Figure 6–11.Further suppose that ON = ND is the maximum daily output of each mineral spring. Thus, the total output of both the springs is OD = ON + ND.

It will be seen from the figure that when the total output OD of both the springs is offered for sale in the market, the price will be zero. It may be noted here that if there was a perfect competition, the long–run equilibrium price would have been zero and actual output produced equal to OD. This is because cost of production being assumed to be zero; price must also be zero so as to provide a zero profit long–run equilibrium under perfect competition.

Assume for the moment that one producer A of the mineral water starts the business first. Thus, to begin with he will be the monopolist. He will then produce daily ON output because his profits will be maximum at output ON' and will be equal to ONKP (since the costs are zero, the whole of total revenue ONKP will represent profits).

The price which that producer will charge will be OP. Suppose now that the owner of the other spring enters into the business and starts operating his spring. This new producer B sees that the former producer A is producing ON amount of output.

According to the assumption made by Cournot, the producer B believes that the former producer A will continue producing ON (= 1/2 OD) amount of output, regardless of what output he himself decides to produce. Given this belief, the best that the new producer B can do is to regard segment KD as the demand curve confronting him. With his demand curve KD, and corresponding marginal revenue curve

MRB, the producer B will produce NH (= 1/2 ND) amount of output. The total output will now be ON + NH = OH, and as a result the price will fall to OP' or HL per unit.

The total profits made by the two producers will be OHLP' which are less than ONKP. Out of total profits OHLP', profits of producer A will be ONGP' and profits of producer B will be NHLG. Thus, entry into the market by producer B and producing output NH by him, the producer A's profits has been reduced.

A will therefore reconsider the situation. But he will assume that producer B will continue to produce output NH. With producer B producing output NH, the best that the producer A can do is to produce 1/2 (OD –NH). He, will, therefore, reduce his output.

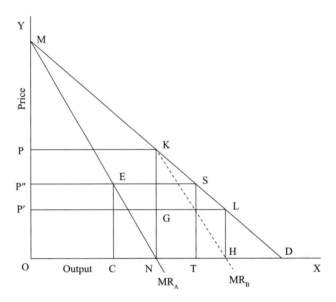

Figure 6–11   Output Cournot's Duopoly Solution

Now that the producer B has been surprised by the reduction of output by producer A and will also find that his share of total profits is less than that of producer A, he will reconsider his situation. Learning nothing from his earlier experience and believing that producer A will continue producing its new current level of output, the producer B will find that he will now be making maximum profits by producing output equal to 1/2 (OD — New output of A).

Producer B, accordingly, will increase his output. With this move of producer B, producer A will find his profits reduced. The producer A will therefore again reconsider his position and will find that he can increase his profits by producing output equal to 1/2 (OD — Current output of producer B).

This process of adjustment and readjustment will continue and producer A being forced gradually to reduce his output and producer B being able to increase his output gradually until the total output OT is produced (OT = 2/3 OD) and each is producing the same amount of output equal to 1/3 OD.

In this final position, producer A produces OC amount of output and producer B produces CT amount of output, and OC = CT. Throughout this process of adjustment and readjustment, each producer assumes that the other will keep his output constant at the present level and then always finds his maximum profits by producing output equal to 1/2, (OD – the present output of the other).

As seen above, producer A starts by producing ON = (1/2 OD) and continuously reduces his output until he produces OC. The final output OC of producer A will be equal to 1/3 OD (= 1/2 OT). On the other hand, producer B begins by producing 1/4th of OD and continuously increases his output until he produces CT. His final output CT will be equal to 1/3 OD (= 1/2 OT). Thus, the two producers together will produce total output equal to 1/3 OD + 1/3 OD= 2/3 OD (= OT).

Cournot's Duopoly Equilibrium:

It will be seen from Figure 6–11 that when each producer is producing 1/3 OD (that is, when producer A is producing OC and producer B equal to CT), the best that his rival can do is to produce 1/2 (OD – 1/3 OD) which is equal to 1/3 OD = OC – CT. Thus, when each producer is producing 1/3 OD so that the total output of the two together is 2/3 OD, no one will expect to increase his profits by making any– further adjustment in output. Thus, in Cournot's model of duopoly, stable equilibrium is reached when total output produced is 2/3rd of OD and each producer is producing 1/3rd of OD.

It will be useful to compare the Cournot's duopoly equilibrium with the monopolistic and the purely competitive equilibriums. If the two producers had combined and formed a coalition, then the output produced by them together will be the monopoly output ON and. therefore, the price set will be the monopoly price OP.

Monopoly output ON produced in case of coalition is much less than the output OT produced in Cournot's duopoly equilibrium. Further, the monopoly price OP charged in case of coalition is much greater than the price OP" determined in Cournot's duopoly equilibrium.

In case of coalition, they will enjoy the monopoly profits ONKP which are maximum possible joint profits, given the demand curve MD. These monopoly or maximum joint profits can be shared equally by them. It will be seen from Figure 6-11. that these monopoly profits ONKP made in case of coalition are much greater than the total profits OTSP" made by them in Cournot's duopoly equilibrium.

It is thus clear that in case of the duopolists competing with each other as conceived by Cournot's duopoly solution, the price and the profits are lower and output is greater than if they had combined together and formed a monopoly.

On the other hand, if the market were perfectly competitive, the output would have been OD and price would have been zero. This is because with assumed marginal cost being equal to zero, perfectly competitive equilibrium will be reached at the output level where price is equal to zero. That is, perfectly competitive solution would have resulted in greater output and lower price than under Cournot's duopoly equilibrium.

To sum up, under Cournot's duopoly equilibrium, output is two thirds of the maximum possible output (i.e., perfectly competitive output) and price is two-thirds of the most profitable price (i.e., monopoly price).

Following Cournot, the cost of production in the above discussion of Cournot's oligopoly solution has been taken to be zero. However, it should be noted that above conclusions will not change if the cost curves with positive cost of production are introduced into the discussion.

Reaction Functions and Cournot Duopoly Solution:

Cournot solution of duopoly problem can also be obtained with reaction functions of the two firms. An output reaction function depicts the profit-maximizing output of a firm, on the assumption that the other firm's output remains constant.

We have seen above that the profit-maximizing output of a Cournot's duopolist is one-half of the difference between the other firm's output and the market demand for output at which price equals marginal cost.

6.6.2 Sweeyz model

The kinked demand curve of oligopoly was developed by Paul M. Sweezy in 1939. Instead of laying emphasis on price-output determination, the model explains the behavior of oligopolistic organizations. The model advocates that the behavior of oligopolistic organizations remain stable when the price and output are determined.

This implies that an oligopolistic market is characterized by a certain degree of price rigidity or stability, especially when there is a change in prices in downward direction. For example, if an organization under oligopoly reduces price of products, the competitor organizations would also follow it and neutralize the expected gain from the price reduction.

On the other hand, if the organization increases the price, the competitor organizations would also cut down their prices. In such a case, the organization that has raised its prices would lose some part of its market share.

The kinked demand curve model seeks to explain the reason of price rigidity under oligopolistic market situations. Therefore, to understand the kinked demand curve model, it is important to note the reactions of rival organizations on the price changes made by respective oligopolistic organizations.

There can be two possible reactions of rival organizations when there are changes in the price of a particular oligopolistic organization. The rival organizations would either follow price cuts, but not price hikes or they may not follow changes in prices at all.

A kinked demand curve represents the behavior pattern of oligopolistic organizations in which rival organizations lower down the prices to secure their market share, but restrict an increase in the prices.

The assumptions of this model are:

(i) There are only a few firms in an oligopolistic market.

(ii) The firms are producing close–substitute products.

(iii) The quality of the products remains constant and the firms do not spend on advertising.

(iv) A set of prices of the product has already been determined and these prices prevail in the market at present.

(v) Each firm believes that if it reduces the price of its product, the rival firms would follow suit, but if it increases the price, then the rivals would not follow it, they would simply keep their prices unchanged. We shall see presently that, because of this asymmetric reaction pattern of the rivals, the demand curve of each firm would have a kink at the prevailing price of its product.

The slope of a kinked demand curve differs in different conditions, such as price increase and price decrease. In this model, every organization faces two demand curves. In case of high prices, an oligopolistic organization faces highly elastic demand curve, which is dd' in Figure 6–12.

On the other hand, in case of low prices, the oligopolistic organization faces inelastic demand curve, which is DD'(Figure 6–12). Suppose the prevailing price of a product is PQ, as shown in Figure 6–12. If one of the oligopolistic organizations makes changes in its prices, then there can be three reactions of rival organizations.

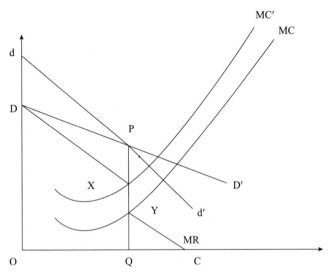

Figure 6–12   Kinked Demand Curve Model

Firstly, when the oligopolistic organization would increase its prices, its demand curve would shift to dd' from DD'. In such a case, consumers would switch to rivals, which would lead to fall in the sales of the oligopolistic organization. In addition, the dP portion of dd' would be more elastic, which lies above the prevailing price.

On the other hand, if price falls, the rivals would also reduce their prices, thus, the sales of the oligopolistic organization would be less. In such a case, the demand curve faced by the oligopolistic organization is PD',which lies below the prevailing price.

Secondly, rival organizations will not react with respect to changes in the price of the oligopolistic organization. In such a case, the oligopolistic organization would face DD'demand curve.

Thirdly, the rival organizations may follow price cut, but not price hike. If the oligopolistic organization increases the price and rivals do not follow it, then consumers may switch to rivals. Thus, the rivals would gain control over the market. Thus, the oligopolistic organization would be forced from dP demand curve to DP demand curve, so that it can prevent losing its customers.

This would result in producing the kinked demand curve. On the other hand, if the oligopolistic organization reduces the price, the rival organizations would also reduce prices for securing their customers. Here, the relevant demand curve is Pd'. The two parts of the demand curve are DP and Pd', which is DPd' with a kink at point P.

Let us draw the MR curve of the oligopolistic organization. The MR curve would take the discontinuous shape, which is DXYC, where DX and YC correspond directly to DP and Pd' segments of the kinked demand curve. The equilibrium point is attained when MR = MC. In Figure 6-12, the MC curve intersects MR at point Y where at output OQ.

At point Y, the organization would achieve maximum profit. Now, if cost increases, the MC curve would move upwards to MC. In such a case, the oligopolistic organization cannot increase the prices. This is because if the organization would increase the prices, the rival organizations would decrease their prices and gain the market share. Moreover, the profits would remain same between point X and Y. Thus, there is no motivation for increasing or decreasing prices. Therefore, price and output would remain stable.

However, kinked demand curve model is criticized by various economists.

Some of the major points of criticism are as follows:

（i）Lays emphasis on price rigidity, but does not explain price itself.

（ii）Assumes that rival organizations only follow price decrease, which does not hold true empirically.

（iii）Ignores non-price competition among organizations. Non-price competition can be in terms of product differentiation, advertising, and other tools used by organizations to promote their sales.

6.6.3　Other models

6.6.3.1　Stackelberg Model

A Stackelberg oligopoly is one in which one firm is a leader and other firms are followers. This model applies where: (a) A firms sell homogeneous products,

(b) competition is based on output, (c) firms choose their output sequentially and not simultaneously.

The leader is typically a first–mover who chooses its output before other firms can do it. Since other firms must set their output decision given the leader's output decision, the leader in a Stackelberg oligopoly typically has a bigger market share and higher profit than other firms in the oligopoly.

6.6.3.2 Bertrand Model

There are two versions of Bertrand model depending on whether the products are homogeneous or differentiated.

The homogeneous–products Bertrand model of oligopoly applies when firms in the oligopoly produce standardized products at same marginal cost. When the marginal cost is same, it is in the best interest of each firm in oligopoly to undercut its rival (i.e. beat its price), because the other firms are also trying to beat it. This price war leads to a situation at which market price is equal to the marginal cost. The output and price level in a Bertrand oligopoly is the same as in perfect competition.

The differentiated–products Bertrand model contends that when an oligopoly produces differentiated products, price competition doesn't necessarily lead to a competitive outcome. It is because when each firm produces a differentiated product, its demand doesn't become zero when it raises its price. In fact, the Bertrand model concludes that if one firm increases it price, the other firms in a differentiated oligopoly should also increase theirs because this will increase its profit.

6.6.3.3 Contestable Market Theory

Contestable market theory posits that when the initial investment required in an oligopoly is not a sunk cost i.e. where most of the investment can be recovered if a firm decides to leave the market, the industry functions more like a perfect competition. It is because the recoverability of the investment encourages new firms to get a go at the industry and this eliminates any positive economic profit.

The following matrix compares different aspects of the common oligopoly models:

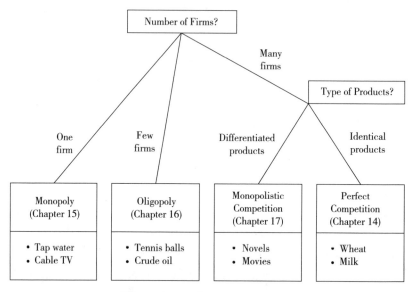

Figure 6-13 Comparision chart

Conclusion

Monopolies can use their market power to hold price above the level that would prevail in acompetitive market, turning consumer surplus into positive economic profits. This poses a tricky problem for policy-makers, who want to regulate orbreak up monopolies to increase welfare. Practically speaking, it can be difficult to accomplish this goal without causing more inefficiency. Policies designed to address the problemsassociated with monopolies run the risk of setting prices at the wrong level or raising costsby breaking up a natural monopoly.

Learn about imperfect competition and the characteristics of industries that fall into the categories of monopolistic competition and oligopoly. Knowing about these market structures helps business owners make optimal decisions about production and pricing.Market structure can tell us a lot about how firms make decisions, but there are still anumber of other factors that we haven't explored yet. Up until now, we've focused on theamount of any given good that firms choose to produce.

Key Term

Monopoly   Oligopoly

Natural Monopoly   Monopolistic Competition

Price Discrimination   Product Differentiation

Review Questions

1. A monopolist is producing at a point at which marginal cost exceeds marginal revenue. How should it adjust its output to increase profit?

2. We write the percentage markup of price over marginal cost as(P–MC)/P. For a profit–maximizing monopolist, how does this markup depend on the elasticity of demand?Why can this markup be viewed as a measure of monopoly power?

3. Why will a monopolist's output increase if the government forces it to lower its price?If the governmentwants to set a price ceiling that maximizes the monopolist's output,what price should it set?

4. Why is there no market supply curve under conditions of monopoly?

5. Why might a firm have monopoly power even if it is not the only producer in the market?

6. What are some of the different types of barriers to entry that give rise to monopoly power? Give an example of each.

7. What factors determine the amount of monopoly power an individual firm is likely to have? Explain each one briefly.

8. What are the characteristics of a monopolistically competitive market? What happens to the equilibrium price and quantity in such a market if one firm introduces a new,improved product?

9. Why is the firm's demand curve flatter than the total market demand curve in monopolistic competition? Suppose a monopolistically competitive firm is making a profit in the short run.What will happen to its demand curve in the long run?

Some experts have argued that too many brands of breakfast cereal are on themarket.

Give an argument to support this view.Give an argument against it.

10. Why is the Cournot equilibrium stable?(i.e., Why don't firms have any incentive to change their output levels once in equilibrium?) Even if they can't

collude, why don't firms set their outputs at the joint profit–maximizing levels (i.e., the levels they would have chosen had they colluded)?

11. In the Stackelberg model, the firm that sets output first has an advantage. Explain why.

12. What do the Cournot and Bertrand models have in common? What is different about the two models?

13. Explain the meaning of a Nash equilibrium when firms are competing with respect to price. Why is the equilibrium stable? Why don't the firms raise prices to the level that maximizes joint profits?

Application

1. Will an increase in the demand for a monopolist's product always result in a higher price? Explain. Will an increase in the supply facing a monopsonist buyer always result in a lower price? Explain.

2. Caterpillar Tractor, one of the largest producers of farm machinery in the world, has hired you to advise it on pricing policy. One of the things the company would like to know is how much a 5–percent increase in price is likely to reduce sales. What would you need to know to help the company with this problem? Explain why these facts are important.

3. A firm faces the following average revenue(demand)curve:

$P=120-0.02Q$

where Q is weekly production and P is price, measured in cents per unit. The firm's cost function is given by $C=60Q+25000$. Assume that the firm maximizes profits.

a. What is the level of production, price, and total profit per week?

b. If the government decides to levy a tax of 14 cents per unit on this product, what will be the new level of production, price, and profit?

4. Suppose all firms in a monopolistically competitive industry were merged into one large firm. Would that new firm produce as many different brands? Would it produce only a single brand? Explain.

5. Consider two firms facing the demand curve $P=50-5Q$, where $Q=Q_1+Q_2$. The firms' cost functions are $C_1(Q_1)=20+10Q_1$, and $C_2(Q_2)=10+12Q_2$.

a. Suppose both firms have entered the industry. What is the joint profit–

maximizing level of output? How much will each firm produce? How would your answer change if the firms have not yet entered the industry?

b. What is each firm's equilibrium output and profit if they behave noncooperatively? Use the Cournot model. Draw the firms' reaction curves and show the equilibrium.

c. How much should Firm 1 be willing to pay to purchase Firm 2 if collusion is illegal but a takeover is not?

6. Suppose that two competing firms,A and B, produce a homogeneous good. Both firms have a marginal cost of MC=¥50. Describe what would happen to output and price in each of the following situations if the firms are at(i) Cournot equilibrium,(ii) collusive equilibrium, and(iii) Bertrand equilibrium.

a. Because Firm A must increase wages, its MC increases to ¥80.

b. The marginal cost of both firms increases.

c. The demand curve shifts to the right.

7. Suppose the market for tennis shoes has one dominant firm and five fringe firms. The market demand is Q=400−2 P. The dominant firm has a constant marginal cost of 20. The fringe firms each have a marginal cost of MC=20+5q.

a. Verify that the total supply curve for the five fringe firms is Q.=P−20.

b. Find the dominant firm's demand curve.

c. Find the profit−maximizing quantity producedand price charged by the dominant firm, and the quantity produced and price charged by each of the fringe firms.

d. Suppose there are 10 fringe firms instead of five.How does this change your results?

e. Suppose there continue to be five fringe firms but that each manages to reduce its marginal cost to MC=20+2g. How does this change your results?

7

Factors of Production

Learning Objectives

LO 7.1   Define factors of production and describe how they contribute to output.

LO 7.2   Graph the demand curve for a factor of production, and explain its relationship to marginal productivity.

LO 7.3   Explain how to find the equilibrium price and quantity for a factor of production.Use graphs to demonstrate the effect of a shift in supply or demand and describe what causes these curves to shift.

LO 7.4   Define human capital, and justify its importance in the labor market.

LO 7.5   Describe the similarities and differences between the markets for land and capital and the market for labor.

LO 7.6   Identify two reasons why a wage might rise above the market equilibrium, and describe their effect on the labor market.

LO 7.7   Describe several causes of imperfectly competitive labor markets and their effect on workers and employers.

In this chapter, we'll discuss the markets for factors of production. Economists usually lump the factors of production into three categories—labor, land, and capital. We'll see how prices in these markets are determined by markets for consumer goods, as well as by public policy. Seeing how supply and demand govern factor markets allows us to understand how firms make decisions about how much of which factors to use. This choice is important for any business owner: Is it worth buying a new machine or hiring another employee? How can you know?

When you finish school, your income will be determined largely by what kind of job you take. If you become a computer programmer, you will earn more than if you become a gas station attendant. This fact is not surprising, but it is not obvious why it is true. No law requires that computer programmers be paid more than gas station attendants. No ethical principle says that programmers are more deserving. What then determines which job will pay you the higher wage?

7.1   Define factors of production and describe how they contribute to output

What do you pay for building a house? We need to input workers, building materials, time and so on. When a firm design a building, it uses architects' time (labor), the physical space on which it sits (land), and an equipment and other building materials (capital). Similarly, when a bookstore sells books, it uses the physical space (land), attendants' time (labor), and the books and bookshelf(capital). These ingredients to produce goods and services are collectively called *factors of production.* Economists think that there are three types of factors:labor, land, and capital. labor is the time employees spend working, and **land** is the place where they work. **Capital** refers to manufactured goods that are used to produce new goods.

Understanding factor markets—particularly labor markets—is also a key to explaining people's income. We'll describe how ownership of different factors of production affects income and why people earn different amounts. This chapter is thus a building block for understanding income inequality. Since the majority of people make their living primarily by selling their labor, we'll focus on understanding the differences between the wages people earn. What differentiates Albert Pujols from a farm worker, or a professional racquetball player, or a plumber, or you? This chapter will leave you with tools for understanding labor markets as a worker, a boss, or a voter.

7.2   The nature of factor demands

The demand for factors differs from that for consumption goods in two important respects: ① Factor demands are derived demands, ② factor demands are interdependent demands.

（1） *Demands for factors are derived demands*. Considering the demand for dormitory by a firm which produces computer software. A software company will rent office space for its programmers, customer service representatives, and other workers. Similarly, other companies like pizza shops or banks will need space for their activities. In each region, there will be a downward–sloping demand curve for office space linking the rental being charged by landlords to the amount of office space desired by companies—the lower the price, the more space companies will want to rent.

But there is an important difference between ordinary demands by consumers and the demand by firms for inputs. Consumers demand final goods like computer games or pizzas because of the direct enjoyment or utility these consumption   goods provide. By contrast, a business does not pay for inputs like office space because they yield direct satisfaction. Rather, it buys inputs because of the production and revenue that it can gain from employment of those factors.

Satisfactions are in the picture for inputs—but at one stage removed. The satisfaction that consumers get from playing computer games determines how many games the software company can sell, how many clerks it needs, and how much office space it must rent. The more successful its software, the greater its demand for office space. An accurate analysis of the demand for inputs must, therefore, recognize that consumer demands do ultimately determine business demands for office space.

This analysis is not limited to office space. Consumer demands determine the demand for all inputs, including farmland, oil, and pizza ovens. Can you see how the demand for professors of economics is ultimately determined by the demand for economics courses by students?

The firm's demand for inputs is derived indirectly from the consumer demand for its final product. Economists therefore speak of the demand for productive factors as a derived demand. This means that when firms demand an input, they do so because that input permits them to produce a good which consumer desire now or in the future. Figure 7-1 shows how the demand for a given input, such as fertile cornland, must be regarded as being derived from the consumer demand curve for corn. In the same way, the demand for office space is derived from the consumer demand for software and all the other products and services provided by the companies that rent office space.

(2) *Demands for factors are interdependent*. Production is a team effort. A chain saw by itself is useless for cutting down a tree. A worker with empty hands is equally worthless. Together, the worker and the saw can cut the tree very nicely. In other words, the productivity of one factor, such aslabor, depends upon the number of other factors available to work with.

Therefore, it is generally impossible to say how much output has been created by a single input taken by itself. Asking which factor is more important is like asking whether a mother or a father is more essential in producing a baby.

The demand for a factor of production is a derived demand. It is the interdependence of productivities of land, labor, and capital that makes the distribution of income a complex topic. Suppose that you were in charge of determining the income distribution of a country. If land had by itself produced so much, andlabor had by itself produced so much, and machinery had by itself produced the rest, distribution would be easy. Moreover, under supply and demand, if each factor produced a certain amount by itself, it could enjoy the undivided fruits of its own work.

7.3　Distribution theory and marginal revenue product

The fundamental point about distribution theory is that the demands for the various factors of production are derived from the revenues that each factor yields on its marginal product. Before showing this result, we begin by defining some new terms.

Marginal revenue product

We can use the tools of production theory to devise a key concept, marginal revenue product (MRP). Suppose we are operating a giant shirt factory. We know how many shirts each additional worker produces. But the firm wants to maximize profits measured in dollars, for it pays salaries and dividends with money, not with shirts. We therefore need a concept that measures the additional dollars each additional unit of input produces. Economists give the name "marginal revenue product" to the money value of the additional output generated by an extra unit of input.

Equation 7-1

$$MRPL=MPL \times P$$

The **marginal revenue product** of input A is the additional revenue produced by an additional unit of input A.

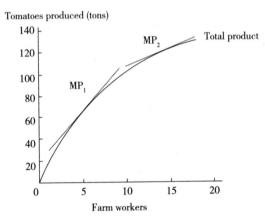

The more workers a farm employs, the more tomatoes the farm can harvest. Hiring an additional farm worker adds fewer tomatoes to the harvest than the previous worker.

Figure 7–1   Marginal product of labor

In some cases, firms can choose what combination of factors to use, substituting one for another. For instance, picking tomatoes can be done either by hand or by machine. A farmer can choose to hire many workers and buy no machinery, or hire fewer workers and buy more machinery. *Note that this doesn't work for all goods: You can't choose to produce a baseball game by having fewer players and more bats.*

A profit–seeking firm will choose the combination of inputs that maximizes profit, based on the local price of each factor of production. The price of farm machinery is similar all over the world, but the cost of farmlabor varies more widely.

In poorer economies, labor is usually cheap, so farmers tend to hire lots of workers and buy fewer machines. In rich countries, labor costs more, so farmers tend to hire fewer workers and buy more machines. Another way of saying this is that farming tends to belabor–intensive in poor countries and capital–intensive in rich countries.

7.4   Labor markets and wages

We now have some concepts to use when thinking about the markets for factors of production. We'll use them to take a closer look at the markets for labor and capital. First, we'll consider the demand for labor, and then its supply. To understand labor demand, we need to focus on the firms that hire the labor and use it to produce goods for sale. By examining the link between the production of goods and the demand for labor, we gain insight into the determination of equilibrium wages.

7.4.1   The demand for labor

What causes the labor demand curve to shift?

We now understand the labor demand curve: It is nothing more than a reflection of the value of marginal product of labor. With this insight in mind, let's consider a few of the things that might cause the labor demand curve to shift.

The Output Price   The value of the marginal product is marginal product times the price of the firm's output. Thus, when the output price changes, the value of the marginal product changes, and the labor demand curve shifts. An increase in the price of apples, for instance, raises the value of the marginal product of each worker that picks apples and, therefore, increases labor demand from the firms that supply apples. Conversely, a decrease in the price of apples reduces the value of the marginal product and decreases labor demand.

Equation 7-2

$$VMPL = MPL \times P \text{ of output}$$

Technological Change   Between 1968 and 1998, the amount of output a typical U.S. worker produced in an hour rose by 57 percent. Why? The most important reason is technological progress: Scientists and engineers are constantly figuring out new and better ways of doing things. This has profound implications for the labor market. Technological advance raises the marginal product of labor, which in turn increases the demand forlabor. Such technological advance explains persistently rising employment in face of rising wages: Even though wages (adjusted for inflation) increased by 62 percent over these three decades, firms nonetheless increased by 72 percent the number of workers they employed.

- Technological advance
— Can raise MPL: Increase demand for labor
- Labor–saving technology
— Can reduce MPL: Decrease demand for labor

The Supply of Other Factors. The quantity available of one factor of production can affect the marginal product of other factors. A fall in the supply of ladders, for instance, will reduce the marginal product of apple pickers and thus the demand for apple pickers. We consider this linkage among the factors of pro– duction more fully later in the chapter.

7.4.2 The supply of labor

Consider the choice made by an individual worker—say, a farm worker in Chongqing—who is deciding how many hours to work each week. The main benefit of working is earning a certain wage for every hour of work. Workers can choose to work a lot to earn more money, or they could choose to pass up that chance in order to have more time off.

It is important to know how many hours a worker will be willing to work at different wage rates. When the real wage rate increases, the individual will be pulled in two opposite directions. The real wage rate is the relative price of leisure which has to be given up for doing work to earn income.

（1）*Substitution effect of a rise in wages.* With higher wages, workers will give greater value to working than leisure. With work more profitable, there is a higher opportunity cost of not working. As real wage rate rises, *leisure* becomes relatively more expensive (in terms of income foregone) and this induces the individual to substitute work (or income) for leisure. This is called *substitution effect* of the rise in real wage and induces the individual to work more hours (that is, supply more labor) at a higher wage rate.

（2）*Income effect of a rise in wages.* But the increase in the real wage rate also makes the individual richer, that is, his income increases. This increase in income tends to make the individual to consume more of all commodities including leisure. This is called ***income effect*** of the rise in wage rate which tends to increase leisure and reduce number of work hours (i.e. reduce labor supply). The economists generally believe that substitution effect of a rise in real wage is larger than its income effect and therefore individuals work for more hours (that is, supply more labor) at a higher wage rate.

However, beyond a certain higher real wage and number of hours worked, leisure becomes more desirable and income effect outweighs substitution effect, and as a result supply of labor decreases beyond a certain higher wage rate.

In what follows we shall explain how we derive a supply curve of labor of an individual and of the economy as a whole in all these circumstances. Thus, whether an individual will supply more work–effort or less as a result of the rise in the wage rate depends upon the relative strengths of the income and substitution effects.

The changes in the work–effort or labor supplied by an individual worker due to the changes in the wage rate. To begin with, the wage line is AW_1 the slope of the wage line indicates the wage rate per hour.

With wage line AW_1, the individual is in equilibrium at point Q on indifference curve I_1 and is working AL_1 hours in a week. Suppose the wage rate rises so that the new wage line is AW_2, with wage line AW_2, the individual is in equilibrium at point R on the indifference curve I_2, and is now working AL_2, hours which are more than before.

If the wage rate further rises so that the new wage line is AW_3, the individual moves to the point S on indifference curve I_3 and works AL_3 hours which are more than AL_1 or AL_2. Suppose the wage rate further rises so that the wage line is AW_4. With wage line AW_4, the individual is in equilibrium at point T and works AL_4 hours.

If points Q, R, S and T are connected, we get what is called wage offer curve which shows the number of hours that an individual offer to work at various wage rates. It should be noted that the wage offer curve, strictly speaking, is not the supply curve of labor though it provides the same information as the supply curve of labor.

The supply curve of labor is obtained when the wage rate is directly represented on the Y–axis and labor (i.e. work effort) supplied at various w age rates on the X–axis reading from left to right. In Figure. 7–3 the supply curve of labor has been drawn from the information gained from Figure 7–2. Let the wage line AW_1 represent the wage rate equal to P_1, wage line AW_2, represents wage rate P_2, wage line AW_3 represents wage rate P_3 and wage line AW_4 represent wage rate P_4. It will be seen that as the wage rate rises from P_1 to P_4 and as a result the wage line shifts from AW_1 to AW_4 the number of hours worked, that is, the amount of labor supplied increases from AL_1 to AL_4.

As a result, the supply curve of labor in Figure 7–3 is upward sloping. The indifference map depicted in Figure 7–2 is such that the substitution effect of the rise in the wage rate is stronger than the income effect of the rise in the wage rate so that the work– effort supplied increases as the wage rate rises.

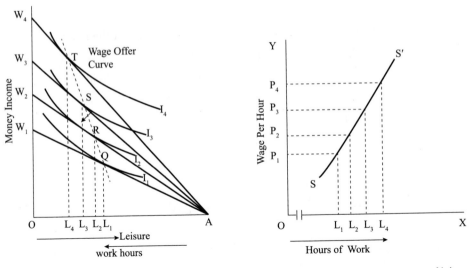

Figure 7–2 Wages offer curve   Figure 7–3 Upward sloping supply curve of labor

Backward–Sloping Supply Curve of Labor:

But the supply curve of labor is not always upward sloping. When an individual prefers leisure to income, then the supply of labor (number of hours worked) by an individual will decrease as the wage rate rises. This is because in such a case income effect which tends to reduce the work effort outweighs the substitution effect which tends to increase the work effort.

In Figure 7–4(a) an indifference map along with a set of wage lines AW_1, AW_2, AW_3 and AW_4 (showing wage rates P_1, P_2, P_3, P_4 respectively) are shown. As the wage rate rises to P_2 and hence the wage line shifts to AW_2 the number of hours worked by the individual per week increases but when the wage rate further rises to P_3 and P_4 and hence the wage line shifts to AW_3 and AW_4, the number of hours worked by the individual decreases. From Figure 7–4(b) it will be explicitly seen that the supply curve of labor slopes upward to the wage rate P_2 (that is, point K) and beyond that it slopes backward.

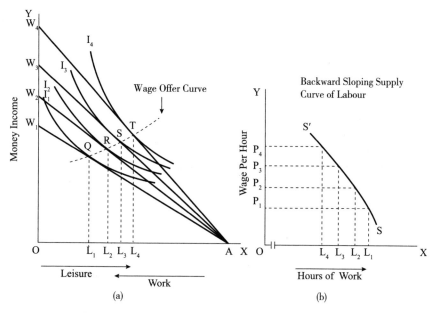

Figure 7–4   Backward sloping supply curve of labor

Supply Curve of Labor for the Economy as a Whole:

The supply curve of labor of a group of individuals or of the whole working force in the economy can be derived by summing up horizontally the supply curves of individuals. It may be noted that the supply curve of labor for the economy as a whole will be upward sloping or backward sloping depending upon whether the relative number of individuals having upward sloping supply curves is greater or less than those having backward sloping supply curves of labor. Further, different individuals will have backward sloping portion in their supply curve at different wage ranges, which creates difficulties in finding the nature of supply curve of the whole work force.

It is generally found that when the wage rate rises from the initially low level to a sufficiently good level, the total supply of labor to the economy as a whole increases (that is, supply curve for the economy as a whole slopes upward to a certain wage rate) and for further increases in the wage rate, the total supply of labor to the economy as a whole decreases (that is, beyond a certain wage rate the total supply curve of labor slopes backward). Thus, the total supply curve of labor for the economy as a whole is generally believed to be the shape depicted in Figure 7–5(b).

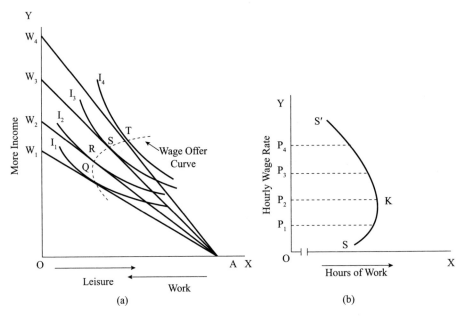

Figure 7–5　Work effort increases with the rise in the wage rate when the substitution effect is greater than the income effect

Up to W_1, the substitution effect is greater than the income effect, and higher wages causes more hours worked.

After W_2, the income effect outweighs the substitution effect. Now people work fewer hours because they can get their target income from a lower number of hours.

What causes the labor supply curve to shift?

The labor supply curve shifts whenever people change the amount, they want to work at a given wage. Let's now consider some of the events that might cause such a shift.

Changes in Tastes　In 1950, 34 percent of women were employed at paid jobs or looking for work. In 1998, the number had risen to 60 percent. There are, of course, many explanations for this development, but one of them is changing tastes, or attitudes toward work. A generation or two ago, it was the norm for women to stay at home while raising children. Today, family sizes are smaller, and more mothers choose to work. The result is an increase in the supply oflabor.

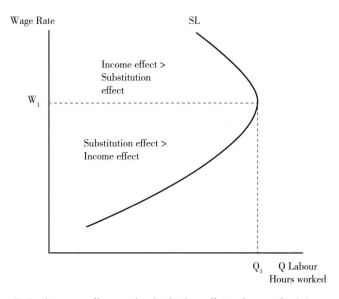

Figure 7-6   Income effect and substitution effect of wage for labor supply

Changes in Alternative Opportunities The supply oflabor in any onelabor market depends on the opportunities available in other labor markets. If the wage earned by pear pickers suddenly rises, some apple pickers may choose to switch occupations. The supply oflabor in the market for apple pickers falls.

Immigration Movements of workers from region to region, or country to country, is an obvious and often important source of shifts inlabor supply. When immigrants come to the United States, for instance, the supply oflabor in the United States increases and the supply oflabor in the immigrants' home countries contracts. In fact, much of the policy debate about immigration centers on its effect onlabor supply and, thereby, equilibrium in thelabor market.

Reaching equilibrium

So far, we have established two facts about how wages are determined in competitive labor markets:

N   The wage adjusts to balance the supply and demand for labor.

N   The wage equals the value of the marginal product of labor.

At first, it might seem surprising that the wage can do both these things at once.

In fact, there is no real puzzle here, but understanding why there is no puzzle is an important step to understanding wage determination.

Figure 7-7 shows the labor market in equilibrium. The wage and the quantity of labor have adjusted to balance supply and demand. When the market is in this equilibrium, each firm has bought as muchlabor as it finds profitable at the equilibrium wage. That is, each firm has followed the rule for profit maximization: It has hired workers until the value of the marginal product equals the wage. Hence, the wage must equal the value of marginal product oflabor once it has brought supply and demand into equilibrium.

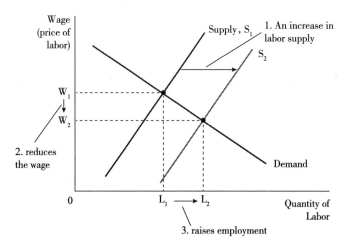

Figure 7-7 A shift in labor supply

This brings us to an important lesson: **Any event that changes the supply or demand forlabor must change the equilibrium wage and the value of the marginal product by the same amount, because these must always be equal.** To see how this works, let's consider some events that shift these curves.

Shifts in labor supply

Suppose that immigration increases the number of workers willing to pick apples. As Figure 7-7 shows, the supply of labor shifts to the right from S_1 to S_2. At the initial wage W_1, the quantity of labor supplied now exceeds the quantity demanded. This surplus of labor puts downward pressure on the wage of apple pickers, and the fall in the wage from W_1 to W_2 in turn makes it profitable for firms to hire more workers. As the number of workers employed in each apple orchard rises, the marginal product of a worker falls, and so does the value of the marginal product. In the new equilibrium, both the wage and the value of the marginal product of labor are lower than they were before the influx of new workers.

Shifts in labor demand

Now suppose that an increase in the popularity of apples causes their price to rise. This price increase does not change the marginal product of labor for any given number of workers, but it does raise the value of the marginal product. With a higher price of apples, hiring more apple pickers is now profitable. As Figure 7-8 shows, when the demand for labor shifts to the right from D_1 to D_2, the equilibrium wage rises from W_1 to W_2, and equilibrium employment rises from L_1 to L_2. Once again, the wage and the value of the marginal product of labor move together.

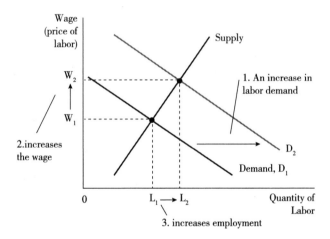

Figure 7-8   A shift in labor demand

This analysis shows that prosperity for firms in an industry is often linked to prosperity for workers in that industry. When the price of apples rises, apple producers make greater profit, and apple pickers earn higher wages. When the price of apples falls, apple producers earn smaller profit, and apple pickers earn lower wages. This lesson is well known to workers in industries with highly volatile prices. Workers in oil fields, for instance, know from experience that their earnings are closely linked to the world price of crude oil.

From these examples, you should now have a good understanding of how wages are set in competitive labor markets.Labor supply and labor demand together determine the equilibrium wage, and shifts in the supply or demand curve for labor cause the equilibrium wage to change. At the same time, profit maximization by the firms that demand labor ensures that the equilibrium wage always equals the value of the marginal product of labor.

7.5 Land and capital

Before we say anything else about the markets for land and capital, we should note one important difference from labor markets: When a firm wants to use land or capital, it has two choices—to buy or rent. When we talk about the price of land or capital, then, we need to distinguish between the **rental price** and the **purchase**. **The rental price** is what a producer pays to use a factor of production for a certain period or task. **The purchase price** is what a producer pays to gain permanent ownership of a factor of production. The rental price and the purchase price are both important concepts for understanding markets for land and capital.

Rental markets. The rental prices of land and capital are determined in the same way as the wage in alabor market. When Walmart hires a full–time cashier, Walmart is actually "renting" the cashier's labor for 40 hours a week. Walmart also is renting when it leases a new building or borrows money. In the case of borrowing, the rental price of capital is the interest paid on loans.

In the markets for factors of production, economists use the phrase *economic rent* to describe the gains that workers and owners of capital receive from supplying theirlabor or machinery in factor markets. In the rental markets shown in Figure 7–9, the area above the supply curve but below the equilibrium rental price is economic rent. It represents the rental price of a factor of production minus the cost of supplying it.

The shaded area in the figure may seem familiar to you: we identified this as *producer surplus.* The concept is the same, but in the markets for factors of production, we use the term economic rent. Later, we'll discuss what role these gains (as part of something called the factor distribution of income) play in the economy.

Purchase markets. Renting land or capital allows a firm to use it for a certain period without worrying about its long–term value. In contrast, buying land or capital requires potential owners to think about an asset's long–run productivity. To determine the price, they should pay for land or capital, potential buyers must forecast what its marginal product is likely to be over time. They can then assess the value of the expected future flows of income in order to compare them to the cost of the asset. Smart sellers will make similar calculations in order to calculate their own notion of a reasonable price.

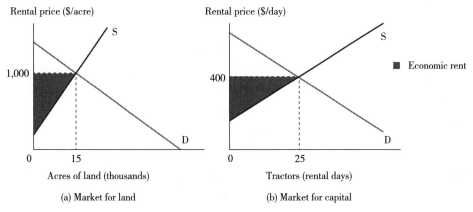

Just as in the labor market, the rental markets for land and capital reach an equilibrium price and quantity at the point where the supply curve intersects the dem and curve. The area above the supply curve and below equilibrium rental price is called *economic rent.*

Figure 7–9   Economic rent in rental markets for land and capital

7.6   The factor distribution of income

We can now explain how much income goes to labor, how much goes to landowners, and how much goes to the owners of capital. As long as the firms using the factors of production are competitive and profit–maximizing, each factor's rental price must equal the value of the marginal product for that factor. labor, land, and capital each earn the value of their marginal contribution to the production process.

Economists refer to the pattern of income that people derive from different factors of production as **the factor distribution of income**. In other words, the factor distribution of income shows how much income people get from labor compared to land and capital. Now consider the purchase price of land and capital. The rental price and the purchase price are obviously related: Buyers are willing to pay more to buy a piece of land or capital if it produces a valuable stream of rental income. And, as we have just seen, the equilibrium rental income at any point in time equals the value of that factor's marginal product. Therefore, the equilibrium purchase price of a piece of land or capital depends on both the current value of the marginal product and the value of the marginal product expected to prevail in the future.

Conclusion

Why do some people earn more money than others? That is one of the most fundamental questions in economics and politics. When markets are competitive, everyone earns income in proportion to the productivity of the factors of production they control. For most people, that means their income is based on their own productivity as workers. That's usually closely tied to the skills, education, and other talents that determine our "human capital." For farmers, the productivity of land matters as well. For investors, income is determined by the productivity of their financial capital. Competitive markets have the remarkable ability to reward work according to what is contributed to the economy.

We've seen that we can use the familiar tools of supply and demand to put prices on the factors of production, and we examined how business owners decide how much of each factor to use in producing goods and services. Their choice is driven by both the marginal productivity and the price of each factor. In future chapters we'll return to the markets for land, labor, and capital, to see what happens when we add public policy and collective decision making to the picture.

Key Term

Factors of Production	Efficiency Wage
Human Capital	Capital
Rental Price	Purchase Price
Monopsony	Value of the Marginal Product
Marginal Product	Economic Rent

Review Questions

1. Consider the factors of production that go intoa fast-food restaurant. Give an example of land, labor, and capital.

2. Suppose an auto manufacturer has one factory in the United States and one in Mexico. The auto manufacturer produces the same number of cars and the same models in each factory but hires more workers in Mexico than in the United States.Give an explanation for the discrepancy in the amount of labor hired in each location.

3. Suppose you run a flower–delivery business and employ college students to drive the vans and make deliveries. You are considering hiring an additional worker. What information would you need to know to decide whether doing so would increase or decrease your profit?

4. Christina runs an IT consulting firm in a competitive market. She recently determined that hiring an additional consultant would mean that she would be able to serve five more clients per week. Assuming her goal is to maximize her profits, explain why Christina did not hire another consultant.

5. Suppose your retired grandmother has complained of boredom and is considering taking a part–time job. Use the concept of opportunity cost to advise your grandmother how to decide whether to take the job.

6. Suppose you have inherited a few acres of land from a relative and you are considering what to do with your inheritance.A farmer with land next to yours offers to buy your acres so he can expand his grazing area. How will you decide whether to sell your land to the farmer? What factors should you consider?

7. Large telecom companies like China Telecom and China Mobile routinely send repair technicians to customers' homes. Although they are skilled laborers, they must usually train on the job, so it takes some time for them to reach a high standard of quality. In addition, their work cannot be constantly supervised. Explain why an efficiency wage could help telecom companies to increase the productivity of repair techs.

Application

1. Recently, some college alumni started a moving service for students living on campus. They have three employees and are debating hiring a fourth.The hourly wage for an employee is ¥18 per hour.An average moving job takes three hours. The company currently does three moving jobs per week, but with one more employee,

the company could manage five jobs per week. The company charges ¥80 for a moving job.

a. What would be the new employee's marginal product of labor?

b. What is the value of that marginal product?

c. Should the moving service hire a fourth worker?

2. Sasha has 60 hours a week she can work or have leisure. Wages are ¥8/hour.

a. Graph Sasha's bud get constraint for income and leisure.

b. Suppose wages increase to ¥10/hour. Graph Sasha's new bud get constraint.

c. When wages increase from ¥8/hour to ¥10/hour, Sasha's leisure time decreases from 20 hours to 15 hours. Does her labor supply curve slope upward or downward over this wage increase?

3.Imagine that, faced with budget shortfalls, a government changes its current policy of granting tax credits based on family size to a flat rate tax credit for a family with one or more children.

a. Over time, what will happen to the average age in the population?

b. Over time, what will happen to the size of the workforce?

4. In each scenario, will wages rise above the market equilibrium or fall below it?

a. All but one of the factories in a town go out of business.

b. All the software engineers in Silicon Valley organize into a union and go on strike.

c. A major grocery store chain buys out all the other stores in the city.

8

General Equilibrium and Welfare Economic

The previous chapter was devoted to looking at equilibrium in one market in isolation, known as *partial equilibrium analysis. General equilibrium analysis* gives us a sense of how the various pieces of an economy fit together to work as a whole. Partial equilibrium analysis can lead to bias. Consider the market for DVDs and cinema tickets. The government taxes movie tickets. If we look at partial equilibrium, the supply curve for movie tickets shifts and we are done. If we look at general equilibrium, we consider how this might affect the DVD market (which feed back into the movie ticket market). In this chapter, we study the equilibrium of all markets simultaneously, referred to as general equilibrium analysis. In addition to knowing how the system operates, we also want to find out if it produces "good" results. The second part of the chapter therefore discusses welfare economics, the branch of economics concerned with the social desirability of alternative economic states. Welfare economics provides a set of criteria for evaluating an economic system.

8.1　General equilibrium analysis

Assumptions

The general equilibrium analysis is based on the following assumptions:

(1) There is perfect competition both in the commodity and factor markets.

(2) Tastes and habits of consumers are given and constant.

(3) Incomes of consumers are given and constant.

(4) Factors of production are perfectly mobile between different occupations and places.

(5) There are constant returns to scale.

(6) All firms operate under identical cost conditions.

(7) All units of a productive service are homogeneous.

(8) There are no changes in the techniques of production.

(9) There is full employment of labor and other resources.

Supply and demand curves

General equilibrium spillovers can occur with any market structures. In this chapter, however, our focus is on competitive markets that can be analyzed using the familiar supply and demand model.

General equilibrium demand

Ultimately, demand patterns in an economy are determined by individuals' preferences.

For our simple model we will assume that all individuals have identical preferences, which can be represented by an indifference curve map3 defined over quantities of the two goods, x and y. The benefit of this approach for our purposes is that this indifference curve map shows how individuals rank consumption bundles containing both goods. These rankings are precisely what we mean by "demand" in a general equilibrium context. Of course, we cannot illustrate which bundles of commodities will be chosen until we know the budget constraints that demanders face. Because incomes are generated as individuals supplylabor, capital, and other resources to the production process, we must delay any detailed illustration until we have examined the forces of production and supply in our model.

Developing a notion of general equilibrium supply in this two-good model is a somewhat more complex process than describing the demand side of the market because we have not thus far illustrated production and supply of two goods simultaneously. Our approach is to use the familiar production possibility curve for this purpose. By detailing the way in which this curve is constructed, we can illustrate, in a simple context, the ways in which markets for outputs and inputs are related.

General equilibrium in a pure exchange economy

The analysis of general equilibrium using supply and demand curves provides valuable insights regarding the linkages between competitive markets. However, with its focus on market outcomes, supply and demand analysis tells us little about what is going on at the level of the individual decision maker. Moreover, shifting multiple sets of supply and demand curves is a somewhat unwieldy way to study how the overall set of prices in the economy is determined. To get around these difficulties, we will employ a more fundamental level of analysis.

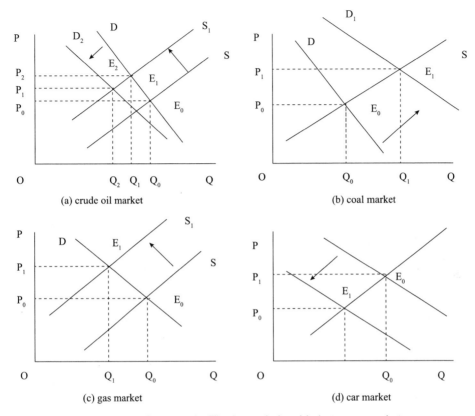

(a) crude oil market

(b) coal market

(c) gas market

(d) car market

Figure 8-1   Case study: The interrelationship between markets

8.2   Economic efficiency

This efficiency criterion was developed by Vilfredo Pareto in his book "Manual of Political Economy", 1906. An allocation of goods is Pareto optimal when there is no possibility of redistribution in a way where at least one individual would be better off while no other individual ends up worse off.

A definition can also be made in two steps:

—A change from situation A to B is a Pareto improvement if at least one individual is better off without making other individuals worse off;

—B is Pareto optimal if there is no possible Pareto improvement.

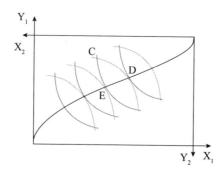

Figure 8-2　Pareto optimal

This can be easily understood using an Edgeworth box. Starting from point C, two Pareto improvements can be made:

—From C to D: Individual 1 would increase its utility, since a further indifference curve would be reached, while individual 2 will remain with the same utility;

—From C to E: Individual 2 would maintain its utility while individual 2 increases theirs.

Once we are at point either D or E, no further Pareto improvements can be made. Therefore, D and E are Pareto optimal.

Following the same steps for every indifference curve, we can say that every point in which indifference curves from different individuals are tangent is Pareto optimal. The curve that links these infinite Pareto optima is called the contract curve.

8.3　General equilibrium analysis

Assumptions

· **Utility maximization** —Everybody is maximizing their utility.

Convex indifference curves—Indifference curves are the usual convex shape (very easy to relax).

Non–satiation—More is better, everybody wants to go as far from their origin as they can.

· **No Interdependence**—Don't care how much the other person gets.

Edgeworth box

Edgeworth box diagram for production Construction of the production possibility curve for two outputs (x and y) begins with the assumption that there are fixed amounts of capital and labor inputs that must be allocated to the production of the two goods. The possible allocations of these inputs can be illustrated with an Edgeworth box diagram with dimensions given by the total amounts of capital and labor available.

In Figure 8–2, the length of the box represents total labor hours, and the height of the box represents total capital–hours. The lower left corner of the box represents the "origin" for measuring capital and labor devoted to production of good x. The upper right corner of the box represents the origin for resources devoted to y. Using these conventions, any point in the box can be regarded as a fully employed allocation of the available resources between goods x and y. Point A, for example, represents an allocation in which the indicated number of labor hours are devoted to x production together with a specified number of hours of capital. Production of good y uses whatever labor and capital are "left over." Point A in Figure 8–2, for example, also shows the exact amount of labor and capital used in the production of good y. Any other point in the box has a similar interpretation. Thus, the Edgeworth box shows every possible way the existing capital and labor might be used to produce x and y. Let's make some assumptions about their tastes

Initial approach:

Let's consider an economy where there are:

Two factors of production: capital (K) and labor (L).

Two goods: Good X and good Y.

Two agents: A and B

The economic problem that is faced needs to find the most adequate allocation of factors of production in order to produce goods X and Y and how these goods will be distributed amongst consumers A and B. This configuration will be such that there will be no other feasible configuration that will allow an increase in any individual's welfare without decreasing the other individual's welfare.

In order to achieve ***Pareto optimality,*** a certain set of assumptions need to be held.

—The production function needs to be continuous, differentiable, and strictly concave. This will result in a convex set of production possibilities, also known as production possibility frontier Its shape shows an increasing opportunity cost as we need to use a higher number of resources in order to produce a larger amount of a certain good.

The dimensions of this diagram are given by the total quantities of labor and capital available. Quantities of these resources devoted to x production are measured from origin O_x; quantities devoted to y are measured from O_y. Any point in the box represents a fully employed allocation of the available resources to the two goods.

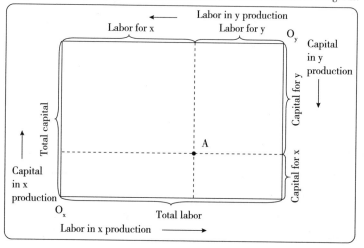

Figure 8–3   Edgeworth box

—Consumers' preferences need to be monotonic, convex and continuous, showing how individuals' welfare increases with a greater amount of goods, but with a decreasing marginal utility.

—Perfect and free availability of information.

—There has to be an absence of externalities and public goods so the utility of individuals depends directly and uniquely from their possession of goods X and Y.

As you can see on the adjacent figure, this PPF (blue curve) slopes downwards. This slope, which equals the marginal rate of transformation between X and Y, shows us how, in order to increase the output X, the quantity of Y must decrease. In fact, the marginal rate of transformation measures the tradeoff of producing more X in terms of Y.

This frontier determines the maximum output (of both X and Y) that can be obtained given the technology. Production at point A will produce more quantity of Y and less of X than production at point B. However, both are technically efficient, since they maximize the output. For example, production at point C is technically inefficient because, at any point on the PPF, more combined output is produced using given the technology. Also, point D is unattainable given the technology, being this is the reason why it is outside the PPF.

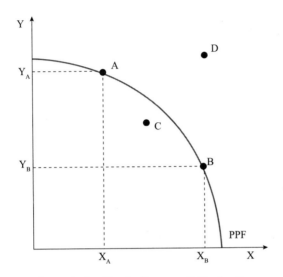

Figure 8–4   Production possibility frontier

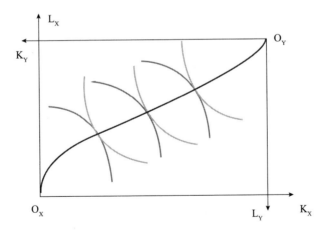

Figure 8–5   Edgeworth box

Production possibility frontier – Edgeworth box. ThePPF can be derived from the contract curve on an Edgeworth box. In this box, we see the quantity of inputs (K, L) being used in the production of each good (X,Y). In fact, we can see how, for each quantity of each product, the quantity of each input can change. The isoquants (green curve for X, red for Y) determine how much a certain input has to increase in order to compensate the decrease in the other input, maintaining the quantity of output produced unaltered. The slope of these curves is given by the marginal rate of technical substitution of each output.

The points where the isoquants of different outputs combination intersect, which are Pareto–optimal, allow us to draw the contract curve, from which the PPF can be derived. Since the technology is given, only one PPF can be derived from the contract curve (as opposed to the case of the utility possibility frontier).

8.3.1 Production optimization

The optimizationproblem in production relies in the maximization of total output production taking into consideration that it is subject to a limited amount of capital and labor. Analytically,

Equation 8-1

$$\text{Max } X(K_X, L_X) + Y(K_Y, L_Y)$$
$$\text{s.t. } K_X + K_Y = \overline{K}; \ L_X + L_Y = \overline{L}$$

We can start by looking at the production of goods X and Y as two different optimization problems. The firm will have to decide what quantity of capital and labor allocate to the production of good X, as shown on the left side of the diagram below, but also what quantity of capital and labor assign to the production of good Y, as shown on the right. These curves are the isoquants corresponding to each production process.

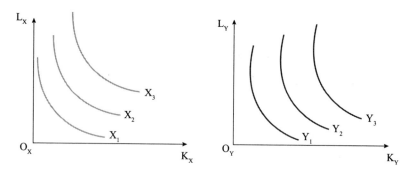

Figure 8–6   General equilibrium – Production optimization – Two products

These two diagrams can be plotted together using what is known as the Edgeworth box, which makes it easier to compare quantities of capital and labor used, while also comparing quantities of goods X and Y being produced. Indeed, it's not only easier to analyze, but also makes more sense, since the total available quantities of capital and labor are given.

The solution to this problem is related to the marginal rate of technical substitution (MRTS). A higher efficiency will be achieved if the reallocation of a unit of labor or capital from one good to other leads to a higher production of the former. When the marginal rate of technical substitution is equal for both goods, it means that all available inputs are being used, which translates into a purely efficient production process.

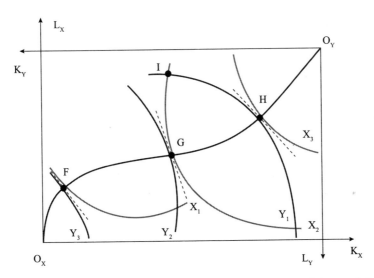

Figure 8-7   General equilibrium – Production optimization – Edgeworth box

Equation 8-2

$$MRTS_{KL}(X)=\frac{MP^X_K}{MP^X_L}=\frac{MP^Y_K}{MP^Y_L}=MRTS_{KL}(Y)$$

formula–General–equilibrium–Efficient–production

Graphically, if we plot all these points, we construct what is known as the contract curve (blue curve in the Edgeworth box). These represent all Pareto efficient distributions, such as F, G or H. I is not Pareto efficient, since going from I to either G or H would result in an increase in the production of one of the goods without giving up the production of the other. From this curve we can derive the production possibility frontier, which shows the quantities of goods X and Y being produced, as shown in the following diagram. It must be noted that both the contract curve and its derivative, the production possibility frontier, show all the solutions that are Pareto efficient from the firm's point of view. Only when considering input and output prices will we be able to determine a unique solution (because of the concavity of the production possibility frontier).

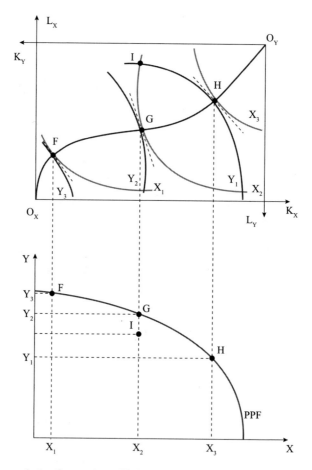

Figure 8-8　General equilibrium – Production possibility frontier

8.3.2   Consumption optimization

Bundles of goods cannot be ranked in a reliable way without knowledge of the distribution of the products, especially if a bundle has different amounts of each good. There may be some bundles that have more products of a good but less of another. The optimization problem will be to maximize the utility of individuals A and B subject to a limited total amount of goods X and Y. Analytically,

Equation 8-3

$$Max\ U_A\ (X_A, Y_A) + U_B(X_B, Y_B)$$
$$s.t.\ X_A + X_B = \overline{X};\ Y_A + Y_B = \overline{Y}$$

formula–General–equilibrium–Consumption–optimization

In this case we have to achieve the optimal distribution of two, already produced goods (X and Y) between two individuals (A and B). We can follow the same step by step method used before. Here, we'll plot indifference curves corresponding to the amounts of goods X and Y consumed by A (on the left), and the amounts of goods consumed by B (on the right).

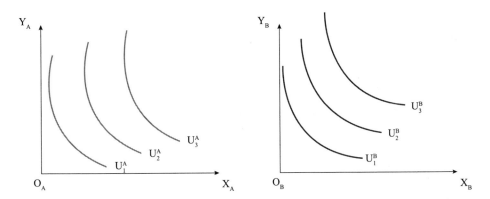

Figure 8-9   General equilibrium – Consumption optimization – Two products

Again, we use the Edgeworth box to graph the different distributions that can be given between two individuals, A and B, and two goods, X and Y. The further the indifference curve is from the origin, the higher the level of utility enjoyed by the consumer.

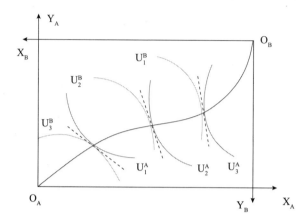

Figure 8–10   General equilibrium – Consumption optimization – Edgeworth box

Although all the points in the graphic are feasible, not all are efficient, given the utilities and preferences of consumers. The indifference curves join all the points that give consumers the same level of utility. By connecting all points of tangency between the indifference curves of both individuals, the contract curve is constructed and represents all Pareto efficient allocations. The tangency between indifference curves is the point where both consumers have an equal marginal rate of substitution for goods X and Y, and are therefore not willing to trade between them, as it would result in a lower utility.

$$MRS^A_{XY} = \frac{U'^A_X}{U'^A_Y} = \frac{U'^B_X}{U'^B_Y} = MRS^B_{XY}$$

formula–General–equilibrium–Consumption–efficiency

8.3.3   Global optimum

Until now we have only considered different parts of the economy, and not the economy as a whole. The optimization problem faced this time is similar to the previous one, although this time an additional restriction is added, since we are here considering both production and consumption: The production level also needs to be efficient.

Equation 8-4

$$Max\ U_A(X_A,Y_A) + U_B(X_B, Y_B)$$
$$s.t.\ X_A+X_B=\overline{X};\ Y_A+Y_B=\overline{Y}$$

$$\overline{X}+\overline{Y}= PPF$$

formula–General–equilibrium–Production–and–consumption–optimisation

As this optimizationproblem is based on the previous one, we have the same marginal rate of substitution equalization, but also these two must be equal to the marginal rate of transformation, the PPF's slope,

Equation 8-5

$$MRT_{XY}=MRS^{A}_{XY}=MRS^{B}_{XY}$$

formula–General–equilibrium–Production–and–consumption–efficiency

These solutions are multiple, since there are various points where the condition holds. However, if we consider output prices (given by the consideration of input prices mentioned before), we are able to consider a unique solution. In the adjacent diagram, if output prices were to be P_X and P_Y, the equilibrium would be point E. However, if output prices were instead P'_X and P'_Y, the equilibrium would be point E'.

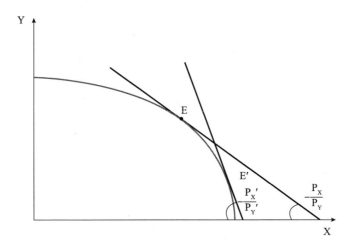

Figure 8–11　Global optimum

Let's say that prices are set at P_X and P_Y, and that the equilibrium point is E, as seen in the diagram below. Consumers A and B will consume both goods X and Y in different amounts. These amounts are given by the equilibrium in consumption, point E on the contract curve. We have also equilibrium in the production process, given by point E on the production possibility frontier. We know this is a general equilibrium because the marginal rate of substitution is equal to the marginal rate of transformation; or, in other words, the slopes of the indifference curves are equal to the slopes of the production possibility frontier.

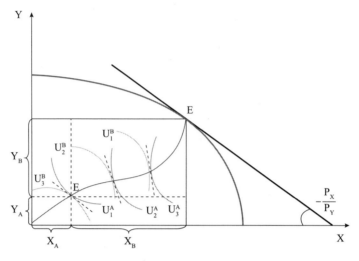

Figure 8-12　General equilibrium

Competitive markets result in an equilibrium position such that it is not possible to make a change in the allocation without making someone else worse-off. In reality there are many Pareto optimums and we cannot state that one is better than the other. Even if one consumer got all of the production and the other one none, we cannot say it is an inefficient distribution if all resources are being used efficiently. This is the reason why some economists believe it is an incomplete criterion. However, there are others, such as Milton Friedman and the advocates of the Chicago School, for whom this proves that the economy will act efficiently without the need of government intervention.

8.4　Welfare economics

This debate demonstrates that we want to know not only how a competitive economy works, but whether the results are in some sense "good". This section introduces *welfare economics*, the branch of economic theory concerned with the social desirability of alternative economic states. Welfare economics provides a framework for distinguishing circumstances under which markets can be expected to perform well from those circumstances under which they will produce undesirable results.

There are two fundamental theorems of welfare economics.

First fundamental theorem of welfare economics (also known as the "Invisible Hand Theorem"):

Any competitive equilibrium leads to a Pareto efficient allocation of resources.

The main idea here is that markets lead to social optimum. Thus, no intervention of the government is required, and it should adopt only "laissez faire" policies. However, those who support government intervention say that the assumptions needed in order for this theorem to work, are rarely seen in real life.

It must be noted that a situation where someone holds every good and the rest of the population holds none, is a Pareto efficient distribution. However, this situation can hardly be considered as perfect under any welfare definition. The second theorem allows a more reliable definition of welfare.

Second fundamental theorem of welfare economics:

Any efficient allocation can be attained by a competitive equilibrium, given the market mechanisms leading to redistribution.

This theorem is important because it allows for a separation of efficiency and distribution matters. Those supporting government intervention will ask for wealth redistribution policies.

Conclusion

This chapter shows how prices and quantities in all markets are simultaneously determined. A second section introduced welfare economics, providing a framework for deter–mining whether the outcomes generated by an economy are in some sense socially desirable. A Pareto–efficient allocation of resources may not be socially desirable if the associated distribution of real income is deemed to be unfair. The social welfare function introduces ethical considerations by showing how society is willing to trade utility among its members.The First Welfare Theorem says that if everyone is a price taker and there is a market for every commodity, then the allocation of resources is Pareto efficient. This chapter discusses externality situations, in which a market may not exist and the allocation of resources may therefore be inefficient.

Key Term

Production Optimization

Consumption Optimization

Pareto Efficiency

Production Possibility Frontier

Welfare Economy

Edgeworth Box

Review Questions

1. Why can feedback effects make a general equilibrium analysis substantially different from a partial equilibrium analysis?

2. In the Edgeworth box diagram, explain how one point can simultaneously represent the market baskets owned by two consumers.

3. In the analysis of exchange using the Edgeworth box diagram, explain why both consumers' marginal rates of substitution are equal at every point on the contract curve.

4. "Because all points on a contract curve are efficient, they are all equally desirable from a social point of view." Do you agree with this statement? Explain.

5. How does the utility possibilities frontier relate to the contract curve?

6. In the Edgeworth production box diagram, what conditions must hold for an allocation to be on the production contract curve? Why is a competitive equilibrium on the contract curve?

7. How is the production possibilities frontier related to the production contract curve?

8. What is the marginal rate of transformation(MRT)? Explain why the MRT of one good for another is equal to the ratio of the marginal costs of producing the two goods.

9. Explain why goods will not be distributed efficiently among consumers if the MRT is not equal to the consumers' marginal rate of substitution.

Application

1. Using general equilibrium analysis, and taking into account feedback effects, analyze the following:

a. The likely effects of outbreaks of disease on chicken farms on the markets for chicken and pork.

b. The effects of increased taxes on airline tickets on travel to major tourist destinations such as Florida and California and on the hotel rooms in those destinations.

2. Jane has 3 liters of soft drinks and 9 sandwiches. Bob, on the other hand, has 8 liters of soft drinks and 4 sandwiches. With these endowments, Jane's marginal rate of substitution(MRS) of soft drinks for sandwiches is 4 and Bob's MRS is equal to 2. Draw an Edgeworth box diagram to show whether this allocation of resources is efficient. If it is, explain why. If it is not, what exchanges will make both parties better off?

3. Jennifer and Drew consume orange juice and coffee. Jennifer's MRS of orange juice for coffee is 1 and Drew's MRS of orange juice for coffee is 3. If the price of orange juice is ¥2 and the price of coffee is ¥3, which market is in excess demand? What do you expect to happen to the prices of the two goods?

4. In the context of our analysis of the Edgeworth production box, suppose that a new invention changes a constant–returns–to–scale food production process into one that exhibits sharply increasing returns. How does this change affect the production contract curve?

5. In the analysis of an exchange between two people, suppose both people have identical preferences. Will the contract curve be a straight line? Explain. Can you think of a counterexample?

6. Give an example of conditions when the production possibilities frontier might not be concave.

Game Theory

9.1　Definition

Players — those who make choices in the game.

Strategies — the possible choices the players can make to achieve their goals.

Payoffs — the returns or profits to different choices.

Payoff matrix — a matrix that shows how different choices affect the payoffs.

For example, suppose that A owns a house that he values at $60 000. B values the same house at $80 000 and has ¥70 000 in cash. Clearly, the possibility of a mutually beneficial exchange exists. There are two possible outcomes:

i. Cooperative Solution = the two parties reach an agreement over price and the mutually beneficial exchange occurs.

Assume that the price = $70 000. In this case A gets $70 000 and B gets the house, worth $80 000. Total value is $150 000.

ii. Non–cooperative Solution = the two parties negotiate but cannot reach an agreement.

over the price so no exchange occurs. How likely is this to happen or do people ever not have a mutually beneficial exchange because they cannot agree on the terms of the exchange?

A keeps the house worth $60 000 while B keeps $70 000. Total value is $130 000.

iii. Cooperative surplus = the extra value gained by cooperating and exchanging thehouse = $20 000.

What does the payoff matrix look like in this example?

You must first decide what are the choices or decisions each of the parties can make. The issue here is bargaining to get more of the cooperative surplus. Both parties want more of the surplus. Therefore, suppose the decision is to bargain hard or soft. Further, suppose that:

If one party bargains hard and the other soft then the one bargaining hard gets all of the cooperative surplus.

If both parties bargain soft then they equally split the cooperative surplus.

If both parties bargain hard then no exchange occurs.

The payoff matrix looks as follows:

			A's choice	
			Hard	Soft
B's choice	Hard		70K, 60K	90K, 60K
	Soft		70K, 80K	80K, 70K

The first number in each cell is person B's payoff while the second number is person A's payoff. Note that an exchange occurs and the cooperative solution is reached in three often four cells. The only cell where the exchange does not occur is when both play hard.

What will the likely outcome be in the game above? To answer this question, look at each individual's choice and assume that they will each act rationally.

· Individual A's choice

If B chooses Soft then A would be better off with hard.

If B chooses Hard then A does not care between hard and soft (gets $60K in– either case.)

As a result, A is likely to choose hard.

· Individual B's choice

If A chooses Soft then B would be better off with hard.

If A chooses Hard then B does not care between hard and soft (gets $60K in either case.)

As a result, B is likely to choose hard.

Notice that even though a cooperative surplus exists the nature of the game itself, the fact that both parties are bargaining for more of the surplus, results in neither getting any of the surplus. Does this ever happen in real life?

This is also called a dominant strategy game. A dominant strategy game is one where each party's choice is not dependent upon what the other party decides.

9.2　Game theory and strategic thinking

Economists use the word game to refer to any situation involving at least to agents that requires these involved to think strategically. The study of how people behave strategically under different circumstances is called game theory.

When the agents look at the trade-offs they face and pursue their goals in the most effective way possible, we can say that they behave rationally. When the trade-offs you face are determined by the choices someone else will make, behaving strategically are involved in behaving rationally. Behaving strategically means acting to achieve a goal by anticipating the interplay between your own and others' decisions.

There are three features associated with all games, namely, rules, strategies, and payoffs. Rules are defined as the actions that are allowed in a game. In cheese, for example, each type of piece is allowed to move only in certain directions. In real life, people's behavior is constrained by laws. Strategies are the plans of action that the players follow to achieve their goals. For example, when two businesses are competing, strategies might include producing a certain quantity of a good. Payoffs are the rewards that come from particular actions. They can be monetary or nonmonetary. In chess game, the payoff is winning, for example.

9.3 Prisoners' dilemma

The classic prisoners' dilemma is a game of strategy in which two people make rational choices that lead to a less-than-ideal result for both. The same ideas can be applied to situations with more than two people, and o organizations rather than individuals.

Let's talk about the story of prisoners' dilemma now. Suppose that you and an accomplice have been arrested on suspicion of committing both a serious crime and a more minor one. The police hold you two in separate cells. A policeman explains to you that he does not have the evidence to convict either of you of the serious crime, but he does have evidence to convict you both of the minor crime. However, he wants to get at least one conviction for the major crime, so he offers you a deal: If you confess that you both did it, and your accomplice does not confess, you will get let off with one year in prison, while your accomplice gets the maximum 20-year term for committing the major crime. If you and your accomplice both confess, the policeman no longer needs your evidence to get a conviction, so the one-year deal is off. Instead, he tells you that you will get some time off the maximum sentence as a reward for cooperating and you will both get 10 years. What if neither of you confesses? The policeman days that you will both be convicted of the minor crime only, and you will both serve three years. The same deal is offered to your accomplice as well.

A thought occurs to you: If my accomplice confesses, then I will get 10 years of I confess and 20 years if I do not. But if may accomplice does not confess, I will get one year if I confess and three years if I do not. Therefore, whatever my accomplice does, I will be better off if I confess. Although you were partners in crime, you soon realize that your accomplice will be using the same logic. This means you will both confess, and you will both get 10 years. Unless you and your accomplice could agree to cooperate by both saying nothing then you could avoid this outcome, and each get away with only serving three years.

Table 9-1 summarizes this predicament in a decision matrix. If your accomplice confesses, your choice is between 10 years in prison and 20 years in prison. If your accomplice does not confess, your choice is between 1 year in prison and 3 years in prison. Your opponent faces the same set of choices as yours. The incentives each of you faces mean that you will both confess and end up in the top-left box, both serving for 10 years in prison. If you could have cooperated with each other, you could have ended up in the bottom-right box, both serving for 3 years.

Table 9-1　The prisoners' dilemma

		You	
		Confess	Don't confess
Your accomplice	Confess	(10, 10)	(1, 20)
	Don't confess	(20, 1)	(3, 3)

9.3.1　Dominant strategy

In the prisoners' dilemma, whatever your accomplice does, you are better off confessing. When a strategy is the best one to follow no matter what strategy other players choose, it is called a dominant strategy. However, not all games feature a dominant strategy for each player. For example, the rock-paper-scissors game. In general, rock beats scissors, scissors beat paper, and paper beats rock. Because both players move at the same time, predicting your opponent's choice is tough. Reading across the rows or down the columns of the decision matrix in Table 9−2 shows that there is no single strategy that will work best for you regardless of what you opponent does.

Table 9−2　A game with no dominant strategy

		Player B		
		Rock	Paper	Scissors
Player A	Rock	Tie	B wins	A wins
	Paper	A wins	Tie	B wins
	Scissors	B wins	A wins	Tie

Here, we will introduce a new concept, Nash equilibrium, which is named after the famous game theorist John Nash. A Nash equilibrium is reached when all players choose the best strategy they can, given the choices of all other players. That is, this is a point in a game when no player has an incentive to change his or her strategy, given what the other players are doing.

There is a possibility for a game like rock–paper–scissors to have no Nash equilibrium. Suppose you are playing with a friend. If your friend plays scissors, and you play rock, you have no incentive to change as rock beats scissors, but your friend would have an incentive to change to paper as paper beats rock. Then if your friend changes to paper, this would give you an incentive to change to scissors since scissors beat paper. This will continue. There is no stable outcome where neither of you would wish to change your strategy once you find out what the other player is doing.

However, there is a stable outcome in the prisons' dilemma problem: you both confess. This outcome gives an implication that an equilibrium outcome to a game is not necessarily a good one for the participants. A noncooperative equilibrium is named after this negative–negative outcome as a result that the participants act independently, pursuing only their individual interests.

Even though everyone is acting in their own self–interest, some games have a stable positive–positive outcome. Consider the game of driving. Suppose you are one of only two motorists in a motor game, and you are driving toward each other. If you decide to drive on the right and the other person drives on the left, you have a head–on collision, and this is the least–preferred payoff for you both. This is not an equilibrium; your decision gives the other driver an incentive to drive on the right instead. When you both drive on the right, you avoid accidents, and this is your most-preferred payoff. In this case, neither of you has an incentive to change. Driving on the right is thus a positive-positive outcome.

Recall the discussion of the prisoners' dilemma, both players of the game would be better off if they could cooperate. But why they choose the less-preferred one? It is not simply because they are being held in separate cells and cannot talk to each other. Nor is the problem of trust. Even if you are completely sure that your accomplice can be trusted not to confess, you would still confess. In this kind of games, prearranged agreements to cooperate are tough to make work as both players have a strong incentive to defect. One solution to this problem is to reduce the players' payoffs by creating a punishment for defecting. This punishment has to be bad enough so that it can outweigh the incentive not to cooperate. For example, in the classic prisoners' dilemma, assume that you and your accomplice signed an agreement that anyone who testifies against another member will be killed in retribution. This will then change the payoff for confessing: A shorter stay in prison, but with the expectation of being killed at the end of it. Given this agreement, you would be better to choose not to confess. Agreements like this are an example of a commitment strategy, where players agree to submit to a penalty in the future if they defect from a given strategy. The agreement to future penalties can allow players to reach a mutually beneficial equilibrium that would otherwise be difficult to maintain by changing the payoffs.

9.3.2 Competition and collusion

Consider a more general example. There are only two gas stations in a town, A and B. Each could choose to charge high prices or low prices. This gives us 4 possible outcomes and payoffs shown in Table 9-3. If both stations charge low prices, they both make low profits, 2 million for example. If both stations charge high prices, they both make high profits, 3 million for example. If A charge high prices and B charge low prices, everyone in town will buy gas from B. Then B makes even higher profits (4 million) and A loses money. If A charges low prices and B charges high prices, the opposite occurs. Then everyone buys gas from A. Station A now makes even higher profits and B loses money.

Table 9-3 The prisoners' dilemma in competition between two firms

		B	
		Low prices	High prices
A	Low prices	(2, 2)	(4, 0)
	High prices	(0, 4)	(3, 3)

This game can be seen as an application of the prisoners' dilemma, with a dominant strategy of charging low prices, which is shown in Table 9-3. Both gas station A and station B will choose low prices, though they would be better off if they could make an agreement to keep prices high. This noncooperative equilibrium is bad for both game players, though it is good for the consumers as they can pay lower prices for their gas.

It is expected that the two gas stations could cooperate and reach an equilibrium where they can make higher profits together. however, the gas consumers will want to prevent this cooperation because they do not want to pay high prices for their gas. This cooperation which will hurt the consumers but benefit the sellers is called collusion, while the noncooperative equilibrium is called competition.

In fact, collusion is a common problem that firms often try to find a way to collude in order to charge higher prices and earn more profits. But governments, on behalf of consumers, try to find a way to make the markets more competitive.

9.3.3   The tit-for-tat strategy

A repeated game is a game that is played more than once. When games are repeated, strategies and incentives often work quite differently. Particularly, players no longer need commitment strategies to reach a mutually beneficial equilibrium. Let's go back to our gas stations example. Imagine you manage the station A. One day when you wake up and think that today I am going to increase my prices. I may lose a little money at first, but it is worth to take the risk because the manager of B station might see the chance for us both to benefit in the longer run. Then, you choose to play a high prices strategy.

Next imagine you manage the station B. Upon seeing that the station B has increased its prices, you might make more money at the first round because people will come to us to buy gas. However, in the second round, you may change your mind that when the station B starts losing money, it will have no choice but to cut price again. But if I also increase my prices, manager of station A might keep his prices high as well, we can both make more profits. Therefore, in round two, both A and B play a high prices strategy. in round three, both gas station managers will have a think. One station could make more money by cutting its prices, if the other station keeps its prices high. However, if one station reduces its prices, the other station will be forced to reduce its price as well. If one station keeps its prices high, the other station will do the same. In later rounds, both gas stations play high prices strategy. Prices remain high, with the two players maintaining cooperation.

The thought processes of the mangers of station A and B are an example of a type of strategy called tit–for–tat. The idea is straightforward. Whatever the other player does, you do the same thing in response. For example, in repeated play of prisoners' dilemma, if the other player makes a cooperative move, then you respond with a cooperative move. If the other player defects with a noncooperative move or competitive move, you respond with a noncooperative move or competitive move. Two players who are both playing tit–for–tat can quickly find their way towards lasting cooperation.

9.3.4　Sequential games

So far, we have talked about games in which players make decisions simultaneously. In games like the Prisoners' dilemma and rock–paper–scissors, each player decides which strategy to adopt before knowing what the other player will do. However, in many real–world situations, one person or company has to make a decision before the other. These are called sequential games as the players move sequentially rather than simultaneously.

In sequential games, the strategic behavior called "think forward, work backward" is particularly important. What does it mean by thinking forward and working backward? First you have to think of all possible outcomes and choose which one you prefer. Then you have to think what choice you would need to make to achieve your preferred outcome. This process of analyzing a problem in reverse, that is starting with the last choice, then the second–to–last choice, and so on, to find the optimal choice, is called backward induction.

Backward induction can be especially useful when your desires are affected by decisions other players will make in response to a decision of your own. One common example is associated with entry into a market. Imagine that McDonald's Corporation is considering opening a new restaurant in a small town that currently has no fast–food restaurant. Suppose that McDonald's (all restaurants) will consider only locations where it expects to get at least a 20 percent rate of return on the investment.

There are two possible locations for company executives to choose between: In the town center, where rental rate is expensive but access for customers is more convenient, or on the outskirts of the town, where land is cheaper, but the customers have to drive there. Provided that the new McDonald's on the outskirts of the town will earn a return of 30 percent, while it will generate a 25 percent return at the downtown. If the executives stopped at this point, it would definitely build the new restaurant on the outskirts of the town.

However, the executives will never stop at this stage, they will consider the probability that KFC could also have a think of entering this town. Then the calculations of McDonald's will change, and they will consider what if there are two similar fast–food restaurants opening, one in the center and the other one on the outskirts. Obviously, the restaurant in the downtown will do much better as most customers won't choose to drive to the outskirts unless they are big fans of the one on the outskirts. It is assumed that the one in the town center will earn a 22 percent rate of return while the one on the outskirts will get only a return of 5 percent. If there are two restaurants competing on the outskirts, each will earn 12 percent; if there are two competing in the downtown, each will earn 8 percent.

Then what should McDonald's do, given the uncertainty about whether KFC will enter the market or not. If McDonald's opens in the town center, it will be confident that KFC will choose not to enter the market. Since a McDonald's has already in the downtown, KFC could get an 8 percent return if it also built in the center, or 5 percent return if it built on the outskirts. It can be predicted that KFC would rather invest its money elsewhere and not enter the market at all. If McDonald's opens on the outskirts, it can expect KFC to build in the downtown, attracted by a return of 22 percent. This would reduce McDonald's rate of return to only 5 percent.

Here we will use a new tool, decision trees, to analyze the sequential games. The decision tree that describes the decision process of McDonald's is shown in

Figure 9-1.

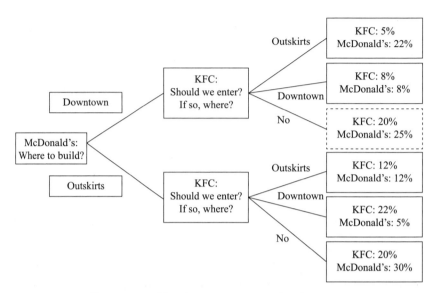

Figure 9-1　The decision process of McDonald's

Since McDonald's is the first mover in this game, the first decision node shows its choice to open in the town center or on the outskirts. Regardless of the choice made by McDonald's, KFC can then make its own decision. It has three options: Open in the downtown, open on the outskirts, not open at all, which are represented at the second nodes of the tree.

We can use backward induction to determine the best course of action for McDonald's. Starting from the right side of the tree, given that McDonald's has opened on the outskirts, KFC will definitely choose to open in the downtown. But if McDonald's has already opened in the town center, then KFC will not enter the market at all. Then the choice of McDonald's is between a 25 percent return in the downtown and a 5 percent return on the outskirts. Even though opening in the town center is not the best choice for McDonald's if there is no competition, it is the optimal decision because it deters other competitors from entering the market.

In this market-entry game, first-mover McDonald's ends up with a return of 25 percent while the second-mover KFC is forced to invest elsewhere at a return of 20 percent. If KFC had entered to town first, then McDonald's would lose its chance to enter the market. Therefore, in this game, whoever gets to town first gets a higher return; the company that arrives second settles for less. This is a game with a first–mover advantage, which means the player who chooses first gets a higher payoff than those who follow.

First–mover advantage can be extremely important in one–round sequential games. A typical example is a bargaining game between a company and employees' labor union. They always negotiate over wages, which is the division of surplus. Suppose this was a one–round game. We consider the case that the company moved firstly; it could offer only 1 percent of the surplus to the labor union. Then the union would have to make a choice: Accept the offer or reject it by going on strike. If the union chooses to go on a strike, both the company and the union would share zero surplus. One percent is always better than nothing, the union would have no choice but accept the offer.

However, if the union moved firstly, things will go to the opposite that the union could require 99 percent of the surplus. Then the company would have to choose between paying the amount and taking the risk that its employees would go on a strike. Also, if the union would go on a strike, the company would make no money with no doubt. Finally, the company would rather make a payment than take the risk.

The above example is called an ultimatum game: One player makes an offer and the other player has the simple choice of whether to accept or reject. But everything will be changed if we move to repeated games. Repeated play can also change the outcome in sequential games by reducing the first–mover advantage. The ability to make counteroffers transforming bargaining from a game in which first mover advantage trumps everything to a game in which patience is the winning strategy. Consider the time value of money that the value of a given sum in the future is less than the value of that same sum now. Bargaining takes time; the value of the surplus goes down for every round of bargaining. Hence, the more patient player, who places more value on money in the future relative to the money in the present, has more bargaining power, and so receives a better payoff. If each player knows how patient the other is, the two sides do not need to play all the rounds. In the example of wage negotiation, the company can simply offer the split that would eventually occur if the two sides played all the rounds. In that case, the surplus will be divided in proportion to the patience of each player.

Recall that in simultaneous games such as the prisoners' dilemma, making a credible commitment can change the payoffs and influence the strategy of the other players. It stays true in sequential games.

Conclusion

The insights of game theory pervade economics, the social sciences, business, and everyday life. In economics, for example, game theory can help explain trade wars as well as price wars.

Game theory can also suggest why foreign competition may lead to greater price competition. Whathappens when Chinese or Japanese firms enter a U.S. market where domestic firms had tacitly colluded on a strategy that led to high oligopolistic prices? The foreign firms may "refuse to play the game." They did not agree to the rules, so they may cut prices to increase their share of the market. Collusion among the domestic firms may break down because they must lower prices to compete effectively with the foreign firms.

A key feature in many games is the attempt on behalf of players to build credibility. You are credible if you can be expected to keep your promises and carry out your threats. But you cannot gain credibility simply by making promises. Credibility must be consistent with the incentives of the game.

Key Term

Game Theory	Sequencegame
Dominant Theory	Prisoner's Dilemma
Nush Equilibrium	The Tit–for–tat Strategy

Review Questions

1. Taking an exam can be considered a game.Describe a rule, a strategy, and payoff for this game.

2. Why is strategic behavior required to win a presidential election? Describe some of the rules, strategies, and payoffs that define this game in the real world.

3. What is the difference between a cooperative and a noncooperative game? Give an example of each.

4. What is a dominant strategy? Why is an equilibrium stable in dominant

strategies?

5. Explain the meaning of a Nash equilibrium. How does it differ from an equilibrium in dominant strategies?

6. How does a Nash equilibrium differ from a game's maximin solution? When is a maximin solution a more likely outcome than a Nash equilibrium?

7. What is a "tit–for–tat" strategy? Why is it a rational strategy for the infinitely repeated prisoners' dilemma?

8. Consider a game in which the prisoners' dilemma is repeated 10 times and both players are rational and fully informed. Is a tit–for–tat strategy optimal in this case? Under what conditions would such a strategy be optimal?

9. What is meant by "first–mover advantage"? Give an example of a gaming situation with a first–mover advantage.

10. What is a "strategic move"? How can the development of a certain kind of reputation be a strategic move?

11. Can the threat of a price war deter entry by potential competitors? What actions might a firm take to make this threat credible?

12. A strategic move limits one's flexibility and yet gives one an advantage. Why? How might a strategic move give one an advantage in bargaining?

13. Why is the winner's curse potentially a problem for a bidder in a common–value auction but not in a private–value auction?

Application

1. In many oligopolistic industries, the same firms compete over a long period of time, setting prices and observing each other's behavior repeatedly. Given the large number of repetitions, why don't collusive out–comes typically result?

2. Many industries are often plagued by overcapacity: Firms simultaneously invest in capacity expansion, so that total capacity far exceeds demand. This happens not only in industries in which demand is highly volatile and unpredictable, but also in industries in which demand is fairly stable. What factors lead to overcapacity? Explain each briefly.

3. Two firms are in the chocolate market. Each can choose to go for the high end of the market(high quality) or the low end(low quality). Resulting profits are

given by the following payoff matrix:

		Firm 2	
		Low	High
Firm 1	Low	−20, −30	900,600
	High	100,80	50,50

a. What outcomes, if any, are Nash equilibria?

b. If the managers of both firms are conservative and each follows a maximin strategy,what will be the outcome?

c. What is the cooperative outcome?

d. Which firm benefits most from the cooperative outcome? How much would that firm need to offer the other to persuade it to collude?

4. Two competing firms are each planning to introduce a new product. Each will decide whether to produce Product A, Product B, or Product C. They will make their choices at the same time. The resulting payoffs are shown below.

		Firm 2		
		A	B	C
Firm 1	A	−10, −10	0,10	10,20
	B	10,0	−20, −20	−5,15
	C	20,10	15,−5	−30,30

a. Are there any Nash equilibria in pure strategies? If so, what are they?

b. If both firms use maximin strategies, what outcome will result?

c. If Firm 1 uses a maximin strategy and Firm 2 knows this, what will Firm 2 do?

Market Failure and Microeconomic Policy

Market failure means that the optimal allocation of resources cannot be achieved through market allocation. Generally speaking, the causes of market failure include monopoly, externality, public goods and incomplete information. For example, where the supply of a product is not related to the level of demand for it: Protecting car production in the face of market failure has, far from helping them, locked the people of the area into an economy which cannot sustain itself.

Market failure occurs when there is a state of disequilibrium in the market due to market distortion. For example, it may take place when the quantity of goods or services supplied is not equal to the quantity of goods or services demanded. Some of the distortions that may affect the free market may include monopoly power, price limits, minimum wage requirements, and government regulations.

10.1   Incomplete competitive market

When a market is incomplete, it typically fails to make the optimal allocation of assets. That is, the First Welfare Theorem no longer holds. The competitive equilibrium in an Incomplete Market is generally constrained suboptimal. The notion of constrained suboptimality was formalized by Geanakoplos and Polemarchakis.

10.1.1   Inefficiency in a monopoly

In a monopoly, the firm will set a specific price for a good that is available to all consumers. The quantity of the good will be less and the price will be higher (this is what makes the good a commodity). The monopoly pricing creates a deadweight loss because the firm forgoes transactions with the consumers. The deadweight loss is the potential gains that did not go to the producer or the consumer. As a result of the deadweight loss, the combined surplus (wealth) of the monopoly and the consumers is less than that obtained by consumers in a competitive market. A monopoly is less efficient in total gains from trade than a competitive market.

Monopolies can become inefficient and less innovative over time because they do not have to compete with other producers in a marketplace. For private monopolies, complacency can create room for potential competitors to overcome entry barriers and enter the market. Also, long term substitutes in other markets can take control when a monopoly becomes inefficient.

When a market fails to allocate its resources efficiently, market failure occurs. In the case of monopolies, abuse of power can lead to market failure. Market failure occurs when the price mechanism fails to take into account all of the costs and/or benefits of providing and consuming a good. As a result, the market fails to supply the socially optimal amount of the good. A monopoly is an imperfect market that restricts output in an attempt to maximize profit. Market failure in a monopoly can occur because not enough of the good is made available and/or the price of the good is too high. Without the presence of market competitors, it can be challenging for a monopoly to self–regulate and remain competitive over time.

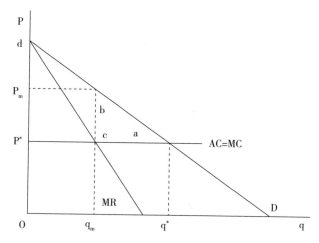

Figure 10–1   Monopoly and low efficiency

10.1.1.1   Rent seeking

Rent seeking is one of the most important insights in the last fifty years of economics and, unfortunately, one of the most inappropriately labeled. Rent seeking (or rent–seeking) is an economic concept that occurs when an entity seeks to gain added wealth without any reciprocal contribution of productivity. Typically, it revolves around government–funded social services and social service programs. Entities therefore, will take rent seeking steps to obtain economic rent that requires no reciprocal contribution of production. Oftentimes, this can mean using a particular status to gain economic rent from the government through social service grants. People are said to seek rents when they try to obtain benefits for themselves through the political arena. They typically do so by getting a subsidy for a good they produce or for being in a particular class of people, by getting a tariff on a good they produce, or by getting a special regulation that hampers their competitors. Elderly people, for example, often seek higher Social Security payments; steel producers often seek restrictions on imports of steel; and licensed electricians and doctors often lobby to keep regulations in place that restrict competition from unlicensed electricians or doctors.

Rent seeking is a byproduct of political legislation and government funding. Politicians decide the laws, regulations, and funding allocations that govern industries and government subsidy distributions. These legislations and actions therefore manifest rent seeking behaviors by offering economic rent with little or no reciprocity.

Issues Arising from Rent Seeking. Rent seeking can disrupt market efficiencies and create pricing disadvantages for market participants. It has been known to cause limited competition and high barriers to entry. Expenditures on lobbying for privileges are costly and that these expenditures, therefore, dissipate some of the gains to the beneficiaries and cause inefficiency. If, for example, a steel firm spends one million dollars lobbying and advertising for restrictions on steel imports, whatever money it gains by succeeding, presumably more than one million, is not a net gain. From this gain must be subtracted the one–million–dollar cost of seeking the restrictions. Although such an expenditure is rational from the narrow viewpoint of the firm that spends it, it represents a use of real resources to get a transfer from others and is therefore a pure loss to the economy as a whole.

10.1.1.2   Market control

Occurs when either the buyer or the seller possesses the power to determine the price of goods or services in a market. The power prevents the natural forces of demand and supply from setting the prices of goods in the market. On the supply side, the sellers may control the prices of goods and services if there are only a few large sellers (oligopoly) or a single large seller (monopoly). The sellers may collude to set higher prices to maximize their returns. The sellers may also control the quantity of goods produced in the market and may collude to create scarcity and increase the prices of commodities.

On the demand side, the buyers possess the power to control the prices of goods if the market only comprises a single large buyer (monopsony) or a few large buyers (oligopsony). If there is only a single or a handful of large buyers, the buyers may exercise their dominance by colluding to set the price at which they are willing to buy the products from the producers. The practice prevents the market from equating the supply of goods and services to their demand.

10.1.2　Antitrust laws

If market power leads to inefficiency then what is the correct solution to that market power? U.S. public policy has focused on either anti-monopoly laws that make firms having or attempting to gain monopoly power illegal or regulation of markets to make them legal. Recall our discussion of the exceptions to the idea that monopoly power leads to inefficiency in the chapter titles "Monopoly and Perfect Competition Compared" . There we suggested that in the real world the simply conclusion that market power leads to inefficiency was not always correct. Regulation, then, theoretically would be used for those situations.

Antitrust law also referred to as competition laws, is the broad category of federal and state laws that are meant to keep business operating honest and fairly. Antitrust laws regulate the way companies do business. The goal is to level the playing the field in the free market and prevent businesses from having too much power. For the purposes of antitrust law, a trust is a large group of businesses that work together or combine in order to form a monopoly or control the market. Major antitrust legislation in the United States includes the Interstate Commerce Act of 1887, the Sherman Act of 1890, the Clayton Act of 1914 and the Federal Trade Commission Act of 1914.

Antitrust laws are applied to a wide range of questionable business activities, including but not limited to market allocation, bid rigging, price fixing, and monopolies. Below, we take a look at the activities these laws protect against. If these laws didn't exist, consumers would not benefit from different options or competition in the marketplace. Furthermore, consumers would be forced to pay higher prices and would have access to a limited supply of products and services.

Antitrust laws don't prohibit a company from controlling a large share of the market if they do it by innocent means. What antitrust laws prohibit are acts intended to form a monopoly by using unfair tactics. The courts use what's called the "rule of reason" test in order to determine if an act is unlawful. They consider the effect of the business decision on the market.

Antitrust and Regulation.

10.2 Externality

An externality refers to a cost or benefit resulting from a transaction, and that affects a third party that did not decide to be associated with the benefit or cost. It can be positive or negative. A positive externality provides a positive effect on the third party. For example, providing good public education mainly benefits the students, but the benefits of the public good will spill over to the whole society.

On the other hand, a negative externality is a negative effect resulting from the consumption of a product, and that results in a negative impact on a third party. For example, even though cigarette smoking is harmful to a smoker, it also causes a negative health impact on people around the smoker.

10.2.1 External costs and benefits

Explain how external costs and benefits affect the trade–offs faced by economic decision makers.

To think clearly about externalities, we'll need to introduce some new terminology. When we talk about costs such as gasoline, wear and tear on a car, road tolls, and parking fees, we're talking about costs borne by a driver herself. In general, we call costs that *fall directly on an economic decision maker* **private cost.** The cost of pollution is not a private cost, because individual drivers don't personally bear all—or even most—of the costs of the pollution they produce. Pollution, or any *other cost that is imposed without compensation on someone other than the person* who caused it, is an *external cost.*

When we add private costs to external costs, we call the sum **social cost.** (Why not "total cost" ? Because total cost is a term used to describe costs of production. Also, the term social cost helps make it clear that we are thinking about this idea from society's perspective.) For example, suppose you decide to host a noisy party. The private costs might include food, drink, and any cleanup costs the next day. The external costs would include annoyance felt by neighbors who can't sleep or study because of the noise your party is creating. The social cost would be the sum of these two types of costs.

Externalities are not all bad news, though. There are lots of situations in which a person's behavior helps, rather than hurts, others. Imagine that you have decided to tidy up your messy front yard and paint your house. Clearly, you benefit from this decision: You have the aesthetic pleasure of a tidy yard and a prettier house, and the value of your property increases. These are benefits that accrue directly to the decision maker, called—as you might have guessed—**private benefits.** But your neighbors, too, benefit from your decision to fix up your house. They get the pleasure of living in a nicer–looking neighborhood, and the value of their properties may also increase a bit—all at no cost to them. *A benefit that accrues without compensation to someone other than the person who caused it is called an **external benefit.***

When we add private benefits and external benefits together, the result is called **social benefit.** To take another example, suppose you decide to get vaccinated against the flu and to wash your hands frequently. The private benefit is that you are less likely to get the flu. The external benefit is that you are less likely to transmit the flu to other people. The social benefit is the sum of these two effects—the overall reduction in likelihood of the flu spreading, both to yourself and to others.

External costs and external benefits are collectively referred to as **externalities.** We typically call an external cost a negative externality and an external benefit a *positive externality*. Externalities are an incredibly important concept in economics. They are one of the most common causes of market failure. From this point on, we will use the terms learned in this section to distinguish between choices that are optimal from the perspective of an individual decision maker, and choices that are optimal from the perspective of society as a whole.

The size of the external cost or benefit caused by a particular action may vary based on location, timing, quantity, or many other factors. For instance, driving during the middle of the day in the summer usually contributes more to smog than driving at night or driving during winter (because sunlight is a key ingredient in the formation of smog). Painting the one derelict house in a nice neighborhood is likely to boost neighbors' property values more than painting one house in a neighborhood full of run–down homes. However, for the sake of simplicity, in this chapter we mostly assume that externalities involve a constant, predictable external cost or benefit.

Finally, there is one special type of externality that doesn't neatly fit into the categories we just laid out. A ***network externality*** is the effect that an additional user of a good or participant in an activity has on the value of that good or activity for others. Network externalities imply that people can help or harm others simply by virtue of their participation in a group.

Network externalities can be positive or negative. We've already described one example of a negative network externality—driving in L.A. rush hour. Every additional person who decides to use the L.A. road network imposes a negative network externality on other road users. You may have also experienced negative network externalities on wireless Internet networks, when each additional user draws down bandwidth, slowing the connection for other users.

Positive network externalities are frequently associated with technology, especially communication technology. An important historical example is the telephone. Telephones, like most communication devices, are useful only if other people have them too. When very few people had telephones, having one let you contact only a limited number of people. The more common telephones became, the more people they allowed you to contact, and the more useful they got. Each person who joined the telephone network made telephones more useful for everyone else— a positive network externality.

Social–media networks are a more recent example. The more people who belong to a service such as WeChat, Weibo, or vlog, the higher the benefits of joining. To flip it around: Everyone who joins one of these services makes it more useful for everyone else. The effect of positive network externalities can be so powerful that it may even mean that social networking services like Facebook are effectively natural monopolies. Once they reach a critical mass of users, it becomes extremely hard for competitors to gain a foothold in the market, because users want to be in whatever network everyone else is in.

10.2.1.1   Negative externalities and the problem of "too much"

Calculate the effect of a negative externality on market price and quantity, and measure the resulting change in surplus.

Because air pollution is an external cost, the costs of driving look smaller from the perspective of an individual driver than they actually are from the perspective of society as a whole. Because drivers don't take the external cost into account, they will decide to drive more than they would if they themselves had to bear the full cost of driving (which mostly includes the cost caused by any pollution).

Why is that a problem? It means people drive "too much" —that is, more than they would if they faced the social costs of their actions. Where there are externalities, the free market no longer allocates resources in a way that maximizes total surplus for society as a whole. To understand why this is the case, let's take a closer look at pollution. An enterprise that emits pollution while producing a product certainly benefits the owner of the operation, who is making money off the production. However, pollution also has an unintended effect on the environment and the surrounding community. It affects others who had no choice in the matter and were probably not taken into account in production decisions and is thus a negative externality. How do we quantify the external costs of pollution? It's not easy to put a dollar figure on all of the diffuse effects of variable pollution around the world. Essentially, the question boils down to this: How much would people who are affected by pollution be willing to pay to avoid it? Or, to put it another way, how much would you have to pay the people who are affected by pollution to persuade them to accept it?

10.2.1.2　Positive externalities and the problem of "too little"

Calculate the effect of a positive externality on market price and quantity, and measure the resulting change in surplus.

It is tempting to think that a positive externality must be a good thing. A negative externality decreases surplus, so a positive externality must do the opposite, right? Sadly, that is not the case. A positive externality also pushes quantity away from the efficient equilibrium level, reducing total surplus. Positive externalities come in many forms. Commuting to work by bicycle involves the positive externality of combatting pollution. The commuter, of course, gets a health–related benefit of the bike trip, but the effect this has on traffic congestion and reduced pollution released into the environment because of taking one car off the road is a positive externality of riding a bike to work. The environment and community were not involved in the decision to commute by bike, but both see benefits from that decision.

10.2.2　Dealing with externalities

We've learned that externalities lower total surplus, but that it is possible to address this problem by transforming external costs and benefits into private ones. By taking money from drivers and giving it to pollution sufferers, or forcing citizen to drive bicycles, efficiency can be restored. If it's possible to eliminate the problems created by externalities, why do they persist?

We will see in this section that solving the externality problems is often easier to describe than to implement. External costs and benefits can be diffuse, complex, and hard to control. Solutions must try to ensure that economic decision makers experience costs and benefits that are equal in value to the true social costs and benefits of their choices. If everyone affected has to be involved in the process, that could mean coordinating across millions—or even billions—of people. This is a tricky problem to solve, even for the smartest of policy-makers.

We will also see that there can be a tension between *efficiency* and fairness in finding solutions to externalities. Saying a market works *efficiently* means only that it maximizes surplus. It doesn't say anything at all about the *distribution* of that surplus. Some technically sound solutions might seem unfair (like rewarding people for not polluting, rather than taxing people who pollute), and thus might not get very far in the political arena.

Before we look at how governments try to solve these problems, let's first consider whether governments need to get involved at all. Under certain circumstances, private individuals may be able to deal with externalities, restoring efficiency to the market on their own.

10.2.2.1   Private remedies

Describe how individuals could reach a private solution to an externality, and explain why this doesn't always occur.

Economists usually reserve the term "market failure" for situations in which the actions of private individuals and firms are *insufficient to ensure efficient markets.* An influential economic theory sets out the circumstances under which people should be able to solve externality problems by themselves. The underlying reasoning is actually quite intuitive. The idea of the "invisible hand" tells us that individuals will pursue mutually beneficial trades with other individuals. No mutually beneficial trade should go unexploited, because someone always has something to gain from pursuing it. The result is that when we add up all of the actions of self-interested individuals, every opportunity to gain surplus has been exploited, and total surplus is maximized.

The idea that **individuals can reach an efficient equilibrium through private trades, even in the presence of an externality,** is called the *Coase theorem,* after economist Ronald Coase. Coase theorem refers to the idea that even in the presence of an externality, individuals can reach an efficient equilibrium through private trades, assuming zero transaction costs. However, there are a couple of key assumptions that must hold: People can make enforceable agreements (also known as contracts) to pay one another, and there are no transaction costs. Often, these two assumptions do not hold true. It cannot be imaged that the elaborate organization would bring together plenty of citizens and get each of them to voluntarily pay the amount that avoiding pollution is worth to them personally, redistribute that money to drivers who agreed to drive less, and then monitor those drivers to make sure they actually followed through. Dramatically, there comes a point where the costs of coordination and enforcement are higher than the surplus lost to the externality, and it's not worth doing. *To sum up: The Coase theorem says that private economic actors can solve the problem of externalities among themselves. Whatever the initial distribution of rights, the interested parties can always reach bargain in which everyone is better off and the outcome is efficient.*

Why private solution not always work?

The example illustrates a second drawback of the Coase theorem. The private solution yields an efficient outcome—the surplus–maximizing quantity of gas is bought and sold. But the distribution of that surplus is very different from the solution we imagined earlier, in which the drivers had to pay other citizens ¥10 per gallon to compensate them for pollution. Instead, now the citizens have to pay drivers not to drive. The citizens are still better off than they were under the externality, but nowhere near as well off as they would be if drivers had to pay for their own pollution.

Notice that either solution is efficient, but the assumptions about what is "fair," and who has the "rights" to do what, are different. In one case it's assumed that drivers have a right to pollute, and have to be paid not to. In the other case, it's assumed citizens have a right to live free of pollution and have to be paid to accept pollution. The Coase theorem reminds us that efficiency is all about maximizing total surplus. It says nothing about achieving a "fair" distribution of that surplus.

Despite the appealing logic of the Coase theorem, private actors on their own fail to resolve the problems caused by externalities. The Coase theorem applies only when the interested parties have no trouble reaching and enforcing an agreement. In the real world, however, bargaining does not always work, even when a mutually beneficial agreement is possible. Sometimes the interested parties fail to solve an externality problem because of *transaction costs, the costs that parties incur in the process of agreeing to and following through on a bargain.*

This reasoning explains why it is often more a question of politics, law, and philosophy than of economics to decide who pays whom to solve the market failure. Even when it would make people better off to pay someone else to do, or stop doing, something that affects them, they often feel that it is not "fair" to do so. People usually care not only about reaching an efficient equilibrium, but also about how we get there and who benefits. When private bargaining does not work, the government can sometimes play a role. The government is an institution designed for collective action. In this example, the government can act on behalf of the fishermen, even when it is impractical for the fishermen to act for themselves. In the next section, we examine how the government can try to remedy the problem of externalities.

10.2.2.2 Public policy toward externality

Taxes and subsidies Because of the cost and difficulty of coordinating private solutions, people often turn to public policy for solutions to externalities. Earlier in the chapter, we described how the effect of forcing decision makers to consider social costs and benefits looked similar to the effects of taxes and subsidies, respectively. It's no surprise, then, that the most basic public policy remedy to an externality problem involves counterbalancing the externality with a tax or subsidy.

Countering a negative externality with a tax. Let's return to the problem of air pollution from driving. Earlier, we imagined solving the externality problem of air pollution in Beijing by taking ¥10 from drivers every time they used a gallon of gas, and using that money to compensate sufferers from pollution. In fact, many governments around the world do use taxes to force drivers to consider social costs. Oregon was the first U.S. state to implement a gas tax, in 1909, and the federal government has taxed gas since the 1930s. While the motive for government taxation of gasoline also included raising general revenues to pay for roads, these taxes also counteract the negative externalities of driving.

A tax meant to counter the effect of a negative externality is called a *Pigouvian tax,* after an economist named Arthur Pigou. Other Pigouvian taxes include the "sin taxes" on alcohol and cigarettes as well as carbon taxes. However, Pigouvian taxes are not a perfect solution to externalities. There are two problems. **The first is setting the tax at the right level.** As we have seen, it is not always easy to put a dollar–and–cents value on external costs. In our example, we estimated the external cost associated with burning a gallon of gas to be ¥10, so we would choose an optimal Pigouvian tax of ¥10 per gallon. If our estimate is wrong and the external cost is higher, then the tax is set too low. In that case, the market will move closer to the efficient equilibrium, but remain somewhat inefficient. If our estimate is too high, then the tax is set too high, and the market will overshoot—the new equilibrium quantity will be inefficient because it is too low, rather than too high. **Second, while taxes are effective at transferring surplus away from consumers and producers and toward the government, there is no guarantee that the government can or will then do anything to help the people who are bearing the external cost.** The revenue collected from a Pigouvian tax is sometimes used as compensation, but often it is not. It might seem "fair" for Beijing gas taxes to be used to build centers for treating people suffering from breathing disorders. But, whether or not the revenue is redistributed to pollution sufferers in this way, the tax still maximizes total surplus in society as a whole, by moving the gas market to the efficient equilibrium. Remember, the distribution of surplus is an entirely separate question from maximizing total surplus.

Capturing a positive externality with a subsidy. Just as a tax can counterbalance an external cost, a subsidy can help consumers or producers capture the benefits of positive externalities. As with a Pigouvian tax, using a subsidy to increase efficiency does not necessarily equal fairness. Such a subsidy would maximize total surplus in society. But the distribution of that surplus depends on where the government gets the money to pay for the subsidies. It might seem more "fair" if the subsidies were paid for out of property taxes, as property owners have the most to gain from pretty neighborhoods, but total surplus would still be maximized if the money was collected from general taxation.

Public policies that use subsidies to solve externality problems are sometimes less noticeable than taxes, but are extremely widespread and important if you know where to look. One example is education. If parents had to pay to send their children to school, many might decide the trade–off wasn't worth it. Yet educating children has all sorts of external benefits: With education, children are more likely to become economically productive members of society and engaged citizens. That's why most governments offer public schools, which subsidize the cost of education. As with taxes, solving a positive externality through subsidies requires quantifying the external cost or benefit accurately. If the subsidy is set too low, then the number of houses painted will remain inefficiently low. If the subsidy is set too high, then total surplus will not be maximized either.

10.2.2.3   Quotas and regulations

Show how quantity regulations can be used to counteract an externality, and discuss the pros and cons of such a solution.

If we know the socially optimal quantity of something—for instance, how much pollution we are willing to tolerate—why not simply regulate quantity rather than taxing? Beijing could calculate the efficient quantity of gas, and limit each citizen's gas purchases to his or her share of that amount. In terms of controlling the amount of pollution, this approach would achieve the same end result as a tax.

However, perhaps surprisingly, limiting total consumption to the efficient quantity does not make the market efficient. The real magic of the invisible hand in a market is not just that it drives price and quantity to the efficient level, but that it does so by allocating resources to those with the greatest willingness to pay for them. Maximizing surplus depends not only on how much gas is bought and sold, but also on who buys and sells it. A tax allows the market to sort itself out in this way; a quota does not.

10.2.2.4   Tradable allowances

Show how tradable allowances can be used to counteract an externality, and discuss the pros and cons of such a solution.

You may have spotted an obvious way to improve the quota system described above. The fact that the two drivers have a different willingness to pay for the next gallon of gas implies that there is a missed opportunity for a mutually beneficial trade: The driver of the Range Rover could pay the Prius driver some amount more than ¥0.80 and less than ¥1.33 in exchange for the rights to one more gallon, and both would end up better off. Why not set a quota, but then allow people to buy and sell their quota allowances? This solution allows policy–makers to choose a quantity rather than set a tax rate, while still ensuring that the quota is allocated to the people with the highest willingness to pay. A production or consumption quota that can be bought and sold is called a tradable allowance.

Just as with a quota, a system of tradable allowances will result in the efficient quantity of a good being bought and sold (as long as the total quota is set at the right quantity, of course). Like a tax, tradable allowances maximize surplus. There is one important difference, though, between a Pigouvian tax and a tradable allowance: The Pigouvian tax results in revenue collected by the government, whereas the tradable allowance creates a market in which quota rights are bought and sold among private parties. The government could collect revenue by selling the initial quotas, but in cases where such programs have been implemented, they are more usually allocated for free to consumers or producers, who then trade among themselves.

10.2.3 Targeting externalities with public policy

When economists propose taxes or tradable allowances as a way to tackle externalities, they try to propose taxes based on the externality itself, rather than on the action that generates it. In this chapter, we've talked a lot about gas taxes, which are targeted at a good that generates pollution, rather than at pollution itself. Ideally, environmental policy would target the end product—carbon emissions—directly. That way, the policy would apply to all the thousands of different activities that generate an external cost through carbon emissions, from raising livestock, to operating a power plant, to lighting a wood fire in a fireplace. However, measuring emissions from all these different sources is extremely difficult, logistically speaking. Taxing gasoline, rather than pollution, is a second–best solution; the first–best solution may simply be unattainable.

Because of the difficulty of measuring pollution directly, many policies do target individual goods and processes. For instance, cars are generally required to have catalytic converters, a specific technology that reduces emissions of nitrous oxides, carbon monoxide, and unburnt hydrocarbons. Local governments often subsidize energy–saving light bulbs or recycling, or they ban wood fires during smoggy times of the year or when dry conditions make fires especially dangerous. The downside of targeting individual activities is that it risks misaligning the incentives that consumers and producers face with the goal of minimizing the externality.

For example, in 1975 the U.S. government–imposed fuel–efficiency standards on cars, called the CAFE standards. The goal was to reduce pollution. But the regulations were designed in such a way that "light trucks" were subject to looser standards. The result? Auto manufacturers started producing cars that were big and heavy enough to be classed as a "light truck," and didn't have to meet the standards for cars. Average fuel efficiency of cars actually fell rather than increased.

A policy that directly targets pollution encourages the development of cleaner technology and processes, and doesn't give clever companies the chance to find ways around it. In fact, consumers and producers have an incentive to find new ways of doing things that don't generate pollution. This allows them to avoid having to pay for a tax or the rights to an allowance, aligning their incentives with the end goal of the policy. Since it is very difficult to monitor private citizens' carbon footprint, and relatively easy to monitor the pollution caused by large factories, the idea of a carbon tax or a tradable carbon allowance makes more sense on a corporate level than a personal one.

10.3   Public goods and common resources

10.3.1   Define different types of goods in terms of rivalry and excludability

What types of goods tend to go the way of the rhino, suffering from overuse? River water, but not orange juice. Fish in the sea, but not chickens on the farm. Computers at the public library, but not personal laptops. What is the common thread? The first thing to notice is that river water, fish in the sea, and public–library computers are not usually owned by a private individual. Instead, they are held collectively by a community or country.

In thinking about the various goods in the economy, it is useful to group them according to two characteristics:

N Is the good **excludable**? Can people be prevented from using the good?

N Is the good **rival**? Does one person's use of the good diminish another person's enjoyment of it?

Most of the goods we've discussed in this book are private goods, which are both excludable and rival in consumption. Many goods, however, lack one or both of these characteristics. Before describing these types of goods, we'll explore the ideas of excludability and "rivalness" a bit further. *Excludability* means the property of a good whereby a person can be prevented from using it. *Rivalness* means the property of a good whereby one person's use diminishes other people's use.

Using these two characteristics,table 10-1 divides goods into four categories:

（1）**Private goods** are both excludable and rival. Consider an ice-cream cone, for example. An ice-cream cone is excludable because it is possible to prevent someone from eating an ice-cream cone—you just don't give it to him. An ice-cream cone is rival because if one person eats an ice-cream cone, another person cannot eat the same cone. Most goods in the economy are private goods like ice-cream cones. When we analyzed supply and demand in and the efficiency of markets，we implicitly assumed that goods were both excludable and rival.

（2）**Public goods** are neither excludable nor rival. *That is, people cannot be prevented from using a public good, and one person's enjoyment of a public good does not reduce another person's enjoyment of it.* For example, national defense is a typically public good. Once the country is defended from foreign aggressors, it is impossible to prevent any single person from enjoying the benefit of this defense. Moreover, when one person enjoys the benefit of national defense, he does not reduce the benefit to anyone else.

（3）**Common resources** are rival but not excludable. For example, fish in the ocean are a rival good: When one person catches fish, there are fewer fish for the next person to catch. Yet these fish are not an excludable good because it is difficult to charge fishermen for the fish that they catch.

（4）When a good is excludable but not rival, it is an example of a **natural monopoly**. For instance, consider fire protection in a small town. It is easy to exclude people from enjoying this good: The fire department can just let their house burn down. Yet fire protection is not rival. Firefighters spend much of their time waiting for a fire, so protecting an extra house is unlikely to reduce the protection available to others. In other words, once a town has paid for the fire department, the additional cost of protecting one more house is small.

Table 10–1   Example of public goods and common resources

Private Goods	Natural Monopolies
• Ice–cream cones	• Fire protection
• Clothing	• Cable TV
Common Resources	Public Goods
• Fish in the ocean	• National defense
• The environment	• Knowledge

10.3.2   The problems with public goods and common resources

10.3.2.1   The free–rider problem

Free–rider problem occurs when people can benefit from a good/service without paying anything towards it. It also occurs, if people can get away with making only a token contribution (Something less than overall benefit) If enough people can enjoy a good without paying for the cost then there is a danger that, in a free market, the good will be under–provided or not provided at all.

It is good to reduce our production of landfill rubbish. However, if one person in a city of five million produces less rubbish, it makes little difference. There is an incentive to free–ride on efforts of other people to recycle and make less effort yourself. In other words, we free ride on the efforts of others to recycle. If someone builds a lighthouse, all sailors will benefit from its illumination – even if they don't pay towards its upkeep. Cleaning a common kitchen area. It would be good if we all contributed to cleaning the kitchen but there is a temptation to leave for someone else – who will do it all for us.

10.3.2.2   The tragedy of the commons

Tragedy of the commons is a parable that illustrates why common resources get used more than is desirable from the standpoint of society as a whole. As we have seen, rhinos are not a public good, because they are rival—if someone shoots a rhino, it is definitely not there for the next person to enjoy. Usually, when you consume a rival good, you have to compensate the person who owns it. When you want to eat chicken, you pay the grocery store, or the restaurant, or the chicken farmer. But historically, before land was divided into private pieces, when you hunted a wild animal such as a rhino or buffalo or elephant, you didn't have to pay anyone. No one owned the wildlife, so no one could force you to pay. In other words, wildlife was typically rival, but also nonexcludable—a common resource. Clean air and water, oil pools, as well as congested roads are typically common resources.

10.3.3 Dealing with public goods and common resources

We've seen that problems with undersupply of public goods and overdemand for common resources lead to an inefficient quantity of production and consumption. In other words, both types of goods are subject to market failures. There are many possible solutions, which generally fall under three categories: *Social norms, government regulation and provision, and private property rights.*

In some cases, society tries to get people to act in the interest of society by shifting social norms. For example, campaigns to embarrass litterers, may change people's opinions on what is individually optimal. *In other cases*, the government tries to fix the market failure through regulation or direct provision. Such approaches attempt to adjust the quantity of a good that is produced or consumed by either restricting private production (if a good is overproduced) or expanding production (if a good is underproduced). *Finally*, some solutions involve creating property rights that turn a nonexcludable good into an excludable one. As with government regulation and provision, such approaches attempt to solve the market failure by converting social costs to private costs. Thus, when individuals act optimally, the socially optimal outcome is achieved.

As we discuss each solution, think about how it changes the trade-off between costs and benefits that people face when supplying or consuming a public good or common resource. We'll see that the range of solutions to these two problems is related to externalities.

10.3.3.1 Social norms

Dirty public spaces arise because littering is easy. Littering saves you the trouble of finding a garbage can, and is very unlikely to incur any real punishment or cost, so there is little incentive to take into account the negative externality imposed on others. But there are many public spaces, especially in close-knit neighborhoods, that stay clean through a simpler mechanism: The expectations and potential disapproval of the community. If you don't litter, we're guessing that it's not primarily because you're afraid of being caught and fined by the police, but simply because you've learned that it's not a nice thing to do. both the free–rider problem and the tragedy of the commons are problems of trade–offs—people are able to enjoy the benefits of something without paying the corresponding costs. Strong social norms can help rebalance the trade–off by imposing "costs" on people who litter, sneak through the back door of the bus, fail to do their bit of snow shoveling, and so on. costs don't have to be financial. Social disapproval or guilt or conflict with those in your community can also be costs.

Some specific "design principles" make informal, community–based solutions to public goods and common–resource problems more effective. These principles include: Clear distinctions between who is and is not allowed to access the resource; the participation of resource users in setting the rules for use; and the ability of users to monitor one another.

10.3.3.2   Bans, quotas, and government provision

What happens when informal institutions and rules are not enough? The management of public goods and common resources is one case in which government intervention can be productive and efficiency enhancing. The reason for this is simple: Often, government bodies have the power to impose limits on how much of a resource is consumed or to make up for inadequate supply, when individuals and informal associations do not. Within that broad justification, however, there are many different ways that governments can intervene, such as direct management of a resource and provision of a public good. We will consider three: *Bans, quotas, and government provision*.

Bans and quotas. When thinking through some of the examples we've discussed, you might feel that we are missing the most obvious solution to the non–excludability problem. Have a problem with keeping public spaces clean? Make littering illegal. Worried about rhinos and other endangered species becoming extinct? Make hunting them illegal, or impose a quota on how many rhinos each poacher is legally allowed to hunt.

Of course, littering usually is illegal, and bans or quotas apply to hunters in many countries. Yet the problems persist, so clearly this is not a perfect solution.

illegal is simply one way of changing the trade–offs that people face, by creating costs for breaking the ban or exceeding the quotas. If the punishment is not severe, or the likelihood of getting caught is low, the cost may not be high enough to change the trade–off. Bans and quotas therefore often fail in situations where it is difficult or costly for authorities to monitor and punish rule–breakers. Poorer countries find it much more difficult to enforce laws against poaching and habitat destruction. Bans on poaching rhinos thus have limited impact in east Africa. In contrast, South Africa has several large and well–managed national parks that protect rhinos and elephants effectively. As a result, the ban on hunting rhinos has proved to be effective. In countries that have the resources to enforce them, bans or quotas that limit the use of common resources are straightforward public–policy approaches to solving the problem of overuse. Especially when the optimal quantity of consumption is zero— for instance, with an endangered species on the brink of extinction—it may be the best approach.

Government provision. Bans and quotas are applied to common–resource problems, to reduce the inefficiency created by overuse. To combat the undersupply of public goods, the more typical regulatory solution is for the government to step in and provide it directly. In the United States and many other wealthy countries, we see government provision of public goods everywhere: in transportation systems, education and research, parks, safety, and much more. To supply a public good, two common issues arise: *First, what is the right amount of the public good to supply? Second, who will pay for it?*

In a functioning market, people will buy a good up to the point where the marginal benefit they enjoy from the last unit is equal to the marginal cost of that unit. If the marginal benefit were greater than the cost, they could increase their utility by buying more. If the cost were greater than the marginal benefit, they could increase their utility by buying less. This same analysis applies to public goods: *If the government is supplying a public good, such as road maintenance, the efficient quantity is the one at which the marginal social benefit equals the cost.*

*What is the **marginal social benefit**?* Each individual who uses the road network gains some marginal benefit from increased road maintenance (more potholes filled, more frequent repaving). When roads are in good repair, everyone who uses them enjoys the benefits. Therefore, the marginal social benefit is actually the sum of the marginal benefit gained by each individual user.

The government should calculate the cost of increased road maintenance, add up the marginal benefit to every user, and supply the quantity of road maintenance at which the two are equal. This cost–benefit analysis is much simpler in theory than it is in practice.

The second issue is figuring out how to pay for government provision of public goods. Determining who will pay depends in part on how easy it is to exclude people who don't pay. In some cases, it is possible to make the good excludable using the power of the government to monitor use and enforce payments among those who actually use them. It is either difficult or undesirable to charge user fees.

10.3.3.3   Property rights

Public goods and common resources are not allocated efficiently by markets, but private goods are. In some cases, the most convenient solution would be to turn everything into a private good. Several hundreds of years ago, the solution to this original tragedy of the commons was surprisingly simple, which is to divide the resource system into parcels (e.g., as volumetric extraction entitlements) as assign them to individuals (as private or individual property). The first step was to institute rules about who got to graze where and when. The ultimate step was to break up the town commons into private lots, so that people had to graze their livestock on their own land.

Tradable allowances. One common way that governments can institute private property rights is through the use of tradable allowances or permits. Remember that quotas can control total quantity, but they don't necessarily allocate supplies in the most efficient way. They can result in undesirable side–effects, such as damaging extraction methods or rushes to get as much of a resource as possible before hitting the quota.

The method of using tradable allowances works the same way for solving a common resource problem as it does for solving an externality problem. A cap is set on the total quantity of the resource that can be used, and shares of that total are allocated to individuals or firms. After the initial allocation, people can buy and sell their shares. Trading ensures that the resource is allocated to those with the highest willingness to pay, while still limiting overall quantity to an efficient level. The people who own shares now have private property rights and an incentive, as owners, to make sure that the common resource does not get overused.

10.4 Information: knowledge is power

In general, to make rational economic choices, people need to know what they are choosing between. When people are fully informed about the choices that they and other relevant economic actors face, we say they have complete information.

Unfortunately, people rarely have perfectly complete information. Often, they have good enough information to makeacceptable choices. But in many cases, people are truly underinformed in ways that matter. You've probably seen people around you make decisions that they later came to regret because they were underinformed. Maybe they bought products that proved to be shoddy, lent money to an acquaintance who turned out to be a deadbeat, or moved to a new apartment with terrible plumbing or a leaky roof.

Of course, some choices are genuinely risky. When you invest in stocks or real estate, you can't have perfectly complete information about how your investment will perform. Despite this, markets can still work well. For example, when you are buying annual insurance against the possibility of flood damage to your house, neither you nor the insurance company can have perfect information about exactly how much heavy rain– fall there is likely to be in the next 12 months.

10.4.1 Information asymmetry

Information asymmetry. A condition in which one person knows more than another. Problems are likely to arise when one person knows more than another, a situation that is called information asymmetry. Let's consider the example of taking your car to a mechanic. The mechanic knows a great deal about the condition of your car, whereas you probably know very little. He could tell you that the entire brake system needs to be replaced, and you'd probably pay for it without ever knowing if he was telling the truth.

To see why such information asymmetries, create problems, consider the wants and constraints of those involved. You want your car fixed at the lowest possible price, but you are constrained by your ignorance of exactly how your car functions or why it broke down. The mechanic wants to make as much money as possible. He is constrained only by his moral scruples and concern about possible damage to his reputation and his business if he turns out to have underestimated your knowledge of the workings of brake systems. in this case, the mechanic may succeed in making more money by charging you for repairs that your car doesn't really require.

Note that this is a problem only because your wants (spend as little as possible) are opposed to the mechanic's (charge as much as possible). If both parties' incentives are aligned, then the information asymmetry doesn't matter. If a mechanically minded friend is fixing your car as a favor, you both want the repair to cost as little as possible. It doesn't matter that you know less than your friend about cars.

Here, we'll discuss two important types of information asymmetry—adverse selection and moral hazard. These asymmetries are common problems for the insurance industry, and we will now see that they plague other markets, too.

10.4.2   Adverse selection and the lemons problem

Adverse selection. A state that occurs when buyers and sellers have different information about the quality of a good or the riskiness of a situation; results in failure to complete transactions that would have been possible if both sides had the same information.

Problem of adverse selection can result. Adverse selection occurs when buyers and sellers have different information about the quality of a good or the riskiness of a situation. As a result, some buyers and sellers can lose out by failing to complete transactions that would have been possible if both sides had the same information.

One well-known example of adverse selection is *the "lemons" problem* in the used-car market. A lemon is a car that breaks down again and again. There is information asymmetry in the used-car market because sellers of used cars know a lot more about the true characteristics of their cars than potential buyers do. A test drive won't necessarily reveal how long the car will run before it breaks down. Buyers of used cars are well aware that they are on the wrong end of this asymmetry: They are always suspicious that a used car could be a lemon, so they won't pay as much for it as they would if they could be certain it was in perfect shape. That means sellers of used cars that are in perfect shape will be underpaid.

Meanwhile, sellers of lemons will still be paid more than their cars are worth. To see why this is true, suppose the used-car market consists of just two types of cars: Lemons and high-quality cars (we'll call them "plums"). If buyers could tell which is which, they would establish one price for plums and another, lower price for lemons. But if buyers can't differentiate between plums and lemons, they will have to offer an average price that reflects the likelihood of getting one or the other. That price will be lower than they'd pay for a guaranteed plum (because there is a chance, they might get a lemon), but higher than they'd pay for a guaranteed lemon (because there is a chance, they might get a plum).

If you know the car you own is a lemon, you'll be attracted by the prospect of selling it at a high price—but if you know the car you own is a plum, you won't want to sell for less than it's worth. Over time, the result will be more lemons and fewer plums on the market. As buyers start to notice they are increasingly likely to get a lemon, they will offer even lower prices, making it even less attractive for plum sellers to enter the market. A vicious cycle ensues in which the selection of cars on the market becomes more and more adverse from the buyer's perspective. This explains why a barely used car that works perfectly is worth a lot less than exactly the same car offered new at a dealership—the buyer of the slightly used car doesn't know whether or not to trust the seller.

Another common example of adverse selection occurs in ***insurance markets*** because of the information asymmetry between insurance companies and their customers. At any given price, drivers who know they are careless will be more eager than careful drivers to buy auto insurance, because they know that they will be more likely to make claims. The selection of customers is adverse from the insurance company's perspective.

10.4.3　Principal–agent problems and moral hazard

Agent, a person who carries out a task on someone else's behalf.

Moral hazard refers the tendency for people to behave in a riskier way or to renege on contracts when they do not face the full consequences of their actions.

Information asymmetries can also cause problems after selection has occurred and the two parties have entered into an agreement. This type of problem often arises when one person entrusts a task to another person. In what is called a principal–agent problem a person called a principal entrusts someone else, called the agent, with a task.

The most basic example of a principal–agent problem that is caused by asymmetric information is the relationship between an employer (the principal) and an employee (the agent). The asymmetry exists because each employee knows how hard he or she works, but the employer does not. Because the principal usually cannot monitor what the agent is doing all the time, the agent may be tempted to put less effort into the task than the principal would want.

In short, employees have an incentive to slack off when the boss isn't watching. Why not play games online or take a few extra coffee breaks, if no one is any the wiser? The tendency for people to behave in a riskier way or to renege on contracts when they do not face the full consequences of their actions is called moral hazard. With moral hazard, people engage in behavior that is considered undesirable by the person who bears the cost of the behavior.

Moral hazard can be avoided by correcting the information asymmetry through better monitoring. If the boss were able to see how much effort employees were really put–ting in, she could adjust their incentives to maintain steady effort. If you knew someone was closely monitoring your workplace computer activity and that your wages could be docked or you could lose your job if you were caught playing games online, it would probably increase your workplace productivity significantly.

It is not always possible to correct such an information asymmetry, however. Not all types of jobs allow bosses to monitor employees closely enough to avoid moral hazard. The same is true of insurance markets, in which moral hazard is a common problem. For instance, if your car is insured against theft, you might not be as careful to park in a safe place and double–check that the door is locked, because you know the insurance.

10.4.4   Moral hazard and adverse selection—avoiding confusion

Sometimes people confuse adverse selection with moral hazard, because they often occur together. Careless drivers are more likely to buy auto insurance voluntarily (adverse selection); drivers with auto insurance may be more likely to be careless (moral hazard). To clarify, remember that:

- Adverse selection relates to unobserved characteristics of people or goods and occurs before the parties have entered into an agreement.

- Moral hazard is about actions and occurs after the parties have voluntarily entered into an agreement.

Although adverse selection and moral hazard can be found at different stages of the same transaction, such as auto insurance, it is possible to have one without the other.

To see how, think back to our chapter–opening example of the student loan program, which involved both problems. Imagine first that the student loan–pooling scheme had been mandatory. That would have eliminated the problem of adverse selection, because students who anticipated high earnings would not have been able to opt out. But it would have left the problem of moral hazard, because it would still have been possible for all participants to evade payment. Now consider an alternative scenario, in which participation remained optional but the IRS agreed to help1 by reporting income to the university so that it could effectively collect against its alumni with higher incomes. This plan would have lessened the moral hazard problem but not the adverse selection. The rest of this chapter will focus on ways in which these problems arising from information asymmetries can be corrected.

10.4.5 Solving information problems

Before we look at ways to solve information problems, we should point out that they are not always worth solving. Sometimes, remaining uninformed is optimal because the cost of acquiring information would be prohibitive. When you pay a mechanic for car repairs that you don't fully understand, for example, it's not as if you couldn't learn how brake systems work if you really wanted to—or hire another mechanic to review the assessment and confirm the repairs are needed. It would just take you a lot of time and effort to do those things. The trade–off isn't worth it. Ask yourself, What's the opportunity cost of acquiring more information? For most of us, the opportunity cost of acquiring mechanical expertise is probably significantly higher than the occasional cost of unnecessary repairs.

Often, however, it is worth the effort to solve problems caused by information asymmetry. In this section, we'll consider some approaches that can be taken by those directly involved in a transaction—screening, signaling, building a reputation, and using statistical discrimination—and two ways in which governments can get involved.

10.4.5.1   Screening

Screening. taking action to reveal private information about someone else.

If you know you are on the wrong end of an information asymmetry, you could always try asking the other party for the information you want. Rather than simply hoping they tell you the truth, you could also look for clever ways to put them in a situation that forces them to reveal, perhaps without even realizing it, the information.

They know and you don't. Taking action to reveal private information about someone else is called screening. In this context, private doesn't necessarily mean personal or embarrassing; it simply means that the information is not public, or available to everyone.

Signaling. taking action to reveal one's own private information.

Screening is useful when people would rather not share private information. Some– times, though, the party with more information would be all too happy to share it. For instance, if I am selling a used car I know is in excellent condition, I would be delighted to share this knowledge with you, the potential buyer. Both of us would prefer to eliminate the information asymmetry that afflicts us. The problem is that we lack a credible way to share information, because somebody selling a lemon will also insist that her car is top quality. Knowing this, you would have no reason to believe me.

When people take action, on purpose or not, to reveal their own private information, they are signaling. Signaling happens in many situations; you may even be doing it by taking an economics course. The signaling theory of education argues that a college degree is like a certificate of quality for used cars: It credibly signals to potential employers that you are intelligent, hardworking, and able to complete assignments. That's why many employers prefer candidates with college degrees, even if what they learned in school has little relevance to the job in question.

10.4.5.2   Reputation

So far, we have focused on asymmetric–information problems affecting one–time interactions, such as a one–off private used–car trade. Often, however, interactions occur over and over, like the repeated games in the "Game Theory and Strategic Thinking" chapter. Used–car dealers, for example, sell used cars every day. This repetition can enable a new solutionto the information problem as people develop a reputation for trustworthiness (or lack thereof).

10.4.5.3 Statistical discrimination

Statistical discrimination. Distinguishing between choices by generalizing based on observable characteristics in order to fill in missing information.

When you don't have time to become fully informed about a specific new situation, you may find yourself relying on a rule of thumb. Suppose you're choosing between having dinner at a Mexican restaurant or the burger place next to it. You know nothing about these two restaurants, and you're too hungry to stop and ask the opinions of locals or search for reviews online. You remember hearing, though, that this neighborhood is known for great Mexican food. It makes sense to choose the Mexican restaurant. Of course, you may be unlucky and find that this particular Mexican restaurant happens to be terrible. Using a generalization here is perfectly rational, though: If the neighborhood has a reputation for great Mexican food, you have a reasonably good chance that this particular Mexican restaurant will, in fact, be great.

Filling gaps in your information by generalizing based on observable characteristics is called statistical discrimination. It's something most of us do all the time. Suppose you are choosing between an action movie starring Keanu Reeves, a romantic comedy starring Tom Hanks, or a psychological drama starring Philip Seymour Hoffman. You may know little about the particular movies but still be able to tell which you are likely to enjoy most, based on knowing which type of movie you typically like best. To return to the lemons problem you may prefer to buy one particular used car over another because you know that, in general, cars of that brand tend to age well. As with the Mexican restaurant, you may be unlucky—the particular car you buy may turn out to be a lemon. But generalizing in this way is a rational response to being on the wrong end of an information asymmetry.

10.4.5.4 Regulation and education

When parties to a transaction can't resolve information asymmetry problems on their own, and they have a negative effect on sufficiently large numbers of people, government will sometimes step in.

Government can help to solve information asymmetry problems in two ways. One is to provide the missing information to the less–informed party, or require the more– informed party to reveal it. For example, almost every packaged–food item you can buy in the United States lists its ingredients and nutritional content. This is the result of Food and Drug Administration (FDA) regulations that force food producers to divulge otherwise–private information. These regulations correct an information asymmetry that is important (consumers want to know what they're eating) and hard to solve without government intervention.

10.5   Income inequality and poverty

In this part, we discuss the distribution of income. As we shall see, this topic raises some fundamental questions about the role of economic policy. The invisible hand of the marketplace acts to allocate resources efficiently, but it does not necessarily ensure that resources are allocated fairly. As a result, many economists—though not all—believe that the government should redistribute income to achieve greater equality. In doing so, however, the government runs into one of the Ten Principles of Economics put forward by Mankiw: People face tradeoffs. When the government enacts policies to make the distribution of income more equitable, it distorts incentives, alters behavior, and makes the allocation of resources less efficient.

Our discussion of the distribution of income proceeds in three steps. First, we assess how much inequality there is in our society. Second, we consider some different views about what role the government should play in altering the distribution of income. Third, we discuss various public policies aimed at helping society's poorest members.

10.5.1   Poverty

Economics is the study of how people manage their resources. A certain amount of goods and services are necessary for the survival of individuals and families; the living conditions of people and families who lack the economic resources or economic capacity to obtain these goods and services are *poverty*.

Of course, poverty is of concern for less intellectual reasons as well. It can be upsetting to see people struggling to support themselves or even to stay alive. Without financial resources, it's difficult to access many of the basic goods that make life livable—food, shelter, health—and certainly those that make life comfortable. Economic thinking can suggest ways to make life better for those in need, both at home and around the world.

Several ideas will come up over and over again in this chapter. Is poverty a problem only when it represents an absolute deprivation, such as not having enough to eat? Or is poverty best defined in relative terms? Should people be considered to be "poor" when they have enough to live on, but still have much less than others in society?

Another theme to follow is that the causes of poverty may not always be obvious. For instance, around the world, being poor often comes along with having less education. But does a lack of education make people poor, or are poor people less able or willing to access education? The patterns of poverty over decades or generations are also critical. How hard is it to start out poor and become rich, or vice versa? If your parents are poor, how does that affect you and your chances in life? Keep these under–lying questions in mind as we discuss the measurement of, causes of, and solutions to poverty.

Measuring poverty

Relative and absolute measures. When defining poverty, the first important distinction to make is between absolute and relative measures. ***An absolute poverty line*** defines poverty as income below a certain amount, fixed at a given point in time. According to statistics, there are about 30 million rural poor people in China with the poverty line of annual net income of 2300 yuan per capita. According to the previous annual poverty reduction rate of more than 10 million, by 2020, China will enter an era without absolute poverty.

Rather than measuring absolute deprivations, ***the relative poverty line*** defines poverty in relation to the income of the rest of the population. In the United Kingdom, for instance, the poverty line is set at 60 percent of the median income. The median income is the level earned by the household exactly in the middle of the national income distribution. (That is, compared to that household, half of the population earns less and half earns more.) The use of a relative poverty line can lead to some surprising patterns. Imagine that in the United Kingdom, for example, economic growth raises the incomes of poor house– holds by 5 percent. This growth helps poor families, but it won't necessarily reduce the official ***poverty rate—the percentage of the population*** that falls below the absolute poverty line. In fact, the official poverty rate might even rise if the income of the median household grows faster than 5 percent.

Internationally, India, South Africa, Indonesia and other developing countries mostly adopt the absolute poverty standard, while the developed countries except the United States generally adopt the relative poverty standard, that is, use 50% or 60% of the median income as the relative poverty line.

Measuring international poverty

International poverty line standard is actually a method of income proportion. It is obviously based on the concept of relative poverty. In early October 2015, the world bank announced that according to purchasing power parity, the international poverty line standard was raised to $1.9 from $1.25 per person per day before. The sharp increase means that the number of poor people in the world has increased significantly. *purchasing power parity (PPP)* is index that describes the overall difference in prices of goods between countries. To create the PPP index, economists collect data on prices in every country and develop an index that describes the overall difference in prices between countries.

Why are people poor?

If economists and policy–makers want to design policies that can attack poverty at its roots, rather than just dealing with its consequences, we need to understand not only who is poor but also why they are poor.

Of course, the real world is an incredibly complex place and so the reasons for poverty are varied. Poverty can be a matter of bad circumstances, bad choices, bad luck, or a combination. But we know from observation that some common factors make falling into poverty more likely, and climbing out of it harder.

Poverty from generation to generation. People who grow up in poor families are more likely to be poor themselves. One reason is straightforward: Poor parents tend to have limited money to bequeath to the next generation. Two other economic ideas—human capital and social networks—capture somewhat more subtle mechanisms:

Human capital are the set of skills, knowledge, experience, and talent that determine the productivity of workers. It is often difficult to tell cause from effect: Does low human capital cause poverty (because people with low human capital are less productive in jobs and therefore likely to earn less money)? Or does poverty cause low human capital (because growing up in a poor community can reduce access to education, health care, and informal learning opportunities)? Likely, the causality runs both ways, creating a negative cycle of poverty and low human capital. To the extent that low human capital causes poverty, policies that break this cycle by improving schools, offering

271

training in job skills, and providing health care can help.

Poverty creates poverty. You may have heard the saying, "the rich get richer and the poor get poorer." We've just described how difficulties in acquiring human capital or finding job opportunities might cause this to be true. But there can also be self-reinforcing mechanisms that make it hard for individuals to break out of poverty once they are already poor, regardless of family background. These mechanisms are called *poverty traps,* and they can help illuminate why the poor often stay poor.

Banks will lend money only if the borrower can pledge a valuable asset as collateral (in case the investment turns out badly). The problem for poor borrowers is that they often lack the assets to pledge as collateral. So, even if they have great ideas, they can't get a loan to put their ideas into action. This poverty trap is called a *credit constraint*—the inability to get a loan even though a person expects to be able to repay the loan plus interest. Credit constraints are another way that poverty itself can make it harder to get ahead.

Poverty in the community. In some places in the world, there are opportunities to earn more money and live in greater comfort, even if they may be difficult to come by. In others, these opportunities may not exist, at least not for the majority of the population. What is it like to live in a society where a third or a half of the population is poor and most of the people you know struggle to find jobs?

Even in wealthy countries, communitywide poverty creates problems beyond those faced by individuals. In these communities, transportation may be limited, jobs scarce, and schools below average. When most of the region is poor, it's hard for local governments to raise money through taxes; that makes it harder in turn for the region as a whole to invest in infrastructure, jobs, and schools. Long-term solutions to poverty must, then, involve ways to grow the economy and expand the range of opportunities available to the population.

10.5.2　Inequality

The measurement of inequality

We begin our study of the distribution of income by addressing four questions of measurement :

N　How much inequality is there in our society?

N   How many people live in poverty?

N   What problems arise in measuring the amount of inequality?

N   How often do people move among income classes?

These measurement questions are the natural starting point from which to discuss public policies aimed at changing the distribution of income.

The lorenz curve and the gini coefficient

We can also summarize income inequality visually, using a graph called the *Lorenz curve.* *The Lorenz curve maps the percentage of the population against the cumulative percentage of income earned by those people. It shows the cumulative percentage of the population on the y-axis, and the cumulative percentage of income those people earn on the x-axis.*

The best way to understand the Lorenz curve is to see that if every person earned the exact same amount, the curve would be a straight line with a slope of 1, as shown in panel A of Figure 10–2. That is, 20 percent of the population would earn 20 percent of the income, and 73 percent of the population would earn 73 percent of the income, and so on. However, if income is unequally distributed, the Lorenz curve will be bowed out in a U–shape: The poorest 1 percent of people will earn less than 1 percent of income, and the richest 1 percent will earn more than 1 percent of the income, as shown in panel B.

The Lorenz curve allows us to calculate a final and even more concise inequality metric—*the Gini coefficient. The Gini coefficient a single-number measure of income inequality; ranges from 0 to 1, with higher numbers meaning greater inequality.* Specifically, the Gini coefficient is equal to the area between the Lorenz curve and the line of perfect equality (area A in Figure 10–3) divided by the total area under the line of perfect equality (area A plus area B in the figure). This calculation gives us a single number to describe income inequality.

If everyone earned the same amount and the income distribution were perfectly equal, the Gini coefficient would be zero: The Lorenz curve would be the line of perfect equality, and so the area between them would be 0. If one person earned all of the income and no one else earned anything, the Gini coefficient would be 1. In reality, the distribution is always somewhere between these extremes. The closer the Gini coefficient is to 1, the more unequal the income distribution.

Cumulative share of income

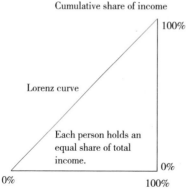

100%

Lorenz curve

Each person holds an
equal share of total
income.

0%

0%   100%

(a) Perfectly equal income distribution

Cumulative share of people

With a perfectly equal income distribution,
each extra 1 percent of the population earns
another 1 percent of income. In that case,
the Lorenz curve forms at a 45-degree angle.

Cumulative share of income

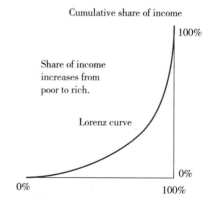

100%

Share of income
increases from
poor to rich.

Lorenz curve

0%

0%   100%

(b) Unequal income distribution

Cumulative share of people

When income is not distributed equally, each extra
percent of poorer segments of the population earn
less than 1 percent of the total income. Among the
richer part of the population, each extra 1 percent
of the population adds more than 1 percent of their
income. This distribution gives the Lorenz curve a
concave shape.

Figure 10-2   The Lorenz curve

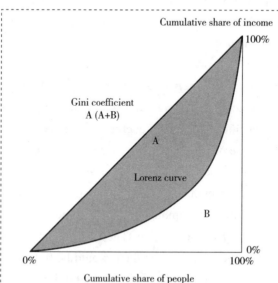

Cumulative share of income

100%

Gini coefficient
A (A+B)

A

Lorenz curve

B

0%

0%   100%

Cumulative share of people

The Gini coefficient is calculated by measuring the area
between the line of perfect equality and the Lorenz curve.
This is represented by Gini coefficient=A/（A+B）. The
greater the inequality,the deeper the U-shape in the Lorenz
curve. The greater the area of A, the higher the Gini coefficient.

Figure 10-3   The Gini coefficient

10.5.3   Policies to reduce poverty and inequality

Most governments, in both rich and poor countries, aim to limit poverty and inequality to some extent. Yet views differ about how to do so. It's also a difficult and controversial area of policy–making. Some people feel that taking from the rich to give to the poor is justice and others feel that it's theft. Some focus on equalizing opportunities rather than outcomes. Others focus on creating a safety net for people who lose their jobs or get sick. Even when people agree on policy goals, they may disagree about how to design the best policies to accomplish those goals.

Public policy goals. We can distinguish among three different types of public policy approaches related to poverty and inequality: Economic development, safety nets, and redistribution. Knowing which goals are being pursued has important implications for designing public policies.

Economic development. Often, policy–makers look for investments that will spur future economic growth. We can group these policies under the category economic development: The goal is not only the immediate effect of the policy on poverty but also the growth it will produce for the entire economy. Common examples include public investments in education, job training, and infrastructure. These policies help reduce poverty indirectly, through increased economic growth and opportunities in the future.

Many of these policies serve dual goals—providing services in the short run and contributing to long–run growth. For instance, education is considered an important good in itself. Most people want their children to have access to education for its own sake. However, from the perspective of the government, it is also a tool for economic development: Better–educated children grow up to be more productive workers who contribute to the economy and who are less likely to be poor and unemployed. Similarly, a plan to revitalize the downtown area of a struggling city may have dual goals: It may make living there more pleasant in the short run. The hope is also that it will attract businesses and new residents, improving the city's economy and reducing poverty in the long run.

Safety nets. Many policies are designed to protect against the temporary hard times that can lead to transient poverty. We can broadly categorize these as *social insurance* programs—*government programs under which people pay into a common pool and are eligible to draw on benefits under certain circumstances.* Under these

275

programs, people pay into a common pool and are in turn eligible to draw on benefits under certain circumstances.

Redistribution. Some policies explicitly seek to redistribute resources with the aim of alleviating the effects of poverty or income inequality. For instance, homeless shelters and food banks don't have much to do with long-run economic development. Instead, they are meant to provide comfort and security to people who face an immediate lack of food and shelter. Similarly, government-subsidized housing, food stamps, Medicaid (health insurance for low-income households), and many other programs offer resources to the poor over the long term. Most people see the primary purpose of these programs as using resources from society's wealthier members to ensure a basic minimum standard of living for its poorer members.

The welfare policy

Progressive taxation. Governments can address poverty and inequality both through how public money is spent and how people are taxed. The design of the U.S. federal income tax system is progressive, which means that the government charges lower tax rates to those with lower incomes. This design has the effect of reducing income inequality: Those with high income tend to pay a larger proportion of their income as taxes than those with low income. The result is that the after-tax gap between rich and poor is smaller than the pre-tax gap.

Income support. Government programs that give money to the poor are commonly referred to as "welfare." It provided financial support to any eligible person, without any restrictions on how the money could be used, which is replaced by *conditional cash transfer a program in which financial support is given only to people who engage in certain actions.* They are designed to help people through temporary hard times rather than provide long-term income support. Conditional cash transfer programs are an increasingly popular antipoverty strategy, both inside and outside the United States.

In-kind transfers. In contrast to cash-transfer programs, many government programs involve in-kind transfers. These programs provide goods or services, rather than cash, directly to needy individuals or households. Often, in-kind transfers take the form of vouchers that are redeemable only for certain items. In-kind transfer programs are, by design, more restrictive than cash-transfer programs. When a poor household receives income support, it can use the money to buy whatever goods and services it wishes. When that same household receives an in-kind transfer, the choice of how to spend the money has already been made. If we believe that people make considered choices to maximize their own well–being, then in–kind transfers are inefficient. After all, cash provides recipients with the flexibility to choose the goods that will do them the most good. Why might a government prefer in–kind transfers? One reason is that it prevents recipients from spending cash on luxury items or on socially disapproved goods such as alcohol or drugs.

Social insurance. Social–insurance programs are designed to help people weather temporary bad periods, but they also help people survive old age, disability, or other long–term conditions. As we noted above, in these programs, the government plays a role similar to that of a private insurance company: It collects contributions from working people in a common pool, defines the circumstances under which people are eligible to draw benefits, and administers and monitors the allocation of those benefits.

The purpose of social preferential treatment is preferential treatment and pension; the object of social preferential treatment is soldiers and their families; the basic feature of social preferential treatment is preferential treatment for soldiers and their families; the fund source of social preferential treatment is national financial allocation.

Disability and unemployment benefits are examples of social insurance in a straight–forward sense. If you lose your job, or have an injury or medical condition that prevents you from working, the government will step in to provide a small stipend to help cover everyday living expenses.

Retirement benefits are less like private insurance (which is generally used to protect against unexpected events) and more like a collective saving program. Nevertheless, because there is an uncertainty about the circumstances the elderly face—when they will retire, what medical problems they will face, how high the cost of living will be, and how long they will need to live on retirement income—retirement benefits are widely seen as an example of social insurance. They play an important role in reducing poverty among the elderly.

Trade–offs between equity and efficiency. Public welfare programs can be costly and have to be paid for by taxes. higher taxes usually mean larger dead–weight loss. Pursuing equity (that is, greater income equality) thus means accepting some inefficiency due to increased taxation.

Welfare programs themselves can also distort choices and create inefficiencies.

Some government programs that aim to reduce poverty are universal, meaning that everyone qualifies regardless of whether or not they are poor. Public schools are one example.

Many programs, however, are means–tested: They define eligibility for benefits based on recipients' income. The goal of means–testing is to target resources toward those who need them the most. Often, means–testing is more complex than a simple eligible/not- eligible distinction. For instance, under the Earned Income Tax Credit described earlier, the size of the credit at first increases with earned income at very low–income levels and then begins to decrease as income rises past the poverty line. The thinking is that a family with income just under the poverty threshold requires less support to access basic goods and services than a family very far below the line.

Unfortunately, means–testing can create perverse incentives. Imagine a simple means–test: If your income is under the poverty line, you are eligible for a cash transfer of $5 000 per year, but if your income is over the poverty line, you are not. Now imagine you are working part–time and living just under the poverty line. Your boss offers you the opportunity to pick up an extra five hours of work each week. If you accept, your income will increase by $3 000 over the course of the year, pushing you over the poverty line. As a result, you will lose your government transfer of $5 000. On net, you will end up $2 000 poorer. How would you respond to this situation? Would you accept the extra hours? Unless there is some sort of extra benefit we're not considering (gaining experience or favor with your boss that will improve your job opportunities down the road, for example), most people would say no to longer hours for lower income.

It is possible to fix this sort of perverse incentive by designing more nuanced means–tests. For instance, a program could phase out benefits as income increasesrather than use a strict cutoff. That way, there will be no point at which a large amount of benefits is lost from a small increase in income. In general, the more narrowly targeted support is to those with low income, the greater the potential inefficiency caused. These examples show why economists often see a trade–off between equity and efficiency in poverty policy.

This is not to say that poverty policy is always inefficient. Some policies, like those that alleviate credit constraints, can improve both equity and efficiency. In this case, a market failure is being solved, so there is no trade–off. But, understanding the potential for trade–offs and unintended consequences is an important consideration when designing poverty policy.

Conclusion

Typically, we rely on the invisible hand of markets to maximize total surplus by allocatingthe right quantity of goods to the right people. But what happens when one person's choicesimpose costs or benefits on others? Free–market outcomes can be less than ideal, and result in too much or too little of the good or activity in question. Asymmetric information describes a situation in which one side of the market has betterinformation than the other. In this chapter, we have seen that asymmetric information can have dramatic effects on the workings of markets.

Key Term

Information Asymmetry	Externality
Adverse Selection	External Costs
The Lemons Problem	Public Goods
Principal–agent Problems	Common Resources
Moral Hazard	Public Goods
Antitrust Laws	Common Resources
Income Inequality	Poverty

Review Questions

1. Why can asymmetric information between buyers and sellers lead to market failure when a market is otherwise perfectly competitive?

2. If the used car market is a "lemons" market,how would you expect the repair record of used cars that are sold to compare with the repair record of those not sold?measure the opportunity cost of her work?

3. Which of the following describes an externality and which does not?Explain the difference.

a. A policy of restricted petroleum exports in OPEC causes the U.S.price of petroleum to rise–an increase which in turn also causes the price of tea to rise.

b. An advertising blimp distracts a motorist who then hits a telephone pole.

4. When do externalities require government intervention?When is such intervention unlikely to be necessary?

5. If you want to fly between Rome and Munich, you may find that the amount that you have to pay depends on what time of day you want to fly. Compare the motivation for this practice with the practice of charging less if you are willing to make your reservations over a month in advance.

6. Insurance companies increasingly have the ability to test people for their genetic likelihood of suffering from certain diseases. Do you think that this sort of testing is a good idea? Is it efficient? Who gains, and who loses?

7. Consider a market in which a firm has monopoly power.Suppose in addition that the firm produces under the presence of either a positive or a negative externality.Does the externality necessarily lead to a greater misallocation of resources?

8. Externalities arise solely because individuals are unaware of the consequences of their actions. Do you agree or disagree? Explain.

9. Explain why a car manufacturer's willingness to offer a resale guarantee for its cars may serve as a signal of their quality.

Application

1. To promote competition and consumer welfare, the Federal Trade Commission requires firms to advertise truthfully. How does truth in advertising promote competition? Why would a market be less competitive if firms advertised deceptively?

2. An insurance company is considering issuing three types of fire insurance policies: (i) complete insurance coverage, (ii) complete coverage above and beyond a $10000 deductible, (iii) 90 percent coverage of all losses. Which policy is more likelyto create moral hazard problems?

3. A number of firms have located in the western portion of a town after single-family residences took up the eastern portion.Each firm produces the same product and in the process emits noxious fumes that adversely affect the residents of the community.

a. Why is there an externality created by the firms?

b. Do you think that private bargaining can resolve the problem?Explain.

c. How might the community determine the efficient level of air quality?

4. Four firms located at different points on a river dump various quantities of effluent into it. The effluent adversely affects the quality of swimming for home-owners who live downstream. These people can buildswimming pools to avoid swimming in the river, and the firms can purchase filters that eliminate harmful chemicals dumped in the river. As a policy adviser for a regional planning organization, how would you compare and contrast the following options for dealing with the harmful effect of the effluent:

a. An equal-rate effluent fee on firms located on the river.

b. An equal standard per firm on the level of effluent that each can dump.

c. A transferable effluent permit system in which the aggregate level of effluent is fixed and all firms receive identical permits.

5. There are three groups in a community. Their demand curves for public television in hours of programming, T, are given respectively by

$$W_1 = ¥200 - T$$
$$W_2 = ¥240 - 2T$$
$$W_3 = ¥320 - 2T$$

Suppose public television is a pure public good that can be produced at a constant marginal cost of ¥200 per hour.

a. What is the efficient number of hours of public television?

b. How much public television would a competitive private market provide?

6. Determine whether each of the scenarios is possible.

a. A poverty rate based on a relative measure is high, income mobility is low, and there is perfect income equality.

b. A poverty rate based on an absolute measure is high, income mobility is zero, and there is perfect income equality.

c. A poverty rate based on an absolute measure is high, income mobility is high, and there is high income equality.

d. There is no poverty based on a relative measure, income mobility is high, and there is perfect income equality.

7. Imagine a person who makes ¥400 per week working 40 hours per week for 50 weeks of the year.She is currently eligible for a welfare program, available to people with income below ¥21000, that gives her ¥800 a year. No such program

is available to people with income above ¥21000 per year. Her boss offers her a promotion that would increase her wage by 25 cents per hour.

a. What is her total income before the promotion?

b. What is her total income if she accepts the promotion?

c. Should she accept the promotion if she wants to have higher income?

8. Two used car dealerships compete side by side on a main road. The first, Harry's Cars, always sells high-quality cars that it carefully inspects and, if necessary, services. On average, it costs Harry's ¥80000 to buy and service each car that it sells. The second dealership, Lew's Motors, always sells lower-quality cars. On average, it costs Lew's only ¥50000 for each car that it sells. If consumers knew the quality of the used cars they were buying, they would pay ¥100000 on average for Harry's cars and only ¥70000 on average for Lew's cars.

Without more information, consumers do not know the quality of each dealership's cars. In this case, they would figure that they have a 50–50 chance of ending up with a high-quality car and are thus willing to pay ¥8500 for a car.

Harry has an idea: He will offer a bumper-to-bumper warranty for all cars that he sells. He knows that a warranty lasting γ years will cost ¥5000 γ on average, and he also knows that if Lew tries to offer the same warranty, it will cost Lew ¥10000 γ on average.

a. Suppose Harry offers a one-year warranty on all of the cars he sells.

（i）What is Lew's profit if he does not offer a one-year warranty? If he does offer a one-year warranty?

（ii）What is Harry's profit if Lew does not offer a one-year warranty? If he does offer a one-year warranty?

（iii）Will Lew's match Harry's one-year warranty?

（iv）Is it a good idea for Harry to offer a one-year warranty?

b. What if Harry offers a two-year warranty? Will this offer generate a credible signal of quality? What about a three-year warranty?

c. If you were advising Harry, how long a warranty would you urge him to offer? Explain why.